THE ARGENTINE FLYING FORTRESS

THE ARGENTINE FLYING FORTRESS

The Story of the FMA IA-58 Pucará

SANTIAGO RIVAS

AIR WORLD

AIR WORLD

THE ARGENTINE FLYING FORTRESS
The Story of the FMA IA-58 Pucará

First published in Great Britain in 2023 by
Air World
An imprint of
Pen & Sword Books Ltd
Yorkshire – Philadelphia

Copyright © Santiago Rivas, 2023

ISBN: 978 1 39909 792 5

Typeset by SJmagic DESIGN SERVICES, India.
Printed and bound in the UK by CPI Group (UK) Ltd.

Pen & Sword Books Ltd incorporates the imprints of Pen & Sword Archaeology, Air World Books, Atlas, Aviation, Battleground, Discovery, Family History, History, Maritime, Military, Naval, Politics, Social History, Transport, True Crime, Claymore Press, Frontline Books, Praetorian Press, Seaforth Publishing and White Owl

For a complete list of Pen & Sword titles please contact:

PEN & SWORD BOOKS LTD
George House, Units 12 & 13, Beevor Street, Off Pontefract Road,
Barnsley, South Yorkshire, S71 1HN, England.
E-mail: enquiries@pen-and-sword.co.uk
Website: www.pen-and-sword.co.uk

Or

PEN AND SWORD BOOKS,
1950 Lawrence Road, Havertown, PA 19083, USA
E-mail: Uspen-and-sword@casematepublishers.com
Website: www.penandswordbooks.com

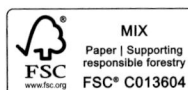

MIX
Paper | Supporting
responsible forestry
FSC® C013604

Contents

Introduction

The Pucará represents the pinnacle of the Argentine aerospace industry, given that it was one of the most manufactured aircraft, the first to enter combat in an international conflict and the first to be sold abroad. Although it was not the most impressive in terms of performance, a place that until today is filled by the I.Ae.33 Pulqui II, the Pucará was the most versatile due to its outstanding capacity in its sector, outperforming its main competitor, the Rockwell OV-10 Bronco, in many respects.

It had its baptism of fire, in a limited way, in the Tucuman jungles against the guerrillas that ravaged the area, and later in the Malvinas/Falklands War, a theatre of operations for which it had not been designed, with little logistics and against an enemy equipped with very sophisticated equipment. However, it successfully fulfilled its mission, becoming a feared strike component against British troops and helicopters.

It also entered combat in other countries, with the Colombian and Sri Lankan air forces, successfully fulfilling its missions. Unfortunately, poor sales management and very poor after-sales service meant that in both countries its operational life was cut short; at the same time it was unable to capture other international clients, apart from the Uruguayan Air Force.

Over the more than 50 years since its first flight, several versions were developed, although only the IA-58A managed to enter service in large quantities. Lack of vision and planning, as well as a scarcity of resources, led to the cancellation of most modernization programmes when it is still a one-of-a-kind type with no suitable replacement.

PART 1

DEVELOPMENT OF THE PUCARÁ

Chapter 1

The Military Aircraft Factory

Argentina was one of the forerunners in the aeronautical industry in Latin America. Argentine military aviation got going around 1912, with airplanes being built in the small facilities of the El Palomar Military Aviation School, near Buenos Aires. From the beginning the plan was to establish an aircraft factory, as there were few facilities for large-scale production at El Palomar. By the early 1920s, the idea was gaining momentum with support from the minister of war, Agustín P. Justo, and in 1924 the state aircraft factory was commissioned in a field at Las Playas, some five kilometres from the city of Córdoba. On 10 November 1926, the cornerstone of the Fábrica Nacional de Aviones (then the Fábrica Militar de Aviones, or FMA) was laid and its facilities were inaugurated on 10 October of the following year. The first model built was the Avro 504, under licence, followed by a series of foreign models such as the Dewoitine D.21 and the rebuilding of several Bristol F.2B Fighters.

However, the original idea was to design their own aircraft, which began with the Ae.C.1 (Ae. = the Aerotechnical Institute which designed the airplanes, C. = Civil and 1 = first model), a three-seater monoplane of which only a prototype was built,

The Avro 504 was the first plane built by the FMA as from 1927, under licence from Avro. (Archive Santiago Rivas)

although it kickstarted a long series of models, for military training, observation, bombing, transport and medical evacuation, as well as civilian models, which in total exceeded 100 units. However, there was much criticism of these designs, and although they remained in service for many years, they led to a return of licensed construction in the late 1930s, with the Curtiss Hawk 75-O and the Focke-Wulf Fw 44J, However the outbreak of the Second World War forced the FMA to take up its own designs: standouts were the I.Ae. DL-22 and I.Ae.24 Calquin, the former for training and the latter for offensive operations.

After the war, many former Axis engineers and technicians were hired to work in Argentina, where they were offered a good job without the worry of arrest. Thanks to them, Argentina managed to become the eighth country in the world and the first in Latin America to manufacture jet aircraft, with the I.Ae.27 Pulqui, designed by Emile Dewoitine.

That era, from 1945 to 1955, was marked by some brilliant developments, but carried out in a loosely organized way, with a large number of unnecessary aircraft being designed. The result was that only one of the important projects of that time, the IA-35 Huanquero, was manufactured in series. During the following period, manufacturing under licence was returned to, with the Beech B-45 Mentor and the Morane Saulnier MS-760 Paris, while some local projects progressed, such as the IA-50 Guaraní II (later G II), which was a turboprop version of the Huanquero, and the civil two-seater IA-46 Ranquel. However, the vast majority of the projects developed by the FMA at the time did not get beyond the drawing board, despite the fact that many of them were totally viable. Lack of political support and FMA mismanagement ensured that the factory was unable to position itself as an important aeronautical manufacturer; it achieved very few sales in the civil sphere and no exports.

From the late 1960s to the early 1980s, the Pucará was the linchpin of FMA production, replaced by the IA-63 Pampa until the FMA was privatized in 1995 and sold to Lockheed, which created Lockheed Aircraft Argentina S.A. (LAASA), which in 1997 became Lockheed Martin Aircraft Argentina (LMAASA). Finally, in 2009, the company returned to the hands of the Argentine state, and was renamed the Argentine Aircraft Factory (FAdeA) Brigadier Juan Ignacio San Martín.

The FMA I.Ae.33 Pulqui II was the most ambitious project undertaken by the factory, designed by a team headed by German engineer Kurt Tank. It flew for the first time in 1951, but the project was abandoned in the late 1950s after many delays. (Archive Santiago Rivas)

Chapter 2

A Counterinsurgency Plane

With the emergence of rural guerrillas after the Second World War, especially in Latin America, the Argentine government began, like the rest of the region, to develop strategies to face this type of unconventional and certainly complex warfare. The armed forces had to modify their fighting strategies where heavy weapons proved, in the main, ineffective. Aviation also had to change its tactics, as the attack aircraft in service at the time were not of much use against small and elusive forces. What was necessary was a slow aircraft, very resistant, with a lot of endurance and with high firepower, equipped with guns, rockets and conventional bombs, without any type of missile. Many countries, including the United States, used older piston aircraft, such as the Douglas A-1 Skyraider, the Douglas C-47, the Douglas A-26 Invader and the North American P-51 Mustang; others tried unsuccessfully to use the airplanes that they had, in the majority of the cases trainers, like the North American T-28 Trojan, the Beech Mentor and the North American Texan.

Only two countries developed and series-produced a counterinsurgency (COIN) aircraft, the United States, with the Rockwell OV-10 Bronco, and Argentina, with the FMA IA-58 Pucará. In Brazil, Neiva designed the Bi Universal de Ataque in the early 1970s, a twin-engine piston with forms quite similar to those that the Pucará would have, but it never got beyond the drawing board as the scale of Brazilian guerrilla activity did not warrant the investment.

In Argentina, the first guerrilla groups appeared in 1959 in the provinces of Salta and Tucumán, in the northwest of the country, in a mountainous and wooded area, although they were quickly dismantled by the Argentine National Gendarmerie, with army support. The first guerrilla group was the so-called Ejército de Liberación

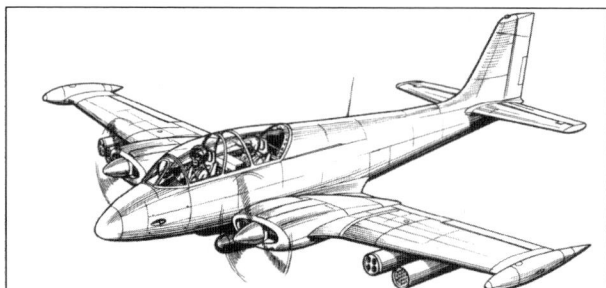

Concept of the Neiva Bi-Universal de Ataque, developed by the Brazilian Navy, using as a basis the Universal trainer and the Pucará, but smaller and with piston engines. (Archive Santiago Rivas)

Right: FMA-built Beech
B-45 Mentor of Grupo 1
Contrainsurgencia, established
in 1966 as the first Argentine
Air Force unit to fight guerrillas.
(Archive Santiago Rivas)

Below: Three views of the version
designed by Grupo de Desarrollos
Aeronáuticos for the IA-55
project. (Archive José Martínez)

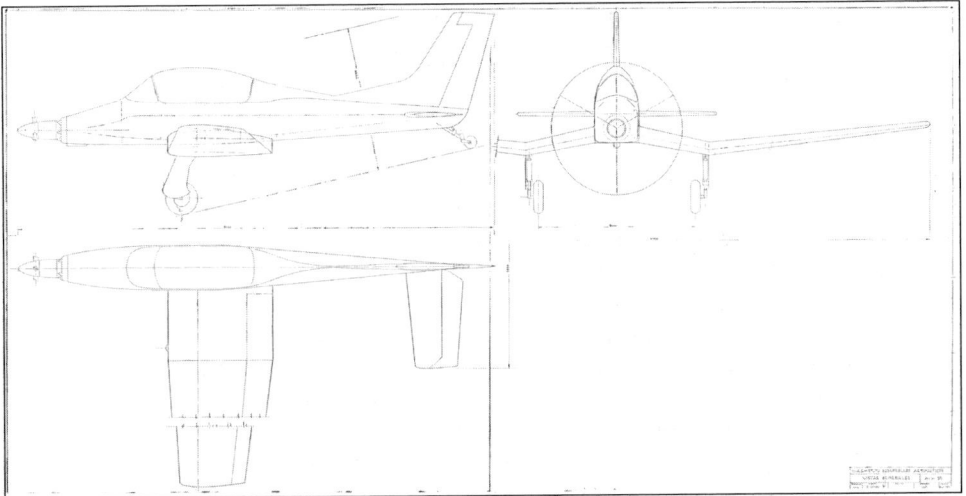

Nacional-Movimiento Peronista de Liberación, known popularly as Uturuncos, which sought the return of General Juan D. Perón. After the majority was captured, the group was dismantled in 1963 but reappeared briefly in Tucumán before dispersing shortly afterwards. That same year the Ejército Guerrillero del Pueblo appeared, created by the Argentine Ernesto 'Ché' Guevara in Cuba and led by Jorge Masetti. The gang was made up of about 30 operators, Argentines and Cubans, and began operating in the Orán area, Salta province, near the Bolivian border, hoping that Guevara would join permanently. However, the group was detected by the National Gendarmerie in March 1964 and all its members were either captured or killed. Despite the quick eradication of such guerrilla groups, the growing threat was clear.

At the same time, practically all of Latin America was shaken by communist-oriented guerrillas, supported by the Soviet Union through Cuba. In Argentina there were moments of institutional crisis, with weak democratic governments, coups, proscribed Peronism and the growth of leftist activities inspired by the Cuban revolution. To deal with the growing threat of guerrilla operations, in 1966 Grupo 1 Contrainsurgencia (G1COIN) was created within the Argentine Air Force, based at I Air Brigade, El Palomar, which was equipped with Beech B-45 Mentors and Sikorsky S-55 helicopters. From 1967 they received the first Bell UH-1D helicopters, which were to replace the old S-55s. Changing their name a year later to Grupo 1 de Ataque (G1A), the unit moved to the VII Air Brigade at Morón, where they received more Bell UH-1Ds and UH-1Hs, Hughes 369s and Hiller SL-4s, in addition to the B-45s already mentioned. None of these aircraft fully fulfilled the COIN function, which is why the design and construction of a true anti-guerrilla plane was essential.

Anticipating a growth in guerrilla activity and also with the objective of equipping other Latin American air forces with an aircraft dedicated exclusively to counterinsurgency operations, the Argentine Air Force (FAA), through DINFIA (Dirección Nacional de Fabricaciones e Investigaciones Aeronáuticas), a body on which the Military Aircraft Factory depended at that time, at the beginning of 1963 held a competition between the Grupo de Desarrollos Aeronáuticos and the Dirección de Fabricación as to who could come up with a suitable aircraft. The decision on who the winner would was to be made by the German engineer Reimar Horten, who had worked for the FMA and lived in Argentina, together with Estanislao Krazinski. Two proposals were presented, one by the Grupo de Desarrollos Aeronáuticos – comprising engineers Commander Ricardo E. Olmedo (head of the department), Commodore Antonio R. Mantel, Federico Seufert and Demetrio J. Díaz – and the other by Commander Héctor Eduardo Ruíz, administrator of Dirección de Fabricación. Both were a tandem, low-wing, conventional two-seat trainer. The former would be equipped with a 675hp Turbomeca Astazou X engine and the latter with a 660hp Astazou XI.

In addition to the Air Force version, a carrier-borne version was envisaged, to operate from the aircraft carrier ARA *Independencia* of the Argentine Navy, in the style of the US Skyraider, replacing the T-28P Fennec as a training and light-attack aircraft. The aircraft would also be used for advanced training in the Air Force, complementing the Mentors and replacing the T-28A. However, the design of both proposals differed greatly, the former being a W-wing design, while the latter was highlighted by a very small section fuselage and an unusually large cockpit dome, which would give great visibility to the pilots, although with reduced protection.

Both, conceptually, were very similar to the Morane Saulnier MS.1500 Epervier, which had first flown in 1958 and of which only two prototypes were produced before it was abandoned, in that they flew both with a 370hp Turbomeca Marcadou, changed for a 650hp Bastan I, then a 700hp Bastan II, a 750hp IIB, an 800hp III, a 986hp Bastan IV, a 1080hp Bastan VI, a 600hp Astazou XIV, a 800hp XVI and finally a 980hp Astazou XVI G, the same one that the Pucará would finally use.

The FMA's close relationship with Turbomeca and the French industry, due in large part to the work with the IA-50 G II, led to the French options being analyzed

Three views of version designed by the Dirección de Fabricación for the IA-55 project. (Archive José Martínez)

Héctor Eduardo Ruiz with a model of his proposal for the IA-55 project. The wing is similar to that of the IA-50 G-II transport, but smaller. (Archive Eduardo Ruiz)

in the development of a local COIN aircraft, especially with regard to the power plant.

Regarding the work at DINFIA, the team evaluated both projects and declared Ricardo Olmedo and his team the winner. The project was named IA-55 and in July 1963, development work began. Although the manufacture of a prototype was announced, the design was not enough to satisfy the requirements of guerrilla warfare, since the armament and armour capacity were limited due to the low engine power, something that had been evidenced in the French competition. In this manner, the IA-55 project was abandoned shortly after.

Huanquero and Guaraní COIN

At that time, the FAA was also evaluating the use of the FMA IA-35 Huanquero for COIN missions. The aircraft, designed in the early 1950s by the German engineer Paul Klages, although it had been conceived as a transport, also had the possibility of carrying weapons. It was initially designed to have two 20mm cannons, 12.7mm machine guns and 250 rounds installed, rechargeable in flight, plus two underwing mounts for four 2.25-inch SCAR or 80mm T-10 rockets in RNA-141 rocket launchers. In addition, it had four pylons under the fuselage for a total of four 50kg bombs or two 100kg bombs in IA-35-35 81 bomb carriers, including napalm of the same weight. It was equipped with a T-2A sight for bombing and a Wild for machine guns and rockets. It was planned to carry luggage containers

FMA IA-35 Huanqueros flying over Tierra del Fuego in the early 1970s, armed with MA-2 70mm rocket launchers that had been received in Argentina in the late 1960s. (Archive Santiago Rivas)

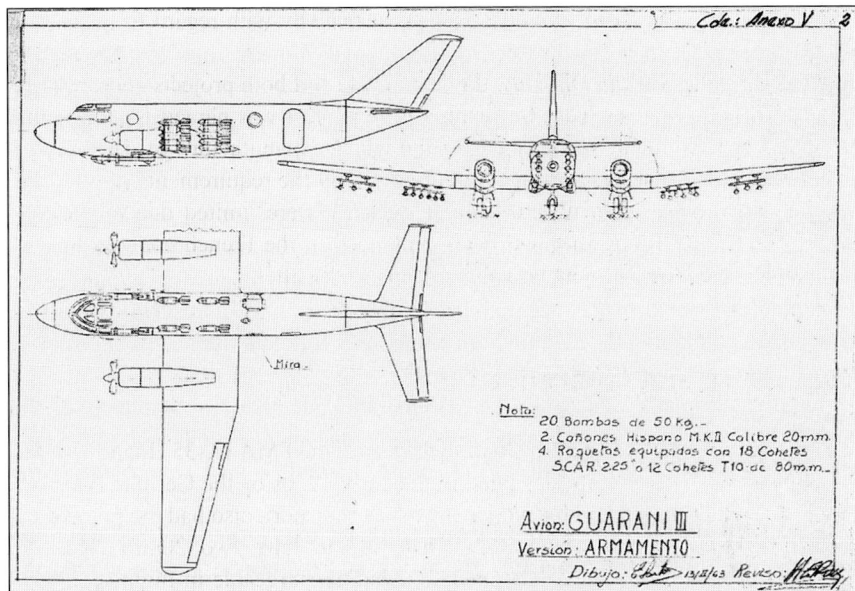

Proposal done in 1963 for an attack version of the IA-50 Guaraní, with provision for guns, a bomb bay and underwing pylons for rockets. (Archive Santiago Rivas)

on the underwing pylons and under the fuselage, in addition to supplementary tanks, carried only by the first example (the first series production Huanquero, the Ea-005) during the tests.

Target practice with the model began on 11 July 1959 by DINFIA at the Military Aviation School, with the participation of the Ea-016, -017 and -018 examples. In the first passage, the I.Ae.35 dropped four 50kg bombs with Arm.139 fuses from 1,300 feet height at 265km/h speed; in the second the Ea-016 and -017 fired their machine guns and the -018 launched eight SCAR rockets in two rounds. In the last passage the -017 fired the rockets in pairs, the -018 fired with its machine guns and the Ea.016 fired all the rockets as a salute. The SCAR rockets for training had been modified by the Departamento Armamento of DINFIA's Instituto Aerotécnico with a TNT warhead.

By the end of the 1960s, the Huanquero were concentrated at II Air Brigade in Paraná, Entre Ríos, and the Base Aérea Militar (BAM, Military Air Base) Reconquista, Santa Fe, and received serials A-301 to -326 (except medical evacuation planes), which indicated its primary use in attack missions, especially for counterinsurgency, all passing to Reconquista before 1972.

In any event, the age of the IA-35, with its piston engines and its glass dome looking like survivors of an old era that had long since disappeared, determined the withdrawal of all examples on 31 December 1973, after more than 15 years of service. In March 1974, the A-316 made the last flight of an FMA IA-35 Huanquero when it was transferred to the National Aeronautics Museum.

9

Meanwhile, in 1960, the national director of DINFIA, Brigadier Mayor Pereira, asked engineer Captain Héctor Eduardo Ruíz, head of the Agrupación Reparación de Aviones, to study the possibility of changing the Huanquero engine for the 870CV Turbomeca Bastan III turboprop. Ruíz worked on the airframe serialled 39, which at that time was being assembled in DINFIA workshops, starting with a modification to the tail, with the access door on the left side, changes to the nose, a new landing gear and, obviously, new facilities for the engines. Given the expectations placed on this version, called IA-35 Guaraní, it was decided to suspend the production of the Huanquero series, which, as planned, would reach 43 examples instead of the original 100. From then on, all the others would be turboprops, continuing the manufacture of the other four that were being assembled, but with the new modifications.

Finally, the plane was called IA-50 Guaraní, but after the first tests of the prototype it was decided to change the tail for one with a single tail and a new horizontal stabilizer, giving rise to the IA-50 Guaraní II, later called simply the G-II.

Back in February 1963 Ruíz had worked on various proposals, including one for antisubmarine warfare and one for attack and counterinsurgency, called the Guaraní III Versión Armamento. It was basically a light bomber, in which the passenger cabin space was allocated to the bomb bay, without the traditional windows and with two portholes per side, and which could carry 20 50kg bombs. In addition, it carried two Hispano Suiza DCA-804 20mm guns in fairings on either of the fuselage and four underwing rocket mounts, with a capacity for 18 SCARs or 12 T-10s. The upward view of the cabin was also improved, with a larger Plexiglas surface. The bombing sight was at the rear of the plane, where the 'bomber' station was also located with two round windows on the sides of the fuselage. This idea was shelved, since the original design of the plane did not make it compatible with the type of war that was already looming in the 1960s and the FAA preferred to aim for a design born for the attack mission.

Chapter 3

The A. X2

Meanwhile, at that time, the IA-53 Mamboretá project was advancing, a light crop duster, which made its first flight on 10 November 1966 under the command of Commander Pedro Luis Rosell. In December, engineer Captain Justo Demetrio Díaz and engineer Billy Juan Mauricio Montico prepared the development of a COIN version of the Mamboretá, using the weight that the crop duster had available to carry the product to be applied with an extra passenger and weapons, although they kept the back seat for shuttle flights or for an observer.

The Mamboretá was equipped with a Lycoming IO-540-B1A5 engine or a Continental IO-520-A, both with six opposed cylinders and 235hp, with a fixed armament capacity of 96kg consisting of four 7.62mm machine guns in underwing pods and 208kg of launchable weapons such as T-10 rockets and 50kg or 100kg bombs on four underwing pylons. The idea was for it to be used for armed reconnaissance and target marking, as well as light attack. In addition, 60kg of armour would be added to the crop duster. While the project was viable and could have nicely complemented the Pucará, continued budget cuts caused the Mamboretá to be abandoned in the early 1970s, when only two prototypes had been built, albeit

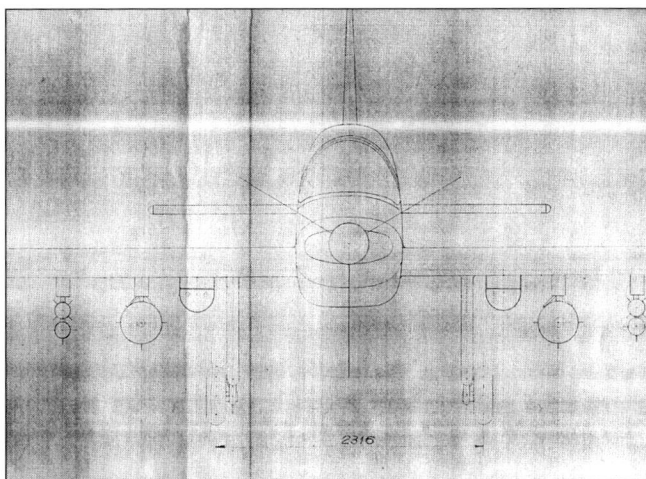

Front view of the proposed armed version of the Mamboretá, with pods for the machine guns, plus pylons for bombs and rockets. (Archive Santiago Rivas)

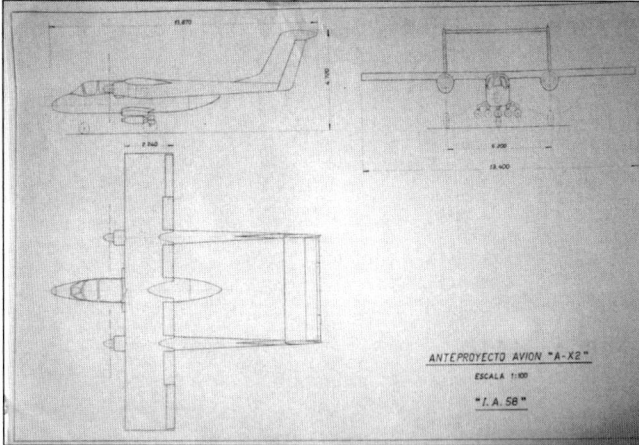

Second design of the A. X2 with the extra weapon sponsons. (Archive Santiago Rivas)

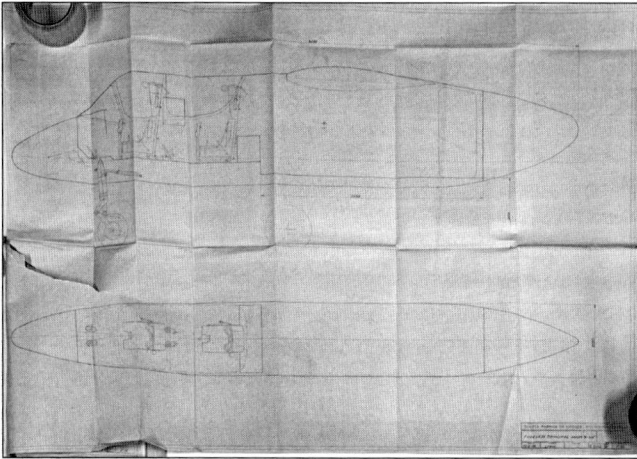

Cabin design of the A. X2 project based on the Bronco, with the pilots' seats, the location for the electronic equipment behind the seats and the cargo cabin. The side door on the back is also visible.

Once the design based on the Bronco was abandoned, engineer Olmedo used the front part of the fuselage with a new wing and tail, as can be seen in this artist's impression. (Archive Eduardo Ruiz)

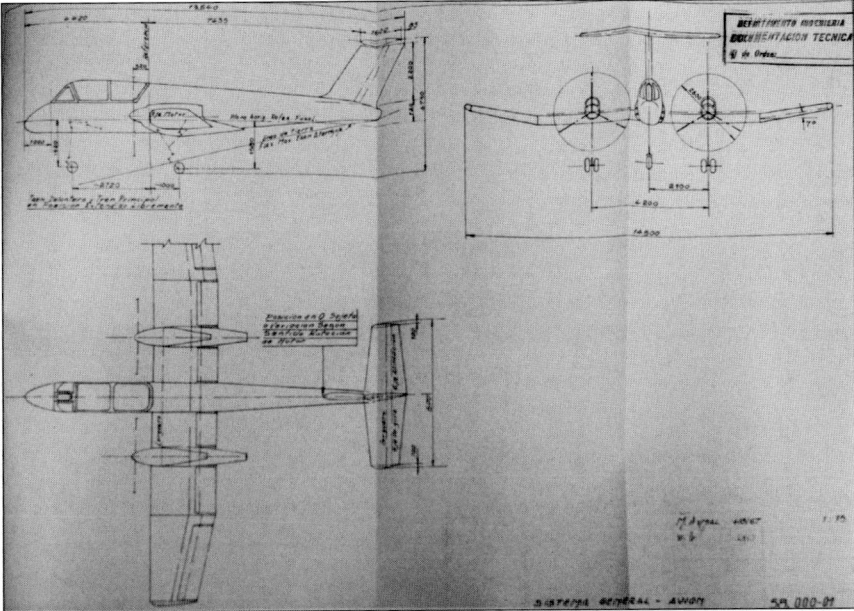

Above: Three views of the A. X2 design by engineer Olmedo. (Archive Eduardo Ruiz)

Right: Planned location for the machine guns for the A. X2, on fairings over the sides of the fuselage. (Archive Eduardo Ruiz)

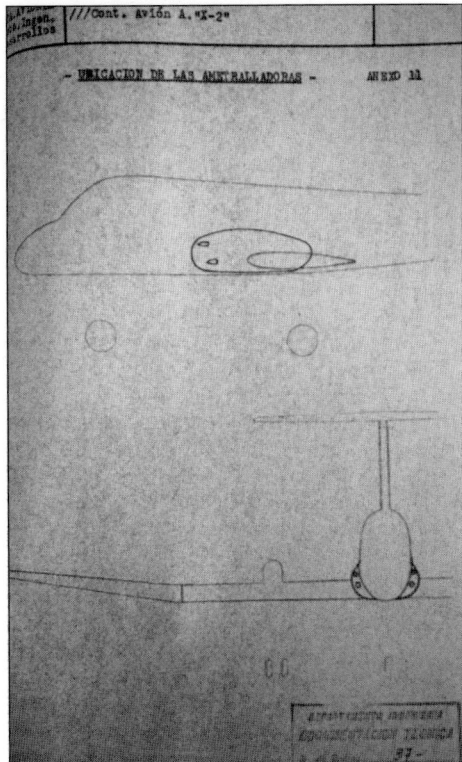

without any COIN capabilities. Another reason why the Mamboretá COIN was cancelled was that these needs were covered with the FMA Beech B-45 Mentor.

At the same time, to cover the need for an aircraft for COIN missions with better performance than the proposed IA-55, in 1965, Commodores Carlos Washington Pastor and Antonio R. Mantel prepared a requirement for a COIN aircraft that would also carry out offensive reconnaissance missions and tactical fire support both on land and at sea, with secondary missions of photographic reconnaissance and training. The project was named A. X2 and shortly thereafter received the designation I.A.58.

In August 1966, the project team of the Grupo de Desarrollos Aeronáuticos of the IIAE (Instituto de Investigaciones Aeronáuticas y Espaciales, part of DINFIA in charge of the designs) was organized, led by Commander Ricardo E. Olmedo, together with Captain Justo Demetrio Díaz and Commander Juan M. Beverina, who directed the Aerodynamics Department of the IIAE.

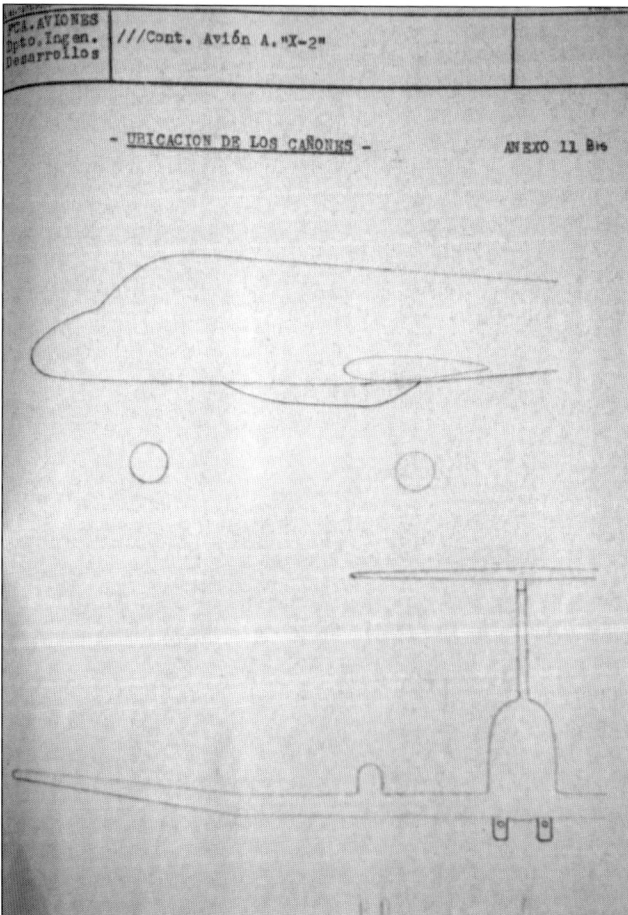

Planned location for the 20mm guns, under the fuselage. (Archive Eduardo Ruiz)

The first wind tunnel model during tests. (Photo FMA)

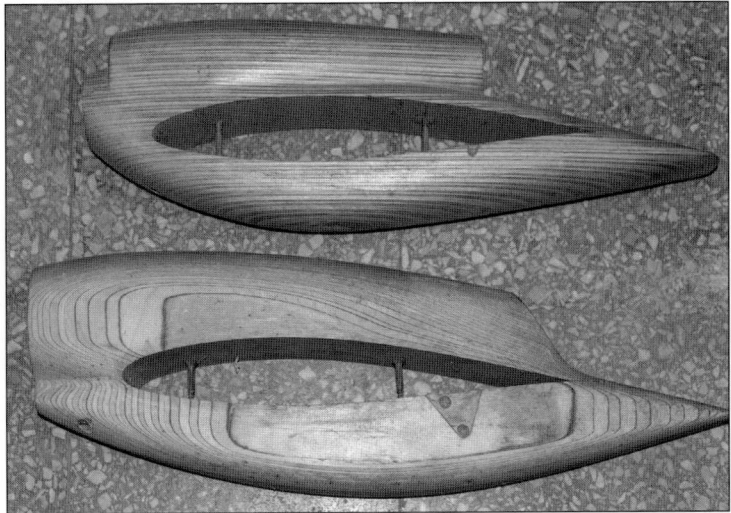

Nacelles for Garrett engines for the first wind tunnel model still stored at the wind tunnel facilities. (Photo Santiago Rivas)

An initial idea

On 11 August of that same year, Captain Díaz presented his preliminary proposal, classifying the A. X2 as an offensive reconnaissance and fire support aircraft on land and sea, and COIN operations, although he also highlighted that it could also perform light transport missions, training and photographic reconnaissance. Dr Reimar Horten stood out among the participants with his advice on aerodynamic issues.

The proposal was based on the OV-10 Bronco, which was entering service in the United States at the time. The project was practically the same, although equipped with two Turbomeca Bastan VI-C of 1,000shp (shaft horsepower) and Ratier Figeac FH 146 propellers of 3.2 metres in diameter and reversible pitch; however, it did not have the same visibility of the North American model. The wing would have four sections of 'double slotted' flaps to improve the STOL characteristics, in addition to the deflection of the propeller flux.

Some deficiencies of the American OV-10 Bronco were taken into account, where the arrangement with blown flaps made it possible for the plane to roll over the axis in case an engine stopped when operating at maximum power with flaps down, such as take-offs. For this reason, the engines had to be interconnected so that, in case one stopped working, the other turned that propeller. The Bastans were unconvincing, although they were used at that time in the IA-50 G-II, which they were known as by the force, because they could not perform inverted flight, being engines for civil use.

Like the US-built aircraft, the A. X2 also had a rear hold with a resistant floor, although larger, in this case being 3.55 metres long by 1 metre wide (with a maximum width of 1.1 metres) and 1.26 metres as a minimum height, to carry up to seven soldiers in the rear hold or three crew members and six paratroopers (the third crew member as jumpmaster). The cargo cabin floor was 1.1 metres high with the plane on the ground, facilitating loading and unloading, counting on the

The OV-10A Bronco at Buenos Aires domestic airport, during the first presentation of the type. (Photo Aeroespacio magazine via Carlos Ay)

Planned position of the pilot on the A. X2, as seen on the wooden mock-up built before the glider. (Archive Eduardo Ruiz)

Air brakes on the rear part of the fuselage of the glider. They were abandoned once the glider was rebuilt. (Archive Eduardo Ruiz)

tail cone as a cargo door, opening to one side, but, unlike the Bronco, it also had a side door on the left side, 0.6 metres wide, for passenger access or paratrooper launching. The floor had anchors for seats and for installing on the side door an XM-5 mount for a 7.62mm Minigun or an XM-75 for a 40mm grenade launcher.

For passenger transport, a configuration with a double seat in the front, four individual seats and an optional basic one was envisaged. For paratrooper transport a longitudinal seat for six troops was envisaged. For cargo, it would have fixed tie-down supports, which would also be used to attach the seats. It could carry packages up to 3.5 metres long, 1.2 metres high and 1 metre wide.

It was planned with a non-pressurized cabin, air conditioning, two VHF sets, an intercom, and a weather radar. The two pilots would have Martin Baker ejection seats, although the model was not determined. Behind the second seat would go the electronic equipment, accessible from the cargo hold. The air conditioning, electrical and hydraulic systems would go in the auxiliary fuselages.

The glider already finished at the FMA. (Archive Eduardo Ruiz)

A cruising speed at maximum continuous power of 460km/h with external loads and 498km/h without loads was expected, although it was estimated that, if a better aerodynamic coefficient was achieved, it could reach 540km/h with external loads. The stall speed with flaps at 45°, two crew members and 350kg of fuel was 91km/h. The take-off run on unpaved runways, with maximum weight and flaps at 30°, was 150 metres. The service ceiling was 31,000 feet and the minimum turning radius at sea level with maximum weight and 30° flaps was 98 metres. The maximum weapons load was estimated at 1,764kg and the maximum range in ferry flight, at 680hp of power in each engine and 20,000 feet above sea level, would be 3,303 kilometres. The empty weight was estimated at 2,770kg, with a payload of 2,230kg and a gross weight of 5,000kg. The plane was expected to be able to operate in temperatures between –30°C and +54.5°C.

It had an internal fuel capacity in the wing of 1,300 litres, plus five additional tanks of 100 gallons (378.5 litres) each or two of 200 and one of 100 gallons. The maximum fuel consumption was 375 litres/hour and the normal 361 litres/hour.

The aircraft had a length of 13.87m, a height of 4.72m, a wingspan of 13.4m, a wheel track of 5.12m and a horizontal tail wingspan of 4.92m. It was planned to equip it with a de-icing system on the wing and tail, engine air intakes and windshield.

The armament would go in five pylons, one under the centre of the fuselage with 1,000kg capacity, two on the sides and another two in supplementary wings, all for 450kg of weapons, similar to those of the Bronco, which could be removed if necessary. The location was close to the plane's centre of gravity, to avoid variations in it when the weapons were dropped.

The glider flying near the FMA. The cables installed to retain the strength of the structure of the tail are visible, as are the brakes on the rear part of the fuselage. (Archive Santiago Rivas)

Four 12.7mm Browning AN-M3 machine guns with 360 rounds each were proposed. Up to six 7.62mm Minigun SUU-12/A were envisaged, five on the weapons pylons and one on an XM-5 mount for shooting from the rear side door. It could also carry up to five AN-M3s in SUU-12/A pods, with 750 cartridges each, one in each pylon. The use of up to two M51 Vulcan 20mm guns, with three or six tubes, was envisaged on the internal side pylons, which pylons could also carry 20mm single-tube guns. It could also carry a 40mm XM-75 grenade launcher on the central pylon and another on the rear side door.

The possibility of equipping it with air-to-air and air-to-surface missiles was foreseen, which should be defined with the Argentine Air Force. Armour to withstand 7.62mm fire from 100 metres away was planned.

It was also planned to be able to install three floats, one central and two lateral, instead of the wheel landing gear, for operations on water, as well as the possibility of installing skis to operate in snow. The installation of JATO units was also envisaged to shorten the take-off distance.

Redesign

Meanwhile, on 11 July 1967 there was a restructuring at the factory, which ceased to be called DINFIA when it was separated from the automobile manufacturing area and became the Area de Material Córdoba (AMC), although it was commonly still called the FMA, dependent on the Air Force Material Command.

Comandante Roberto Starc in the cockpit of the glider. The structure of the fuselage, covered by fabric, is evident. (Archive Eduardo Ruiz)

At that time, both the Grupo de Desarrollos Aeronáuticos and the Grupo Fabricación became part of the Departamento Ingeniería de Desarrollos (Development Engineering Department), leaving the IIAE only for missile and space studies. The engineer Commander Ruíz was appointed as head of this department.

The first results of the studies of Captain Díaz's project showed several deficiencies that led to a complete redesign, which Olmedo presented to Héctor Ruíz in that same month of 1967; this was approved by Ruíz as administrator of the factory and consisted of a more conventional design, low-wing cantilever, maintaining the design of the front part of the fuselage but with a new rear part and with a single T-tail. It would have a retractable tricycle landing gear, powered by two Garrett TPE-331-303s of 845shp (although the possibility of using 1,000shp engines was considered), with a maximum fuel capacity of 2,245 litres (1,950 kilograms) in a fuselage tank and three in each wing (one or two of them self-sealing), with the aim of reaching a maximum ceiling of 31,000 feet, with a ferry range of 3,500 kilometres, a take-off distance of 250 metres and a landing distance of 510 metres, with a minimum turning radius of 150 metres, a minimum control speed of 146km/h and a maximum of about 477km/h, empty weight of 3,070 kilograms and a payload, including fuel and pilots, of 2,130 kilograms or 2,430 with overload, reaching a maximum take-off weight of 5,500 kilograms on prepared runways or 5,200 on unprepared runways.

A maximum capacity of 1,500 kilograms of armament was calculated, including 137 kilograms of internal weapons. The latter would include four 7.62mm Browning

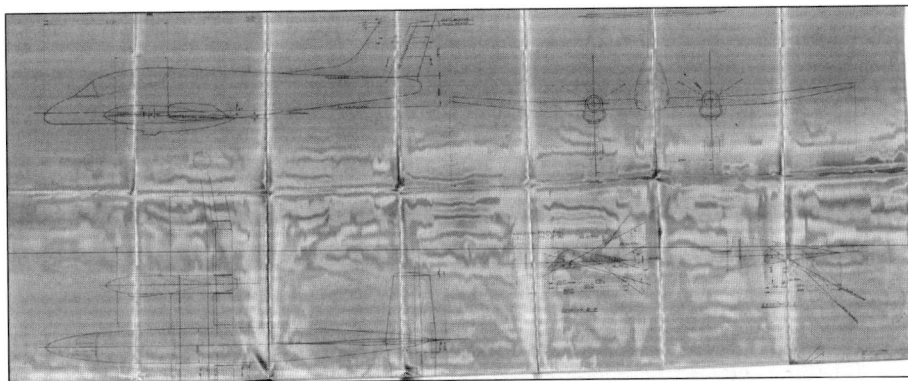

Above: Design of the Pucará with Pratt & Whitney PT6A-32 engines. (Archive Eduardo Ruiz)

Right: Engine nacelle design for the Pucará with Bastan VI engines. (Archive Eduardo Ruiz)

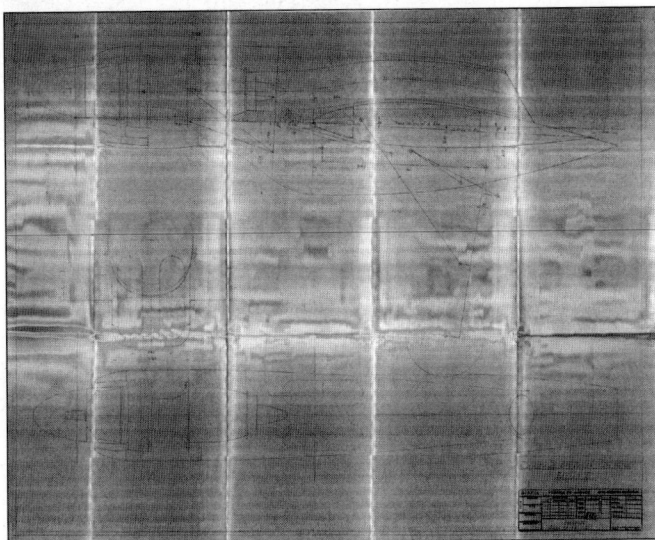

machine guns, two on each side, in a fairing on each side of the fuselage with a total of 2,000 rounds, plus two 20mm guns in removable under-belly fairings with 600 rounds in total. In this way a narrower fuselage was obtained. In addition, it would carry two Aero 7-A1 underwing pylons for 500 kilograms each and one Aero 20-A1 ventral for 1,000kg of weapons, which was expected to include TERs (triple ejector racks) and MERs (multiple ejector racks) and could include 250-, 500- and 1,000-pound bombs, T-10, 2.75-inch or 5-inch rockets, napalm bombs, torpedoes and training bombs.

A weather radar could be installed on the nose and a Librascope-type sight was envisaged. The design also included a $1m^3$ compartment with a reinforced floor, above the wing structure, in the central fuselage, for the transport of equipment, tools, engines, fuel and lubricants or even for the evacuation of personnel. The dimensions were a length of 13.54 metres, wingspan of 14.5 metres and a height of 4.71 metres.

Olmedo's project also contemplated three versions, the I: an attack aircraft with naval capacity, with two Martin Baker 0/100' ejection seats, complete de-icing systems on wings, empennage and engines, oxygen equipment, HF equipment and provision for IFF system and weather radar. Version II was an air-to-ground attack single-seater with an ejection seat, with the possibility of adding a second crew member in a fixed seat, without de-icing system, oxygen for one crew member and also provision to install IFF and radar. Version III was for training, with fixed seats, without de-icing equipment, oxygen, HF radio, nor provision for IFF or radar.

During that year the project was presented to the Commander-in-Chief of the Force, Brigadier General Teodoro Álvarez, who authorized the construction of the prototypes and a glider, despite the opinion of some officers to put it aside and buy the Bronco. This thinking had already prevented the manufacture of national aircraft in other cases, such as when it was decided to buy the F-86 Sabre instead of finishing testing the Pulqui II, with similar performance.

The Bronco in Argentina

As part of a Latin American tour, an OV-10A Bronco (the fifth OV-10A for the US Navy, Bu. No. 155394, constructor number (c/n) 305-5) visited Argentina in November and December of 1968, sponsored by Aerotransportes Wollkopf, an air

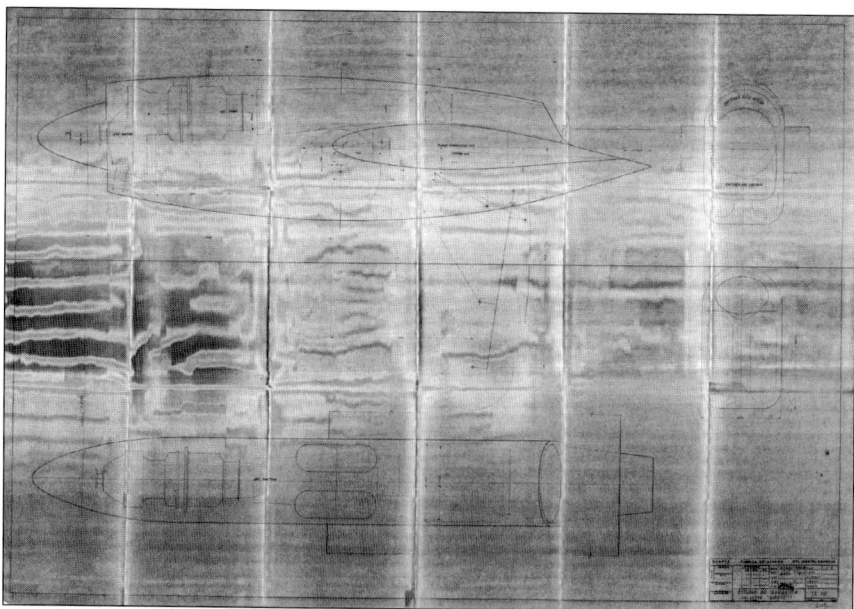

Engine nacelle design for the Garrett installation on the prototype. (Archive Eduardo Ruiz)

First proposal for a jet-engine Pucará for advanced training. (Archive Eduardo Ruiz)

taxi and aeronautical representation company with offices in Buenos Aires and a base of operations at Buenos Aires domestic airport. The Bronco was manned by Edward 'Ed' Gillespie, chief test pilot for the Columbus Division of North American Rockwell in Columbus, Ohio, and Commander Alfredo M. Torinetti, an FAA fighter pilot.

On 22 November, the exhibition was held at Buenos Aires domestic airport, including a 10-minute flight demonstration, and on 3 December, the aircraft was presented at the AMC. The US proposal was based on the fact that the Bronco was already in use in Vietnam, while the Pucará was just in the initial stage of development. However, the evaluation made by the Argentine pilots was negative, mainly due to the poor performance when an engine stopped, which served as a strong support for the continuation of the local project.

Interestingly, the Bronco that visited Argentina was lost on 29 October 1971 in Vietnam, when it was hit by enemy fire over the Vinh Bin province and fell into the sea. Its crew, Lieutenants Segars (pilot) and Smith (observer) ejected and were recovered alive by an army helicopter. 155394 had served with the VAL-4 'Black Ponies' light attack naval air squadron, based in Binh Tuy, since the early 1970s.

Gliders

As soon as the new design of the A. X2 was defined, a full-scale model of the fuselage was built, to specially evaluate the cabin design, while the engineer Reimar Horten

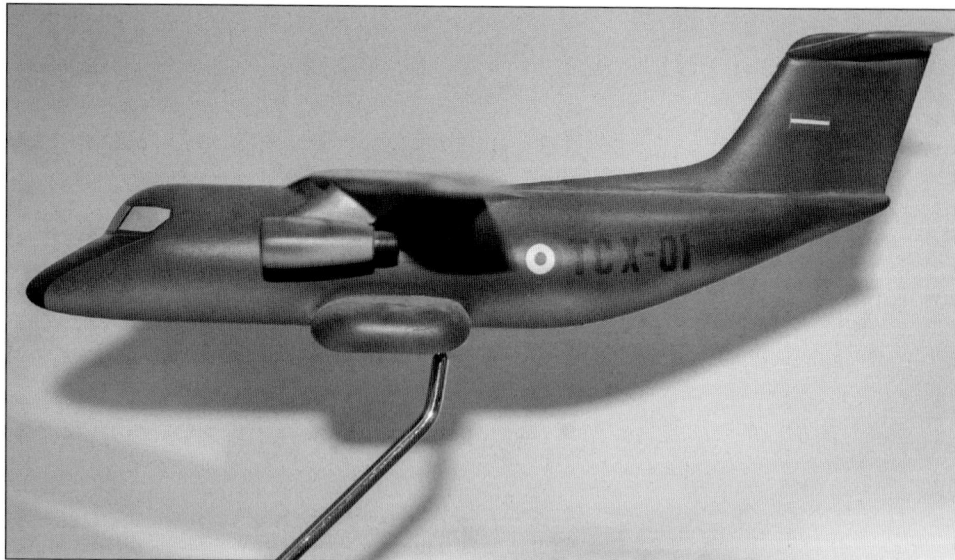

Light jet transport proposal made by engineer Héctor Eduardo Ruiz as part of the family of planes based on the Pucará. This proposal only kept the tail of the original design. (Photo Santiago Rivas)

The second glider flying after modifications to the main landing gear, with faux propellers.

The C-47 towing the glider while an FMA-built Cessna 182 follows them as the chase plane. (Archive Santiago Rivas)

was in charge of building, with staff from the School of Apprentices of the AMC, a wooden glider of the single-seater variant, with a fixed landing gear. In November 1967, the glider, serialled A-X2, was completed and tests began on taxiing, towed by a Kaiser Manhattan automobile loaned by IIAE engineer Apóstoli. After these tests were completed, on 27 December it took flight for the first time under the command of Commander Roberto Starc, towed by the C-47 serialled TC-27 of the AMC Centro de Ensayos en Vuelo (Flight Test Centre), flying for 40 minutes after releasing the tow and then reaching 11,500 feet above sea level. First, evaluations of the general flight conditions were carried out, followed by tests at low speed, flaps, centring, aerodynamic flow tests and flutter. By then, the plane had been internally christened IA-58 'Delfín'. During the evaluation, Captain José B. Videla joined Starc.

The results of the tests were presented in Technical Report No. 26 by engineer Nilo Penazzi, reviewed by Captain Reinaldo Cravero, head of the FMA Technical Department, and approved by Commander Starc. It highlights that in the glider construction stage, the low structural rigidity of the fuselage became evident, which made it necessary to brace the empennage by means of six tensioners plus the need to modify the final configuration of the fuselage. Despite this, it was decided to carry out the first flights to determine corrections to apply. In the first two flights a strong tendency to the right, inefficiency of the aerodynamic brakes and a heavy nose was found. On the third flight, longitudinal instability was found when flying at low speed; it was considered that the control lever was too high and the visibility to the sides was not good due to the width of the cabin. After that flight, the rudder was changed to one with a greater chord, although during the next two flights it was found that the improvement was not sufficient. In addition, stalls

The glider was used after the tests for exhibitions, as in this case during the Aeronautic Week of 1972 when it was displayed in Buenos Aires. It was destroyed some time after that. (Photo Alberto Martín via Hernán Casciani)

were evaluated without flaps, with 15° flaps and with flaps all down. On flights 10 and 11, the aerodynamic flow around the engine nacelles and the wing-fuselage junction were analyzed, finding strong turbulence at the rear of the nacelles. Then, only one additional test flight was made, on 12 March, and the glider was modified with what had been learned. In total, 18:15 hours were reached.

Meanwhile, on 29 January 1968, the general details were presented to the FAA Command according to the requirements and it was decided to rebuild the glider with what had been learned, opting for a complete redesign of the fuselage, tail and engine nacelles.

However, on 15 March of that year, Olmedo left the project after several disagreements with engineer Héctor Ruíz about the configuration of the plane; Ruíz remained in charge of it until its completion.

Under this direction, the glider was redesigned and became a two-seater with a totally new fuselage and tail, with the stabilizer in fixed position, and enlarged engine nacelles, so that they were ahead of the leading edge of the wing. The speed brakes on the tail cone were modified and the position of the second pilot was slightly elevated, to improve his forward visibility. Only the overall wing design remained unchanged. In February, in addition, the design of the powered prototype began, which would not have many significant changes with respect to the previous version of the glider. For this, different engine manufacturers were asked to propose their alternatives to propel the plane.

Selection of motors

As part of that process, on 29 February 1968, United Aircraft Corporation responded to Commodore Horacio Guerra of the FMA by offering two 750shp Pratt & Whitney PT6A-29 engines on loan, one to be delivered in May and the other in November of that year, with repayment (or loan extension) in June 1969. United Aircraft's proposal stated that, if the tests were successful, the company would bring both engines to the PT6A-32 standard (specific for the IA-58, which was never produced in the end) and sell them to the FMA. If not chosen, the agreement stipulated that the engines would be brought up to the PT6A-27 standard and sold to the FAA for use in Twin Otters. The FMA stated that to accept the proposal United Aircraft had to guarantee the delivery of engines with more than 1,000shp, dimensions equal to the -29 and a weight no more than 20 per cent higher, before May 1970.

At the same time, the provision of 1,000shp Bastan VID engines such as those used in the IA-50 G-II as standard was being negotiated with Turbomeca, although, given the aforementioned engine limitations, Turbomeca offered to develop an improved version of the Astazou XVI model, which had better features than the XIV initially offered. In this case, the manufacturer covered development costs; the engine was named Astazou XVIG-01, offering 1,021shp of power with five engines provided free of charge for testing.

As part of this process, Ruíz worked on the design of the nacelles for the four engines that could propel the plane, since the PT6A, the Bastan and the Astazou were joined by the Garrett Airesearch TPE331-O3H-U303, of which the manufacturer delivered the first three engines produced (serial numbers P-04001 to -3). The nacelles for all were designed, but the Bastan was scrapped for the reasons stated along with the PT6 because United Technologies did not yet have the proposed version ready, even though they planned to have the prototypes by December 1968, certification in June or July 1969 for delivery in August 1969. The company promised to be able to modify the -29 engines so that they reached 1,010shp by increasing the temperature of the compressor, which would be modified. In addition, the option of adding two stages to the turbine was proposed, lengthening the engine by 3.5 inches, to reach 1,100shp.

Thus, it was decided to proceed only with the Garrett and Turbomeca options, for which the wind tunnel trials of different bench alternatives began.

Aircraft family

Ruíz, at the same time, began to devise the development of a whole family of aircraft based on the project, but changing the turboprops for two Turbomeca Astafan IV jet engines of 1,200 kilograms of thrust each. The idea was to be able to achieve a higher speed, ideal for the missions that it was expected to fulfil.

On the one hand, the original configuration was adapted, installing an engine on each side of the fuselage, close to the trailing edge of the wing and with the nacelles of the turboprops replaced only by fairings for the landing gear. In this configuration, Ruíz proposed an advanced training aircraft and another for observation and photography.

On the other hand, in a larger modification, with a new and wider fuselage, an observation and light transport aircraft was proposed, with pilot seats side by side, side door and two additional seats, in a pressurized cabin. Of this design, two options were raised with variations in the windows. In addition, he proposed a completely different aircraft, which only kept the Pucará tail, being a cargo transport, with a new high wing and the engines in containers under the wings, with a loading ramp.

They were joined by a proposal for an agricultural aircraft based on the Mamboretá, with the tail assembly of the Cessna A-188, which was produced under licence at the FMA, although it did not inherit anything from the IA-58. In June 1968, he submitted his proposal, working on them throughout 1969. Although he failed to get these projects authorized, he resubmitted them in 1973 and throughout 1974, as described below.

At the same time, Ruíz had abandoned Olmedo's ideas of a single-seater version and a turboprop trainer. Although he had also put aside the naval version, the short take-off run of the plane made a naval version possible. Although it did not have a landing hook, it could operate in the same way in which a Pilatus PC-6 Turbo Porter was tested on board the ARA *25 de Mayo* aircraft carrier. In addition, from the beginning of the design, the possibility of equipping it with two 600-pound torpedoes on the underwing pylons or one of 1,200 on the ventral pylon was envisaged.

The glider flies again

After the modification of the glider, on 25 July 1968 it flew for the first time under the command of Commander Starc, towed by the Douglas C-47 serialled TC-27, freeing itself from the C-47 at 11,500 feet above sea level. The tests carried out were similar to the previous ones, reaching 104 flights with a total of 61:10 hours. On the seventh flight, on 5 August, 10 pressure taps were added to the fuselage, connected to alcohol tubes located in the rear cabin, with which the pressures reached were measured. On the tenth flight, a camera was added to take images of these tubes during the flight. The last flight, with Starc at the controls, was on 8 May 1969. During the tests, segments of the propeller blades were added in the feather position and the main landing gear was modified with dual wheels, for better performance on unprepared runways. The results of these evaluations were included in Technical Report No. 66, signed by the same people who had carried out the previous one.

Chapter 4

Prototypes

To evaluate the performance of the two selected engines, it was decided to equip the first prototype with two Garrett TPE331-O3H-U303 840shp engines and Hamilton Standard 33LF-337 variable pitch three-bladed propellers and the second with the Astazou XVIG-01 and three-bladed Ratier Figeac propellers with reversible pitch, which allowed the elimination of spoilers.

In September 1968, the first prototype began manufacture, serialled A-X2, like the glider. The structure was designed by German engineer Rudolf Freyer, one of the few remaining in the FMA from Kurt Tank's design team. It was also equipped with HSA (Folland) 4GT/1 Type 40 ejection seats.

Although the first flight was planned for 10 August 1969, Air Force Day, the prototype was completed and taken to the FMA runway only on the 16th, and three days later engine and taxi tests began, carrying out the first private flight on the

Construction of the first Pucará protoype. (Archive Santiago Rivas)

Garrett TPE331-O3H-U303 installed on the first prototype of the Pucará, before the first flight. (Archive Eduardo Ruiz)

Official presentation of the Pucará on 10 October 1969. In the background is an FMA IA-46 Ranquel, an FMA IA-35 Huanquero and an FMA-built Cessna A-182, while an FMA-built Morane Saulnier MS-760 Paris can be seen in the foreground. (Archive Eduardo Ruiz)

The Pucará, with the serial A-X2, landing at the FMA on 10 October 1969. (Archive Eduardo Ruiz)

The first prototype, now with the serial AX-01, flying over the plains of eastern Córdoba province. (Archive Eduardo Ruiz)

The first prototype flying over the hills of Córdoba province. (Archive Eduardo Ruiz)

20th, under the command of Major (the rank that had replaced Commander) Starc, taking off from the factory runway. For this case the prototype did not have the internal weapons or the external pylons, the landing gear covers, the rear ejection seat and other elements. The two Hispano Suiza 20mm guns in the lower part of the fuselage and the four Browning Model 1919 7.62x 51mm machine guns on the sides of the fuselage were never installed in this prototype, although they were already defined as the internal armament of the Pucará (the guns that would be used were the remnants of those that had been purchased for the Gloster Meteors, the IAe-33 Pulqui II and the dorsal turret of the Avro Lincolns – there were more than 400 new ones in storage). There would be three weapon pylons, one in the fuselage and two in the wings, at the junction of the central plane with the external sections of each wing, with a total capacity for a maximum of 1,500kg. Unlike Olmedo's initial project, the guns would not go in removable ventral fairings, but rather inside the fuselage and would be fixed. In the same way, the machine guns would not be in fairings that would protrude from the sides of the fuselage, but as the fuselage was wider the machine guns were inside. The opening to be able to place an engine in the fuselage and transport it was eliminated, although a cover was placed in the belly to access the fuselage and thus access equipment.

On 21 August 1969, the second flight was made in private in the presence of the Commander-in-Chief of the FAA, Brigadier General Jorge Miguel Martínez

On 27 November 1969 the plane made its first flight with weapons, with two rocket launchers and six loads simulating bombs on a multiple ejector rack. (Archive Eduardo Ruiz)

The second prototype in flight before the installation of the guns. (Archive Eduardo Ruiz)

The second prototype with SCAR 2.25-inch rockets under the wing pylon. Despite being tested, they were not used operationally. (Archive Eduardo Ruiz)

Zuviría, before going to the workshop to make some adjustments based on what was found in the first two flights. In addition, doors were added for the landing gear, the second seat was installed, as were weapon pylons, although the underwing ones did not have the attachments to carry loads or the landing lights in the front.

On 6 October, the aircraft flew again, returning with some minor faults, which were corrected and the next day made its fourth flight without incident. On 8 October, it flew twice, highlighting some faults on the main gear doors and the engine fuel system. The next day a further two flights were made.

On 10 October 1969, the baptism and official in-flight presentation took place before the defence minister, Dr José R. Cáceres Monié, on the forty-second anniversary of the FMA. That day the plane changed its name from Delfín to Pucará, which in the Quichua language of the Incas and Aimará is the name of the fortresses that they had built in ancient times, in northwestern Argentina. The latest factory-overhauled Gloster Meteor and an IA-50 GII equipped with skis to operate in Antarctica were presented alongside the Pucará. Other FMA products were also on display, such as a Huanquero, an IA-46 Ranquel, a Cessna 182 and a Morane Saulnier MS-760 Paris produced under licence.

On 20 October, test flights were resumed, this time in the rain, which made it possible to verify the need for a windshield wiper, in addition to detecting that the cabin gasket was not totally waterproof and water was entering. Shortly after, Major Sergio García and Captain José B. Videla joined the flights.

The AX-02 with an experimental six-tube 70mm rocket launcher, used only for ground tests. (Archive Eduardo Ruiz)

One of the few pictures of the first three prototypes together at the FMA. (Archive Santiago Rivas)

Presentation of the Pucará at Santa Cruz de la Sierra, Bolivia, on 20 March 1975, when the AX-02 made the first international flight of the type. (Archive Santiago Rivas)

The AX-03 seen around early 1977, displaying a smaller-sized serial and the name Pucará on the upper part of the fin. At the rear cockpit, an unknown instrument, most probably for tests, is installed. The size of the serials had been changed in 1975. (Archive Eduardo Ruiz)

The AX-01 together with FMA IA-50 GII that belonged to the factory, flying near the San Roque dam in Córdoba province. (Archive Santiago Rivas)

The Pucará AX-01 taking off using three JATOs. This system was only used for tests and exhibitions, but made it possible to take off in only 50 metres. (Archive Santiago Rivas)

Shortly after, on 28 November, order OPS69-15 was issued for the change of the prototype serial to AX-01 because the AX-2 designation had already been dropped. However, this change became effective only on 18 May 1970. Meanwhile, on 16 February 1970, the model's first long-duration flight was made, reaching 3:30 hours, which was followed by another of 4:48 hours on the 21st of that month.

On 30 March the aircraft reached 100 flight hours, so it went into a check, which lasted until June. On 26 November of that year, the first flight was made with new Hartzell HC-B3TN-5C/T10282 HB propellers and the next day the first flight with weapons was made, with two 19-tube 70mm rocket launchers, one on each underwing pylon, and six loads of 115kg 'bombs' in an MER on the ventral pylon.

At that time, the second prototype began manufacture, with Astazou engines and a 20cm longer fuselage, which made its first taxi on 9 September 1971 and flew for the first time on 15 September with the serial AX-02, with Major García at the controls, completing initially a 15-minute flight, followed that same day by another of half an hour. After all the systems had been fine-tuned, the first test flight (number 17 of the plane) was carried out on 14 October, initiating a preliminary test programme with this aircraft and its engines. In addition, on 23 October it flew to VII Air Brigade at Morón, Buenos Aires, and then to nearby I Air Brigade at El Palomar, where it was exhibited; the next day it flew to Ezeiza International Airport where it was presented to Argentine President General Roberto Levingston, before later returning to I Air Brigade. The next day it started the return to the AMC, but due to bad weather had to land at the airport at Villa María, in the province of Córdoba, but was able to fly to its destination before the end of the day. On 30 October the test flights were resumed, which ended on 6 November after a total of 44 flights (16 of them for tests) with a total of 34:05 hours.

At that time different versions were proposed. On the one hand, Ruíz suggested that some Pucarás be delivered in a single-seater version, eliminating the second seat, the instruments and controls, but with all the anchors to be able to add them if necessary. In a study from around the end of 1971 the weather radar is referred to as optional equipment for the plane, which was installed twice, as will be seen later. This indicates that said installation was something planned from the beginning and not only carried out for those particular cases. It is also interesting, when describing the armament configurations, that a so-called B-2 configuration was included, with the plane carrying a 1,000kg torpedo, as well as rockets and ammunition for the 20mm guns. Although in practice the use of torpedoes was only evaluated at the time of the Malvinas/Falklands War, it was already considered from the outset.

Astazou selection

After the test flights were carried out, in May 1971 the report on the evaluation of the Garrett and Astazou engines was submitted to the Material Command of the Argentine Air Force, to determine which of the two should be finally adopted for the aircraft.

A pilot boarding the AX-03 on the tarmac of the Centro de Ensayos en Vuelo (Flight Test Centre). (Archive José Martínez)

According to the report, the Garrett engine could deliver up to 840shp (for up to five minutes) at take-off and 770 at cruise, with a torque limit of 2,363 pounds/ft^2, and fuel consumption at take-off of 276 litres/hour and at cruise of 264. The weight of the engine was 156 kilograms and, with its accessories and propellers, it reached 355 kilograms.

In turn, the Astazou delivered up to 965shp in take-off (without limitation in terms of time) and 890 in cruise, with a torque limit of 2,575 pounds/ft^2, a consumption in take-off of 294 litres/hour and in cruise of 265. For its part, the engine weighed 143.5 kilograms and, with propellers and accessories, 335.

In the Pucará, the Garrett supported up to 7 g's upwards and 1.5 laterals, while in the Astazou the limits were 10 and 5 respectively.

For its part, while the Garrett engine was widely used, the Astazou XVI-G was a new model and there was little history of its long-term performance.

In the flight tests, the AX-02 showed a service ceiling in attack configuration, armed with bombs, weight equivalent to the guns and machine guns and their ammunition, with two pilots and full internal fuel, with two engines, of 8,280 metres, against 6,680 of the AX-01, 24 per cent higher; of 5,340 metres against 5,000 with one engine, but the tests were done with a bigger fuel load on the AX-02, so the difference was estimated to be even greater. The AX-02 reached a maximum speed at sea level of 482km/h against 432 of the AX-02. The take-off run was 600 metres

Rollout of the first series production Pucará on 15 November 1974. (Archive Eduardo Ruiz)

Presentation of the first series production Pucará, serialled A-501, in front of Hangar 90 of the FMA, 15 November 1974. (Archive Eduardo Ruiz)

on the AX-02 and 830 metres on the AX-01, while the landing run was 440 and 523 metres respectively. In addition, the AX-02 could meet the requirement of a turning radius of 150 metres flying with the internal weapons (not installed, but the equivalent in weight), against 190 in the AX-01 due to its less power.

The range of the AX-02 with an extra tank, totalling 2,580 litres, flying at an altitude of 16,500 feet and 402km/h was verified at 3,400 kilometres, although in the AX-01, with 2,485 litres was between 2,630 and 3,400 kilometres; but it was indicated that the necessary power tests at different heights in said prototype had yet to be completed. The maximum endurance with extra tanks in the AX-02, with a consumption of 116 litres/hour per engine, was 10:10 hours, while in the AX-01, with a consumption of 128 litres/hour per engine, was 9:37 hours.

At the same time, it was found that the power delivered by the Astazou was guaranteed by the manufacturer, which was not the case with the Garrett engines, which, moreover, easily exceeded torque and temperature, which complicated the operation.

On the other hand, given the small number of flights carried out with the AX-02, a margin of error of more or less 10 per cent was estimated and it was suggested at the same time to make a more complete study of both aircraft in all kinds of situations, such as acrobatic flight, inverted, shooting and bombing, training and instruction, to reach between 150 and 200 hours.

On the other hand, the Garrett engines had presented a large number of faults during the tests, delaying them a lot, which ended on 17 March 1971, after 167

The first two series production planes, A-501 and A-502, on the tarmac of the FMA. Note that the markings were changed, with serials in a smaller size and the full 'Fuerza Aérea Argentina' inscription. The wingtips and stabilizers were still in red as were the operations. (Archive Eduardo Ruiz)

flights and a total of 175 hours, without achieving complete tuning of the engines on the plane. That same day the AX-02 reached 87 flights and 85:30 hours, having reached the set-up of the Astazou in the Pucará, for which the two planes entered a check.

Another aspect considered was the cost of the engines and their accessories, estimated at $57,305 for the Astazou and $69,187 for the Garrett.

For all this, the selection of the Astazou engine was recommended, as it was considered to be better adapted to the operation of the aircraft, especially in combat missions, where maximum performance was required. Thus, it was decided that the AX-01 be modified with the installation of said engines and on 21 June the AX-01 made its last flight with Garrett engines, having accumulated 204:30 hours in 190 flights, removing the Garrett engines on the 25th. Since the plane was 20 centimetres shorter, the benches had to be installed further back than in the AX-02, to keep the centre of gravity in the same location. This aircraft received Hamilton Standard 23LF-3335 propellers, with the installation of the new engines finished on 8 February 1972, returning to test flights on 21 April 1972, with its first flight with Astazou at the controls of Vice-Commodore Roberto Camblor.

In May of that year, the first flight of a Pucará outside the country was made when the AX-02 flew to the Asunción del Paraguay International Airport, to demonstrate the model to the Paraguayan Air Force, something carried out on the 15th.

A-501 at Aeroparque Jorge Newbery, Buenos Aires. (Photo Alberto Martín)

Meanwhile, on 3 June 1971, the C-130E Hercules serialled TC-63 took the AX-02 to France to carry out, at the Turbomeca facilities, structure vibration tests with the new engines, returning on the 24th aboard the Hercules.

In addition, that year and after the first evaluations of the Flight Test Centre, the FAA ordered a series of 30 aircraft that was later raised to 100, starting the assembly line in 1972.

The tests continued with the two prototypes during 1972, at the same time that the third (AX-03) began manufacture, also equipped with Astazous and modified nose, adopting the final shape of the plane. In addition, the outer wing tanks were eliminated because of their influence on the roll. This was the first example equipped with full armament from the start, Matra SFOM 83A-3 sight and Bendix AWE-1 firing programmer. Due to budget problems, the completion was delayed and only made its first flight on 8 December 1973, while serial production was postponed.

While this was happening, in 1973, in Hangar 90 of the FMA the manufacture of the first series airplanes was being prepared, the aerodynamic studies were finished and on 31 December 1973, by order 30, at BAM Reconquista, in the province of Santa Fe, the last FMA IA-35 Huanquero was retired, to be replaced by the Pucará. However, budget cuts delayed the start of production of the series until June 1974. The plan called for the delivery of the first before the end of 1974, another four in 1975, 14 in 1976, 36 in 1977 and 1978 and nine in 1979, completion before June 1979.

On 4 April 1973, the AX-02 carried out a JATO take-off and during that year carried out tests with the weapons, including two conventional 115kg bombs,

70mm LAU-60 rockets, T-10 and SCARs rockets and an experimental six-tube rocket launcher for ground tests, while testing the strength of the self-sealing tanks, internal armour and armoured windshield against the impact of different calibre projectiles, demonstrating great resistance to light weapons fire. Given the delay in the completion of the AX-03, during that year the AX-02 was modified to receive the fixed armament of guns and machine guns.

On 16 April 1974, the Pucará AX-01 was presented to President Juan D. Perón at BAM Mariano Moreno, Buenos Aires, including the take-off using JATOs from the platform itself, in just 55 metres, which was carried out by Vice-Commodore Camblor. In May it was also presented to authorities of the Libyan Air Force who were interested in the model and in October to the Bolivian Air Force, one of the forces that showed the greatest interest in Pucará from the start. Shortly thereafter, the AX-01 received a large aerial data probe in its nose to continue testing.

For the Argentine Air Force Day of that year, 10 August, the three prototypes deployed the VII Air Brigade in Morón, Buenos Aires, where they participated in the parade reviewed by the new president, María Estela Martínez (Perón's widow and vice-president until Peron's death on 1 July 1974), in one of the largest exhibitions of the force in its history.

On 15 September, BAM Reconquista, which would be the unit to operate the Pucará, formed the Pucará Task Force under the command of Major José M. Ignes Rosset. On 15 October with Captain José Ignacio Igarzábal and First Lieutenant Hugo Palaver the first training flights began in Córdoba prior to the reception of the first series aircraft, using the AX-01 and 02 prototypes, with the last pilots finishing the adaptation flight on 13 December.

On 8 November 1974, the first series production aircraft flew for the first time, which initially had been manufactured to be the fourth prototype, serialled A-501, at the controls of Vice-Commodore Camblor. Its second flight was carried out on the 13th by Captain Horacio Oréfice and was presented two days later during the 47th anniversary of the factory, before the authorities of the FMA and the Argentine Air Force, the press and the general public. This aircraft, among other differences, had the Martin Baker APO-6A 0-0 ejection seat. Thus began the evaluation flights by the Flight Test Centre, which lasted until 31 July 1975.

Due to the interest shown by Bolivia, which at that time was waging a war against guerrillas who had been formed long before by Ernesto 'Che' Guevara (who died in that country in 1967), on 20 March 1975 the AX-02 was exhibited there, although the purchase was not made in the end. It was once again officially offered to the Argentine Naval Aviation Command as a light naval attack aircraft to replace the T-28 Fennec, without arousing much interest given that at that time the Navy had just received the Douglas A-4Q Skyhawk that together with the Grumman S-2E Tracker fully covered the needs of the Naval Aviation Command in terms of carrier aviation.

Chapter 5

Trials and New Versions

In 1976, 700 flight hours were allocated for the two prototypes that flew at the factory, since in November 1975 the AX-02 had stopped flying and had become a platform for ground structural tests, being subjected to efforts until its destruction, leaving only the forward part of the fuselage preserved for many years at III Air Brigade. In this regard, it must be borne in mind that its airframe had been subjected to structural stresses during the vibration tests in France, which is why it was penalized.

In 1976, work began on a version, called IA-58B, equipped with two DEFA 553 30mm guns with 280 rounds instead of those of 20mm. The idea was that all the examples from the 61st production aircraft were of this variant.

The AX-04 at Reconquista with four rocket launchers used only on ground tests and an MER on the belly. On the ground are 125kg bombs. (Archive Eduardo Ruiz)

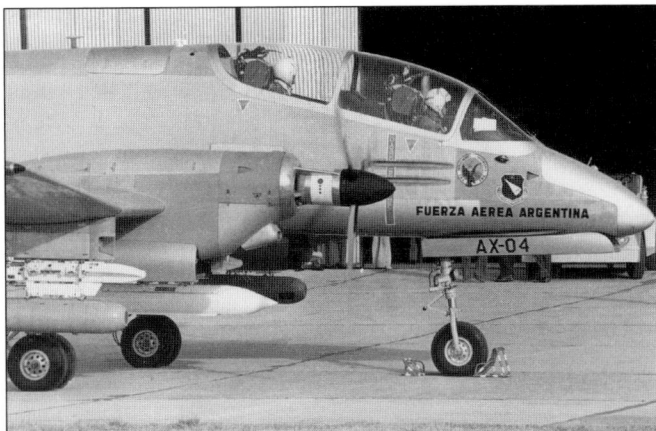

The AX-04 during tests of the Alkan grenade launcher. On the underwing pylons are two camera pods to film the tests. (Archive Eduardo Ruiz)

The AX-04 with two Alkan launchers on an MER under the belly. (Archive Eduardo Ruiz)

Pod developed for a DEFA 552 30mm gun for use on the belly of the Pucará. In the end the pod was not adopted. (Archive Eduardo Ruiz)

On the other hand, due to the loss of the AX-03, A-509, re-serialled AX-04, in November 1977 was assigned to the Flight Test Centre for weapons tests, including a ventral pod with a DEFA 553 30mm gun and the Alkan 530 containers to launch Lacroix 314 anti-vehicle and F130 smoke cartridges.

International exhibitions

As part of the FMA's attempt to sell the aircraft abroad, it was planned to exhibit it at the 32nd Le Bourget Salon in Paris, which would take place between 2 and 12 June 1977. With that goal in mind from 10 to 28 April, tests were carried out with the AX-01 and -03 to evaluate the possibility of taking the Pucará in flight to Europe. With the planes equipped with three additional tanks, they made non-stop flights departing from Córdoba and passing over the cities of Santa Rosa, Neuquén, Bariloche, Bahía Blanca, Ezeiza, Rosario and Paraná to return to Córdoba eight hours later, having travelled 3,200 kilometres. With this, the Pucará's ability to cross the Atlantic in flight was proven, a task carried out by the AX-03 manned by Vice-Commodore García and First Lieutenant Germán Spika, accompanied by the C-130H Hercules serialled TC-64, which carried in its hold A-507. After the flight was authorized by presidential decree No. 1320 of 6 May, it left Córdoba on

The AX-03 preparing to depart for Le Bourget in 1977. Note the radar installed on the nose and one 1,135-litre- and two 320-litre fuel tanks. (Archive José Martínez)

The AX-03 in France. Interestingly, the plane received a normal nose without the radar.

A-507 at Le Bourget, with a Republic A-10 Thunderbolt and the Concorde prototype behind. (Archive Eduardo Ruiz)

14 May at 0830 hours, making the first stopover in Porto Alegre, after flying 2:30 to cover the distance of 1,260 kilometres. The crew then made the first long-duration part, flying directly to Recife, at 2,970 kilometres, which required 7:40 hours of flight and where they had to land by instruments. The crossing of the Atlantic was the riskiest stage, although they were able to complete it without incident, arriving at Salt Island by instruments after another 7:40 hours of flight that required them to cover the 3,070 kilometres' distance. The next leg was also over the sea, although shorter, to Las Palmas, Canary Islands, 1,490 kilometres away, arriving after 3:50 hours of flight and again landing by instruments. From there they continued to Seville to complete the last stretch over the sea, landing 3:20 hours later after flying over 1,335 kilometres. The last leg was to fly to Pau-Uzein in France on 19 May, covering 835 kilometres in two hours and landing at 0930. To accomplish this flight, the aircraft received a VOR/ILS, two ADFs, two VHFs, INS Litton LTL-72, Bendix RUR-160 weather radar in the nose, and Bendix DPR-600 transponder. At the Turbomeca plant in Pau-Uzein, the AX-03 was checked over and A-507 was assembled before flying to Le Bourget, Paris, on 29 May.

After the exhibition, where the Pucará attracted a lot of attention, between 15 and 29 June the AX-03 went to Casaux to homologate the guns and the SC-PT-303 firing programme from the Sistemas y Controles company (which would not later be adopted in further aircraft). In reference to the guns, vibration tests were carried out, one for toxicity of gas emissions from them in the cockpit and one 'explosive'. The latter, according to the report carried out by the French Centre d'essais en vol, CEV, aimed to analyze the risk of gases igniting during shooting,

The AX-03 at the Turbomeca facilities in France.

The Pucará A-19 in flight en route to the United Kingdom.

The Pucará at Farnborough '78.

The IA-58B was an attempt to develop a version of the plane with 30mm DEFA 552 cannons instead of the 20mm Hispano Suiza.

both due to heat and any spark from the aircraft electrical equipment. Twelve tests were carried out on the ground, with bursts of up to 2.5 seconds where no risk of gas explosion was detected, both with the barrel ventilation system open and closed. Then two test flights were made, at 5,000 feet of altitude and at speeds between 150 and 240 knots, making 12 bursts of between 0.7 and 1.9 seconds, in which no risks were detected but the test clarified that it was necessary to view the results cautiously due to the short duration of the bursts. Regarding the cockpit gas tests, high levels of toxic gases were detected when shots were fired over a period of more than 12 seconds. Thus, it was recommended to keep an oxygen mask on, open the vents to the maximum and make some reforms to the ventilation system of the guns. It was indicated that shooting the machine guns generated more vibrations in the instrument panel than with guns, since their muzzles were closer to the instrument panel. Measurements also indicated during shooting the possibility of an untimely disconnect of the connectors of some instruments. It was recommended that tests on the ground were carried out firing of all the ammunition and others in flight with longer bursts. Two flights were also recommended to detect the possibility of ignition of gases at altitudes of up to 11,500 feet and between 130 and 350 knots.

The test report indicates that the aircraft was equipped with two guns and weapon pylons (one Aero 7A-1 ventral and two Aero 20A-1 under the wings), but without the machine guns, which may have been retired before the flight to France.

In addition, the installation of different weapons was tested on the ground, some already homologated by the French Service Technique Aeronautique, others in process and others not homologated. Among the homologated were the general-purpose

In the early 1980s, the AX-04 received a special paint scheme, used until the end of its operational life in 1986.

The AX-04 during tests of a Yaguareté rocket launcher, with six 105mm Pampero rockets.

Ground tests of the Martín Pescador missile on the AX-04 being performed in 1981 at the Centro de Experimentación y Lanzamiento de Proyectiles Autopropulsados (Self-Propelled Projectile Launch and Experimentation Centre) Chamical facilities of the Air Force.

First launch of a Martín Pescador missile from a Pucará, with the plane on the ground and the nosewheel on a small mount to raise the nose of the plane.

A-545 being used for tests of the Martín Pescador in 1982, with the intention of using the missile against British forces in the Malvinas/Falklands War.

bombs SAMP BD 10 of 125kg for training, SAMP model 25 of 250kg, Matra LR-F2 rocket launchers (six tubes of 68mm). Also required were universal adapters AUF-1 for these arms (an adapter for the electrical connection of the plane was needed to be built, since it had 10 connectors against 19 of the AUF-1 and voltage differences) and the Alkan 65 adapter for Lacroix Bavar practice bombs (it also needed an electrical adaptation). Among those in the homologation process were the Alkan Type 530 cartridge launcher for 40 cartridges of 74mm, BLG grenade launchers (later baptized Beluga, with 151 grenades of 1.2kg and 66mm in diameter), Durandal anti-runway bombs of 198kg and Matra LR-F8 rocket launchers, while the unapproved ones were 120kg SAMP and 250kg SAMP EU2 bombs, 125kg super-braked Matra and 36-tube Matra 155 rocket launchers for 68mm SNEB rockets.

The CEV recommended a flight test campaign after the adaptation of the AUF-1 pylon, which was not carried out, as well as the addition of the shot-by-shot option for launching rockets. Only the Alkan 530 was adopted by the FAA (although using MER and TER racks of US origin); the vFrench CEV report advised its use in six launchers, with Lacroix Type 314 anti-vehicle grenades, using the launch of five grenades per second, two containers at a time, at a speed of 240 knots, a height of 60 to 65 metres and a range (if fired sideways on TER or MER racks) of 240 to 250 metres, with a lateral inclination between 0° and 15° to increase or decrease the range of the cartridges. Thus, a coverage of 2,500 x 60 metres of surface was achieved.

Although there are no records to indicate that they had been painted on, a plan was made at the FMA to translate all the external inscriptions of the plane into French, for the tests to be carried out in France.

To replace the AX-04, the plane serialled A-561 was delivered to the Centro de Ensayos en Vuelo in 1986. The plane, which was delivered by the FMA with a camouflage pattern, as were all the planes readied during and shortly after the war, received for some time blue, white and red stripes on the rear part of the fuselage and the tail.

The AX-03 then flew to the Turbomeca factory at Pau-Uzein to test the engine and its performance on the IA-58, beginning the return to Argentina on 10 July, to arrive in Buenos Aires on 18 July.

On its return it was planned to transform it into the IA-58B prototype, although in an accident that occurred on 4 October, the AX-03 was completely destroyed, causing the death of Captain Schmidt.

Given the success of the demonstration at Le Bourget, in 1978 it was planned to send the Pucará to the Farnborough exhibition in the UK, for which the plane serialled A-519, which was being tested by the CEV before its delivery, was modified as it had been the AX-03 for the crossing of the Atlantic. On 18 August it departed with the serial A-19 and manned by Major Carlos Digier and First Lieutenant Germán Spika, supported by the Hercules serial TC-61 and after a successful exhibition between 3 and 10 September, returned on the 20th of that month to Córdoba.

Testing and new versions

In 1979 the AX-01 stopped flying and was used for static displays, being decommissioned in October 1980. Furthermore, the test programme suffered a

The AX-04 with T-10 British-built rockets during tests. The rockets, received by the force with the Gloster Meteors, were never used operationally on the Pucará. (Photo FMA)

severe blow when on 1 June 1979 A-519, with CEV pilots Major Carlos Digier and Captain Germán Spika at the controls, crashed at Cerro Ancasti in Catamarca during tests of the Omega system, causing the death of both pilots. The Omega was planned for installation on the IA-58B, together with the meteorological radar, to take it to Le Bourget. In this way, the CEV had the AX-04 and the AX-05 delivered by the FMA on 14 May, as a prototype of the IA-58B. In addition, A-530 was commissioned to support the ongoing trials with the Pucará.

Other developments in 1981 were the installation of a Garrett cabin heater in A-530, a SEMCA in A-511 and a Hamilton Standard in A-520 to evaluate them and thus improve the comfort of the pilots. This idea was shelved in 1988 and taken up again in 1995 on A-584. A Crossor IFF transponder and later a Simens SIT-4211 were also evaluated, although neither was adopted due to lack of budget.

Finally, the study to install the 'Martín Pescador' short-range, air-surface, radio-guided missile developed by CITEFA (Centro de Investigaciones Técnicas de la Fuerzas Armadas, Centre for Technical Research of the Armed Forces) continued. This had a weight of 150kg, operating range between 2.2km and 9.2 km with a normal range of 6km, whose trajectory was covered in just 11 seconds. It had a 220mm diameter, a length of 3,000mm and a speed of Mach 2.3. The corresponding installation was done on the AX-04 and tests were carried out with successful results.

A-519, marked as A-19, at the FMA before departing for Farnborough in 1978. (Archive José Martínez)

These tests were also carried out on A-545 during the Malvinas/Falklands War, until it crashed in Flor de Oro, Santa Fe, on 2 July 1982. The missile system was never adopted by the Air Force, despite the fact that Naval Aviation had used it since 1973.

In 1983, studies were carried out to install the GGS Mk.IVE air-to-air sight, night sights and the possibility of equipping IX Brigada Aérea planes with Matra R550 Magic air-to-air missiles.

In July 1984, the two experimental vehicles used by the CEV were the AX-04 and the IA-66 serialled AX-06, but the second was decommissioned by the end of the year.

During 1986 A-561 was delivered by the FMA and sent to the CEV for weapons tests, because the AX-04 used for that purpose had gone into a main check that was never finished. Since then, A-561 has always been used by the CEV for different types of tests.

Chapter 6

Proposed Versions

As previously indicated, in 1969, engineer Héctor Ruiz developed a whole family of airplanes, not only based on the Pucará, but also including other projects. In November 1973, he presented the plan again, now including an IA-50 GII version with a pressurized cabin, called GIII, although the project proposed different variants: from one with a capacity slightly higher than that of the GII (for 14 passengers) to one for 25 passengers or about 3 tons of cargo. He also added the IA-60 project for an advanced training and attack jet, also developing a transonic attack aircraft. At the same time, he and Reimar Horten worked on the redesign of their training aircraft proposal, now with smaller dimensions.

Observation and light transport twin jet

Within his 1969 aircraft family proposal, Héctor Ruiz developed a project for an entire family of aircraft based on the Pucará, but in most cases changing the turboprops for two Turbomeca Astafan I turbines, which shared some components of the combustion chamber with the Astazou turboprop, in order to increase the cruising speed and, above all, the service ceiling, to be able to fulfil the intended missions. At that time, Ruiz was working on the study of the pressurized GIII which, keeping the wing and tail, would carry a new fuselage with a pressurized cabin. Based on these studies, he proposed a version of the Pucará jet, but this time, with the wing and tail of the IA-58, and a new, wider fuselage, to carry a pressurized cabin for four seats, with the pilots in tandem and two passengers behind, accessing the cabin through a door and side ladder. In addition, he adopted the landing gear of the IA-50 GII. In total, it was planned to use 40 per cent of the components of the IA-58.

Of this proposal, as seen in the plans, he proposed two versions, where basically only the arrangement of the windows varied, in one case with a three-piece windshield and rectangular side windows, and in the other case with a design similar to the Learjet 21, both for the windshield and the side windows.

These proposals also modified the wing, which increased from 14.55 metres to 18.50 in wingspan, with a wing area of 35.65m^2. A maximum speed at sea level of 610km/h and of 670km/h at 40,000 feet was expected, with a cruising speed of

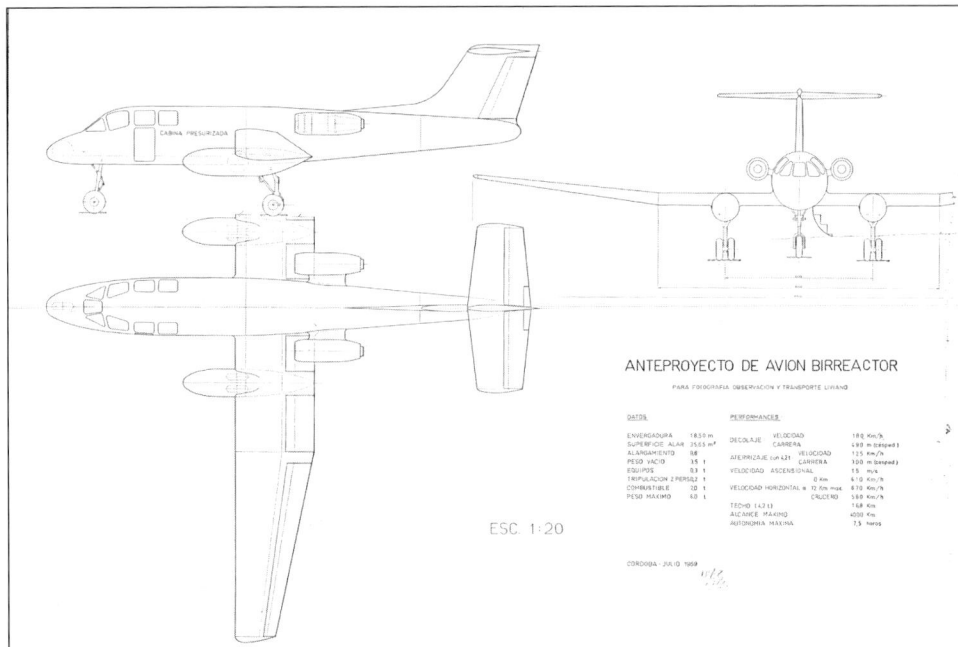

Plans for the initial concept of a light transport and observation airplane based on the Pucará. (Archive Eduardo Ruiz)

580km/h, a maximum ceiling of 55,000 feet, a range of 4,000 kilometres and an endurance of 7.5 hours.

Also, as seen in the document in which Ruiz presented his proposal for a family of airplanes, a version with more seats was planned, possibly for four or five passengers. As Ruiz explained in the work, the objective was to achieve an aircraft similar in performance to the Cesna Citation, but with a lower development cost by using components from the Pucará, the GII and the GIII project.

The plan proposed by Ruiz was to start development during 1976, to have a prototype ready in 1977 and another, in addition to a test cell, in 1978, but the project was not approved.

Assault transport

Under that name, as it appears in Ruiz's proposal for a family of aircraft, or under the name 'Anteproyecto Carguero' as it appears in the plans, the project was developed for a light transport aircraft, which retained only the Pucará's empennage, with a completely new fuselage and high wing, a side-by-side cabin for two pilots and a cargo hold with a rear ramp. Ruiz expected a market of at least 75 to 80 aircraft;

Plans of the light transport and observation plane but with different window design. (Archive Eduardo Ruiz)

he also planned to develop a passenger version to cover regional routes in the civil market.

The aircraft would have an overall length of 22.43 metres, a wingspan of 26.7 metres and a height of 8.12 metres. The cargo cabin would be 8 metres long and the fuselage would be 3.3 metres wide and 2.95 metres high. For its size, the aircraft was slightly larger than a CASA C-212, but with Astafan turbofans and a pressurized cabin, which would give it considerably better performance in terms of speed and service ceiling.

Jet trainer and tandem observation trainer

Another version was intended as a jet trainer, also with Astafan IV, to replace the Morane Saulnier MS-760 Paris in fighter pilot training. The landing gear was located in wing fairings that replaced the nacelles of the turboprops and the jet engines were located on both sides of the fuselage, slightly behind the wing. Preliminary estimated characteristics were an empty weight of 3,500kg, a maximum take-off weight of 6,000kg, a speed of Mach 0.73 or 750km/h at sea level, a cruise speed of 680km/h, a service ceiling of 44,000 feet, 7.5 hours endurance and a

Drawing by Héctor Ruiz of an idea of an executive jet using the wings and tail of the Pucará. Unfortunately, only this drawing was found in his archives. (Archive Eduardo Ruiz)

3,600-kilometre range, thanks to an internal fuel capacity of 2,000 litres. The dimensions were similar to those of the Pucará.

With the same design, he also proposed a version for photography and observation, without too many changes beyond the equipment for camera operation, although the project was abandoned without any studies on the location of the cameras.

Among the existing drawings are some with the engines located further forward, with the air intakes just behind the leading edge of the wing and the exhausts just behind the trailing edge, although these drawings are undated.

In the work plan submitted by Ruiz on 24 September 1969, he envisaged being able to produce a test glider in 1970. In November 1973, this idea, although it did not come to fruition, was again put forward by Ruiz in response to an operational request from the Air Force Air Operations Command, which called for the "preliminary study and preliminary design of an advanced training aircraft suitable for use in aero-tactical procedures". The objective was for the aircraft to replace the Morane Saulnier Paris for advanced training at the Military Aviation School and for the Curso de Estandarización de Procedimientos para Aviadores de Combate (CEPAC, Combat Aviator Procedures Standardization Course), where future fighter pilots completed the last stage of their training before moving on to operational units. In addition, it had to be capable of performing tactical support missions in combat operations in short- and medium-range missions, with the capacity to operate on unprepared runways of up to 1,000 metres, a maximum operational ceiling of no less than 26,000 feet with maximum payload, a flight range of 1,600 nautical miles and a radius of action in hi-lo-hi profile of 600 miles, capable of +7 and –3.5 g's. It was also intended to be a twin-engined, two-seater in tandem, capable of being flown by a single pilot, with 0-0 ejector seats, armoured and pressurized cabin. The fixed armament was to be two 30mm guns and two 7.62mm machine guns internally or in pods, plus five weapons pylons, with at least three of these capable of carrying supplementary tanks. The gunsight was to be of the predictor type, for air-to-air combat and with a depth deflection system for air-to-ground firing, while

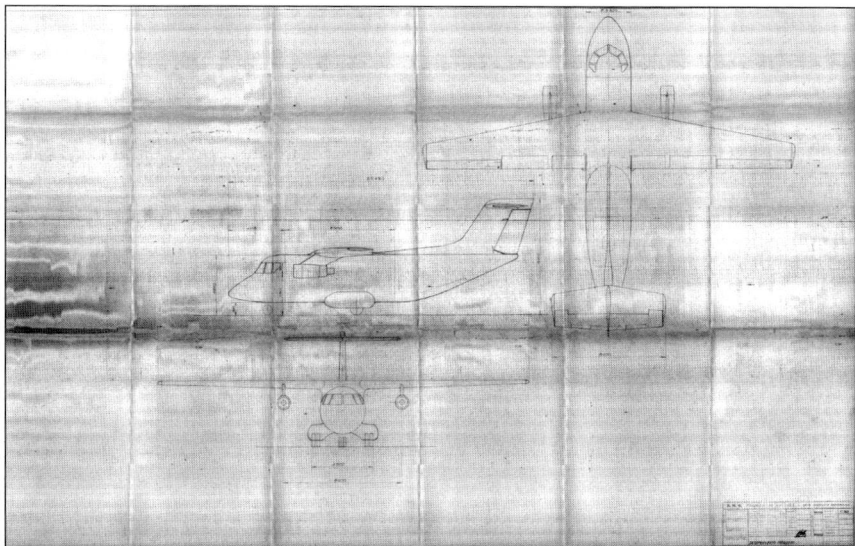

Plan of the assault transport proposed by Héctor Ruiz using the tail of the Pucará. (Archive Eduardo Ruiz)

it was to have mounts for up to four JATO rockets, without affecting the armament pylons. It had to have a flare launcher and be able to carry an air-to-air gun pod on the ventral pylon, as well as a photographic pod. The requirement was for a total of 100 units, to enter service between 1978 and 1980.

In the work plan proposed by Ruiz, the aim was to carry out the development during 1975 in order to have a prototype in 1976, hoping to be able to start series production in 1977. At the request of the FAA, the work was entrusted to Reimar Horten together with Dr José Pedro Tamagno and engineer Carlos Paoletti, who in March 1974 presented their proposal for a new version of the jet trainer. In addition to the change of engine, now for Astafan IVs of 1,200 kilograms of thrust each, with the aim of increasing manoeuvrability, they proposed to reduce the size of the aircraft. Part of the wing between the landing gear nacelle and the outer wing joint would be eliminated, as there was no tapering of the wing. Thus, it would have a wingspan of 11.94 metres instead of the original 14.5 metres, extending the inner wing flap to the outer wing and eliminating the outer flap. The engines were located on the sides of the fuselage as in the 1969 proposal, but the fuselage was shortened by 1.6 metres to 12.4 metres. These changes, however, meant only a 25 per cent alteration to the construction of the aircraft, allowing much of the existing tooling to be used.

It was planned to produce two versions, a two-seat training version with less armour and a single-seat attack version with more armour. The first was expected to weigh 584 kilograms less than the Pucará and the other 573 kilograms less than the IA-58A, making 3,287kg and 3,276kg, respectively, compared to 3,820kg for

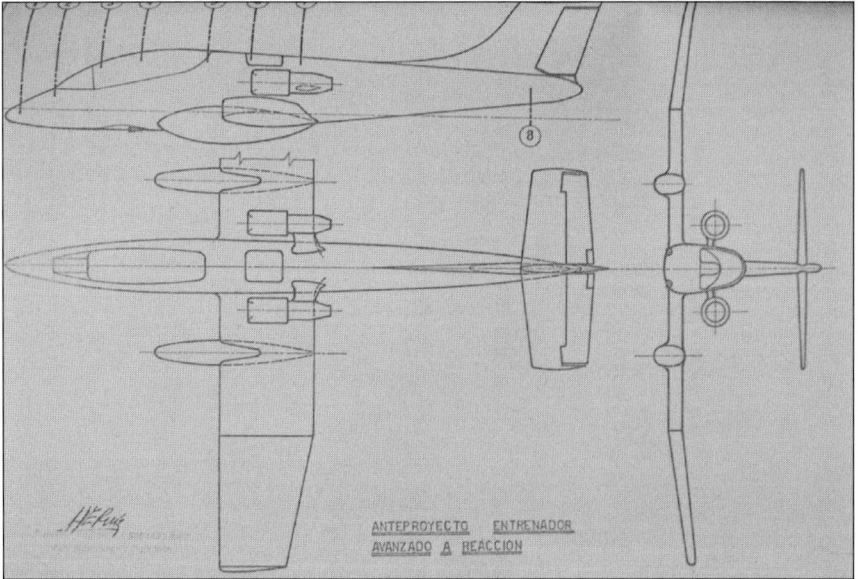

Plan of the jet trainer proposal with the engines installed slightly forward. (Archive Eduardo Ruiz)

the IA-58A. The armament capacity remained the same as the Pucará, with up to 1,560kg, as did the internal armament.

In order to maintain the critical Mach number of the airfoil at Mach 0.64, which had been set until studies could be carried out to achieve Mach 0.68 (with up to Mach 0.70 at certain angles of incidence), air brakes were added to the rear fuselage area.

Finally, the proposed characteristics did not convince the FAA, which was looking for an aircraft with higher performance. This led Ruiz to work on a new idea, also based on the Pucará, which received the name IA-60, described below.

IA-60

Convinced that the Pucará's wing created limitations to the performance of a larger jet, Ruiz began work on a new idea with more radical changes. As he explained in a memorandum dated November 1973, the idea was to make it a subsonic bomber, with a view to later supersonic development, the definitive design of which he hoped to start in 1978, to begin serial production in 1983. There he planned to develop a supersonic version between 1984 and 1988. In a 1974 paper Ruiz changed the dates, expecting to start work in 1976 and have the aircraft ready in 1981. He stated that the supersonic aircraft was expected to reach Mach 1.2 or

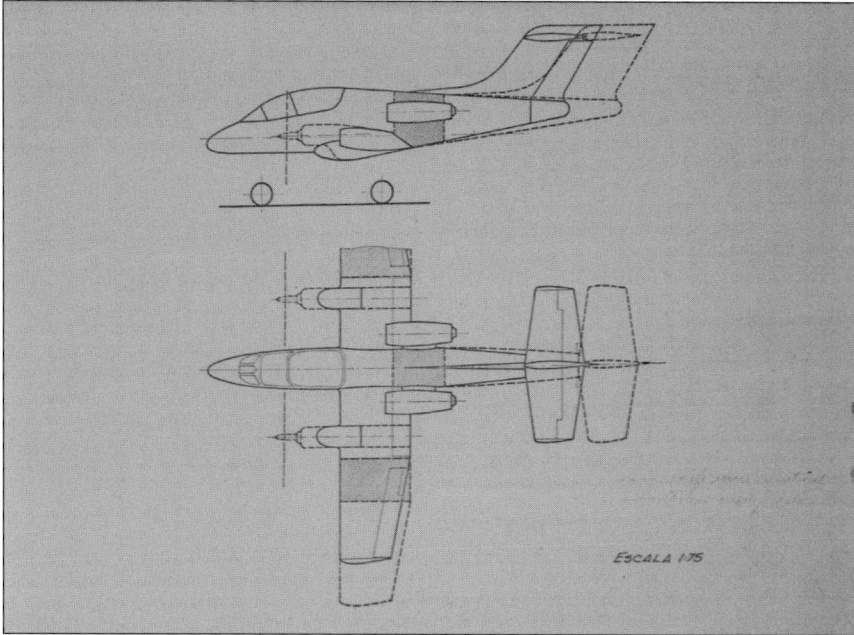

Comparison of the fuselage and wings of the Pucará with the smaller trainer proposed in 1974. (Archive Eduardo Ruiz)

about 1,400km/h, with a weapons capacity of 3,000 kilograms, by changing the planform and profile.

Keeping the fuselage and tail of the Pucará, Ruiz proposed the installation of a single Rolls-Royce/Turbomeca Adour Mk.102 turbofan with 7,305 pounds of take-off thrust, with afterburner, and 3,810 pounds of maximum continuous power. The engine at the time was used by the SEPECAT Jaguar and the Mitsubishi T-2, while the Adour Mk.151 version without afterburner was used by the Hawker Siddeley Hawk, which at the time was just starting its test programme. The engine exhaust would be at the rear of the fuselage, which was cut down from the original Pucará.

In this regard, Ruiz took into account the Hawk's cockpit design to compare it with the Pucará's in terms of visibility, finding that the Pucará had better downward vision in the forward position and sideways vision in both positions.

On the other hand, he decided to go for a completely new arrow wing, adding a fairing on each side of the fuselage, with the engine air intakes at the front and the space for the main landing gear further back, in a configuration similar to that of the IA-63 Pampa.

The planned aircraft, which received the designation IA-60, was intended not only to replace the A-4B and C Skyhawk in the Argentine Air Force, but also to serve as an advanced trainer, replacing the Morane Saulnier Paris.

Among the specifications detailed by Ruiz, the aircraft had to be able to operate from unpaved runways, with a maximum speed of no less than 525

Different weapon configurations planned for the smaller Pucará trainer. Note the plane was expected to have five pylons in total, with two under each wing. The maximum load capacity remained the same, with up to 1,560kg. (Archive Eduardo Ruiz)

Model of the first jet version proposed in 1969, of a smaller size. Note the plane is armed with rockets, as it was also proposed as a light attack aircraft. (Archive Eduardo Ruiz)

knots, approach speed of 110 to 120 knots, maximum dive speed of 540 knots, maximum real speed at 10,000 feet of 475 knots, climb time to 33,000 feet of less than 6 minutes and stall speed at 10,000 feet of 95 knots. The range in clean configuration and with internal fuel had to be greater than 1:40 hours, the take-off distance at sea level, over a 15-metre obstacle, on a grass runway, had to be equal to or less than 1,000 metres and of 1,500 metres at 5,400 feet of altitude. The service ceiling had to be greater than 40,000 feet and, at maximum load, greater than 30,000 feet. The radius of action on hi-lo-hi missions, with maximum load, was to be greater than 600 nautical miles (1,112km), while the range in ferry flight was to be at least 1,600 nautical miles (2,965km). The launchable payload was to be about 2,000 kilograms, it was expected to reach up to 6 g's in manoeuvres, the possibility of carrying a nose camera in a reconnaissance version and up to five extra tanks between four underwing and one ventral pylons.

An empty weight with the crew of 3,850kg or less, a maximum take-off weight of 8,350kg and a maximum landing weight of 5,550kg was envisaged. The operating temperature limits would be –20°C on the ground and –55°C in flight and up to +50°C.

Estimated service life of 4,000 hours and 5,500 take-offs/landings, with a usage of 200 hours per year, with a basic inspection every 100 hours, a structural inspection every two years and a major inspection every six years.

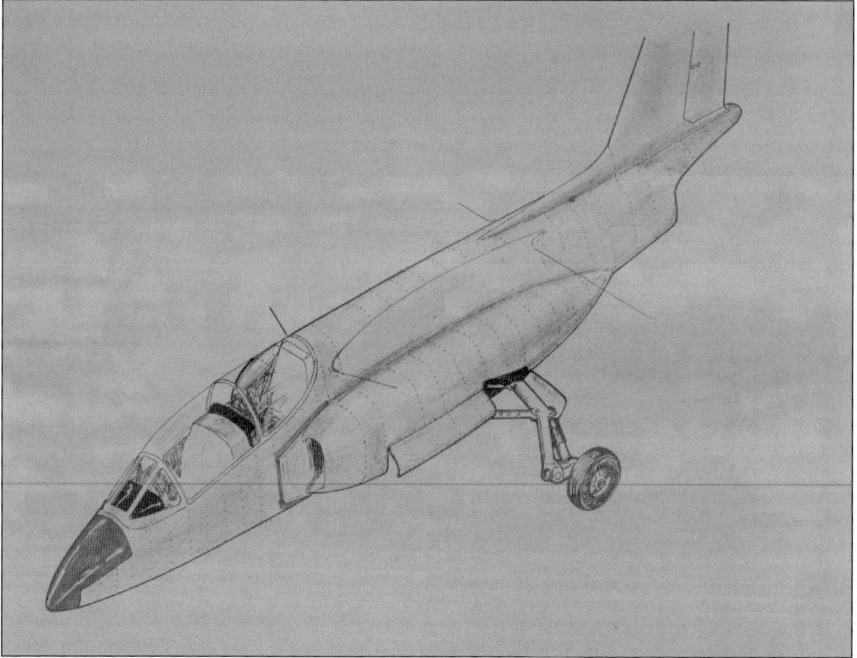

Drawing by Héctor Ruiz of the initial concept of the IA-60. The plane retains the basic Pucará fuselage and tail, with air intakes on the sides of the fuselage, new landing gear and a new wing. The exhaust is under the tail. (Archive Eduardo Ruiz)

The plan was to start engineering work in May 1975, have a mock-up ready in August of that year, a glider in February 1976, commissioning of the prototype in December of that year and first flight in February 1977.

By April 1975 Ruiz had substantially modified the original idea, with a shorter engine exhaust, air intakes directly below the wing and fuselage junction, a redesign of the rear fuselage, some modifications to the forward fuselage design, and a main landing gear with two wheels on each.

He also changed the wing design, working from the A-4 Skyhawk wing, as can be seen from the final design and sketches of the A-4 wing in his files together with the IA-60 documentation. However, the wing finally designed had less chord than that of the A-4, although it retained the initial concept. The installation was on top of the fuselage.

It also modified the design of the horizontal stabilizer, incorporating a 33° arrow, and by June 1975 the entire engine exhaust and the front of the fuselage were again modified, with a larger lower part, as it had been decided to equip it with two DEFA 552 30mm guns. This part was slightly modified again in October of that year. Also, during that year, it was decided to change the engine version to the Adour RT.172-26 or Mk.804, with 8,040lb of maximum thrust with afterburner or 5,320 without afterburner.

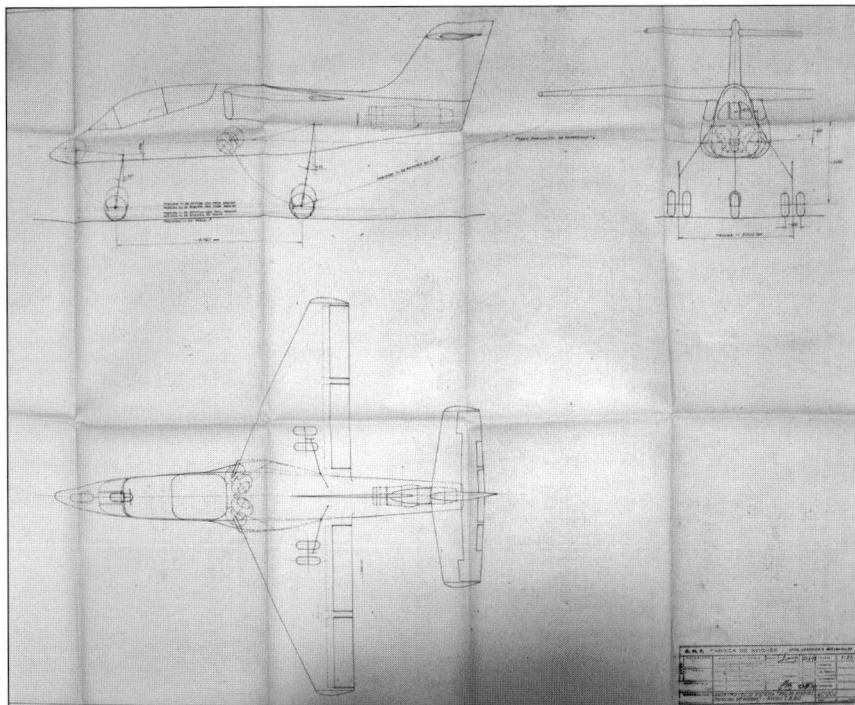

On this plan of April 1975 the IA-60 design received new air intakes; the landing gear was redesigned with two wheels on the main one for operations on unprepared airstrips. The engine exhaust was also modified. (Archive Eduardo Ruiz)

Meanwhile, in August 1975, the Air Force General Staff sent some considerations on the project, including several doubts about the design, such as the fact that, given the size of the aircraft, it was estimated that the actual weight could be higher than planned. In addition, the possibility of incorporating two extra Sidewinder-type missile pylons and that the belly mount could carry 2,000- or 4000lb bombs was also queried. The possibility of carrying a ventral photo pod on the right inner mount and machine-gun pods in the centre pylon or under the wings was also considered. There was consultation on the possibility of considering a carrier-borne version, with no afterburner and single-seat versions, the possibility of towing targets and the possibility of fitting an in-flight refuelling probe.

The next change, in November, was to the air intake, which was moved forward and lower, to the side of the co-pilot's seat, while retaining its rectangular shape. Two wind tunnel models were produced with this configuration, a 1:10 scale model for the subsonic tunnel and a smaller one, with metal wings and stabilizer, for the supersonic tunnel.

During the tests with the larger model, engineer Carlos Paoletti and Dr José P. Tamagno found that there was a loss of lift in the wingtip area, near the ailerons, for angles of attack between 13° and 20° and an appreciable instability at 28°,

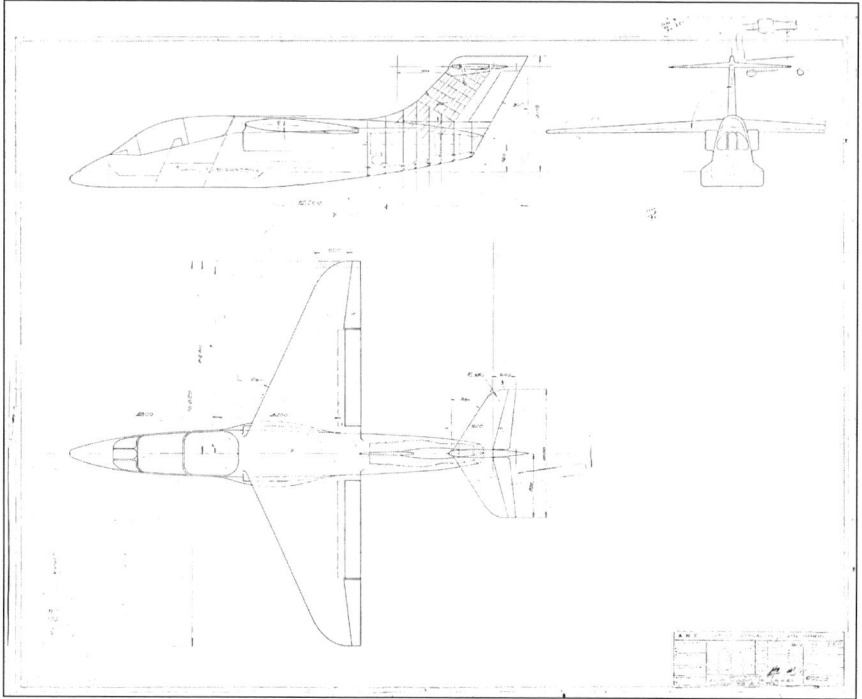

This scheme of the IA-60, of May 1975, shows many other changes, with a new wing based on the A-4 Skyhawk's, a new tailplane, new fairings for the main landing gear and different engine exhaust. (Archive Eduardo Ruiz)

attributable to the loss of effectiveness of the horizontal empennage. This led to the evaluation of different wing configurations. Finally, the problem was solved with a wing combining aerofoils and leading-edge extensions.*

During 1976 the programme progressed very slowly and in September, a report by IIAE advisor Rodolfo Freyer made several criticisms of the project, pointing out that since the I.Ae.33 Pulqui II no work had been done on an aircraft with speeds and characteristics like those expected in the IA-60, and much of the necessary knowledge had been lost. It also indicated the lack of experience in designing a structure such as the one proposed, with openings in the underside for the landing gear and engine installation. The report highlighted the lack of personnel to carry out the design development of the structure, for which there were only eight engineers and 10 design technicians.

The reality that became evident was that the factory did not have the capacity to develop a jet of such characteristics, as, since the end of the Pulqui II project at the

---

* 'The FMA IA-60' by Gonzalo Sebastián Rengel at www.zona-militar.com/2015/08/11/ fma-ia-60/

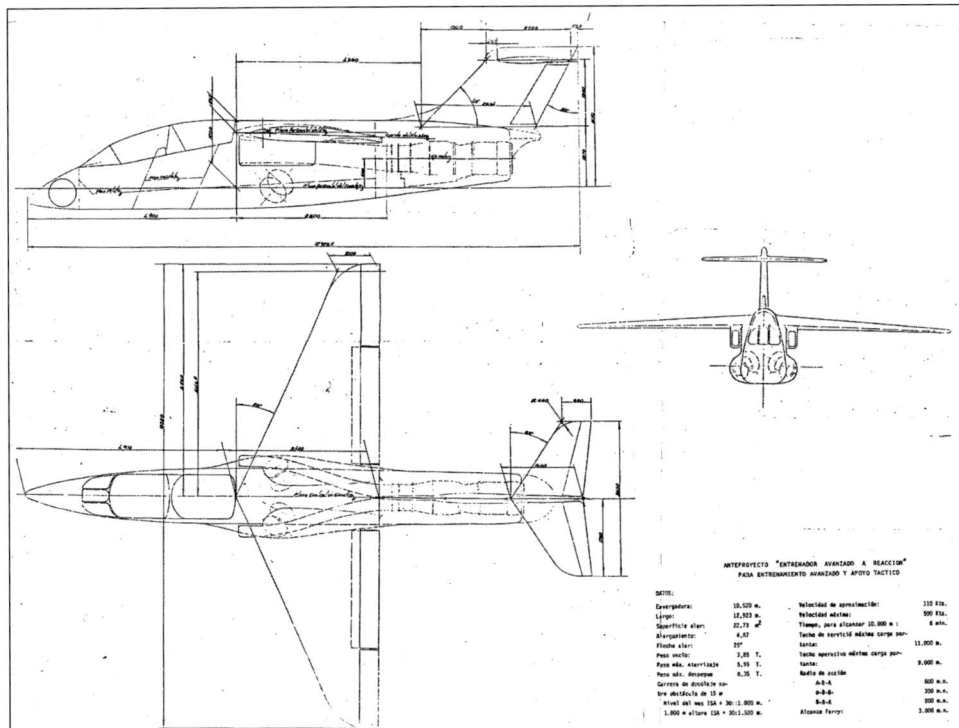

By July 1975, Ruiz had redesigned the fuselage. The nose was bigger as it was planned for 30mm guns instead of 20mm ones. Also, the engine exhaust was changed again. (Archive Eduardo Ruiz)

end of the 1950s, it had only worked on low-performance aircraft projects, which required less precision in manufacture and had less structural stress. This situation, plus the departure of engineer Ruiz from the factory when he was assigned to IV Air Brigade, led to the programme being halted at the end of 1976 and finally abandoned in 1979 when it was decided to work with Dornier for the development of the IA-63 Pampa, since the German company could contribute the knowledge that did not exist at the FMA.

The IA-67 Córdoba

While the FMA was working with Aero Falcon and Volpar Inc. on the development of the IA-66 Pucará, the two partner companies designed a multirole transport aircraft using as many common parts as possible with the IA-66, in order to use the tools and tooling from the Pucará production line, with the same Garrett engines as this version and thus reduce costs, while shortening the design time for the

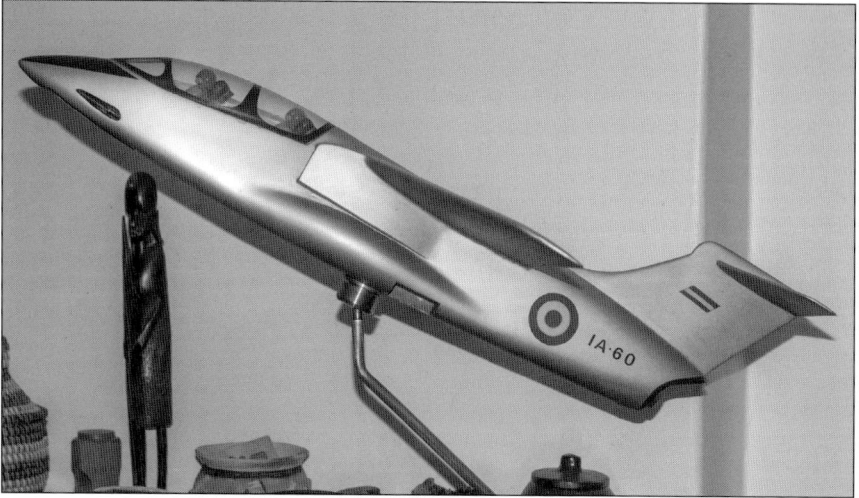

Model of the IA-60 preserved by Héctor Ruiz's family. (Photo Santiago Rivas)

new model. The preliminary study presented in September 1980 by Volpar was called IA-67 Córdoba, and envisaged the construction of three prototypes in just over a year at a cost of only $12 million, with a value for assembly line assembly 36 per cent lower than for a new model (costing $36 million against 50). It would replace the IA-50 G-II and DC-3/C-47 in the Argentine Air Force, as well as being offered to the civilian market and abroad.

The design specified an aircraft with a configuration similar to that adopted by the Israeli IAI Arava, with two tails, using the vertical stabilizer of the Pucará. It also incorporated the wing and engine nacelles of the IA-66. The work presented by Volpar specified a five-stage plan for development, the first of which was a pre-prototype study, a prototype construction programme, a production programme, a certification programme and a final marketing stage.

In response to the proposal, the FMA conducted an analysis and compared the model with the Arava, the CASA C-212, the Embraer Brasilia and the Shorts Skyvan, concluding that their performance was superior and costs were much lower. Volpar subsequently built models for wind tunnel testing and a single-tail version was considered. Although the project was progressing satisfactorily, the FMA decided to shelve it in favour of the ATL, although this too would later be cancelled.

Pucará 2000

As part of the extension contract of the concession that the Argentine government granted in 1999 to Lockheed Martin to operate the FMA, the development of the

Layout of the IA-67 Córdoba proposed by Volpar. (Archive Santiago Rivas)

Pucará 2000 was foreseen, which would consist of the modernization of the aircraft still in service. This plan initially envisaged the replacement of the engines with some variant of the Pratt & Whitney PT6, changes to the avionics, instruments and weapons systems, for which the addition of new pylons was studied. Budget cuts forced the suspension of the engine replacement, although some variants of the PT6 had already been studied, and the programme was finally cancelled at the end of 2001. This plan included the completion of the A-606, -607 and -608 as the first examples. These aircraft would require some minor structural changes that were incorporated into the operational aircraft over the years.

Chapter 7

Produced Variants

IA-58B

In 1976, development began on the IA-58B, which was a Pucará fitted with two 30mm DEFA 553 guns with 280 rounds each, in place of the 20mm Hispano Suiza. It would also have the addition of HF, IFF/SSR, DME, tactical VHF/FM, while the VOR/ILS, DF and VHF equipment were duplicated. Because the guns and ammunition took up more space, the belly of the fuselage had to be modified and the fuselage became bulkier.

During 1978, the production aircraft 025, originally serialled as A-525 and later re-serialled AX-05, was modified as the IA-58B prototype, starting flight tests on 15 March 1979 under the command of Major Carlos Digier.

That same year it was decided to present it at the Le Bourget exhibition, for which it was fitted with Omega navigation equipment and weather radar was planned to be installed to fly it alongside A-519, although the accident of the latter

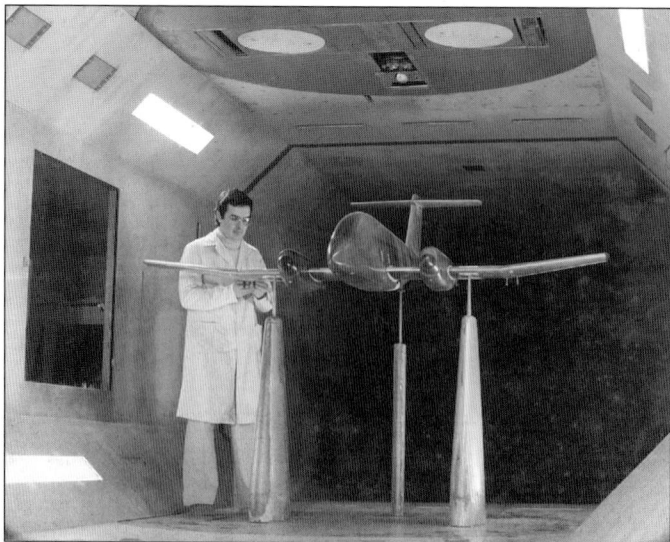

Testing the IA-58B in the wind tunnel. The model has Garrett engines.

Above: The IA-58B during tests at Cazaux, France, where modification evidenced some vibration problems when the guns were fired.

Right: IA-58B cockpit, with the Saab RGS-2 sight. (Photo CEV)

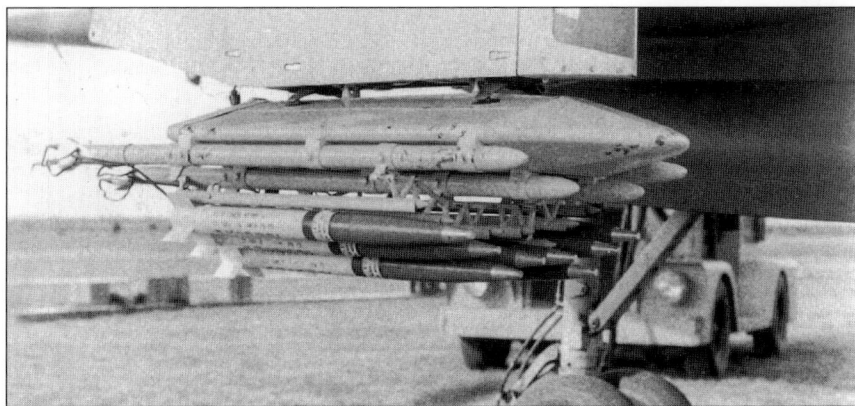

Mount for eight SCAR rockets on the pylon of the IA-58B. This rocket was used as a basis for the development of the IA-C-1057 Aspid 57mm rocket with folding fins by the FMA. (Photo CEV)

on 1 June of that year led to the AX-05 being sent disassembled in a C-130, where it was displayed on the ground between 8 and 17 June. It was then taken to Cazaux for testing of the guns, where results concluded that the guns generated vibrations when fired, although these did not significantly affect the aircraft's controllability, while there were problems with the cabin insulation, into which smoke from the firing of the guns entered. The test schedule would be completed in October 1980, on its return to Argentina after 150 hours of flight. In addition, the cruise speed was 5.5km/h less and the stall speed 115km/h with gear and flaps down.

Rollout of the IA-58C prototype in 1985. (Archive Eduardo Ruiz)

The IA-58C with Major Horacio Orefice at the controls during a test flight. (Archive Eduardo Ruiz)

Instrument panel of the IA-58C prototype.

During 1981, a study was made to install a Saab RGS-2 air-to-air and air-to-surface gunsight on the IA-58B, which was carried out shortly afterwards; it was also planned to install Garrett TPE-331-11U engines, for which tests were carried out in the wind tunnel. The idea of the re-engining was to facilitate marketing, since Venezuela, one of the most interested countries, demanded that the engines be replaced by others other than the Astazou, as they preferred power plants of US origin.

Initially it was thought that the aircraft from c/n 042 would be delivered as IA-58B with Garrett engines, but delays in the installation of these engines led to the decision that only aircraft from 060 would be delivered as IA-58B; in 1981 the programme was finally abandoned because the problems of vibration and smoke ingress in the cabin could not be solved, so this prototype was retired on 7 November 1982. In 1983, the idea was taken up again, but as a rear single-seater, maintaining the IA-58B designation, although it did not go beyond a proposal and was discarded shortly afterwards.

IA-58C

On 12 June 1979, engineer Alberto Yeraci, head of the FMA Fuselage Projects Section, presented a proposal for three possible single-seat variants of the Pucará, all designated IA-58C.

The aim was to achieve a more versatile and lighter aircraft, at a lower cost and whose design would also improve the flight characteristics of two-seater aircraft. Yeraci proposed two alternatives for the location of the pilot's seat, in the pilot's

The IA-58C when it was presented in 1984. Magic missiles were installed on the wing pylons, as the Martín Pescador locally built air-to-surface missile was shown with the plane as part of its weaponry.

The IA-58C prototype approaching to land at the FMA during one of its test flights under the command of Major Horacio Orefice. (Photo FMA)

position in the two-seater or in the co-pilot's position, as it could not be in an intermediate position due to the location of the propellers.

The first alternative, which he called IA-58CI, retained the two-seater configuration and only removed the seat and instruments from the rear seat, but incorporated a new canopy with individual openings for each pilot and a fixed section in the middle. The second, called IA-58CII, involved a single canopy for the pilot and a cover on the co-pilot's seat, so that this could be replaced to accommodate a canopy to revert to the two-seat configuration without major structural changes.

The third configuration, called IA-58CIII, envisaged installing the pilot's position in the rear position, with a cover on the original pilot's station, using the space for avionics or armament.

The first version reduced the weight by 156 kilograms and the cost by $58,500, the second by 171 kilograms and $65,050 and the third by 240 kilograms and $70,000, to which should be added a reduction of about 90 kilograms in the weight of the co-pilot and his equipment.

While the early versions had the advantage that they could be converted back to two-seaters, they did not allow the use of the rear space except for avionics, since the installation of a fuel tank there would lead to variations in the centring of the aircraft as the fuel was consumed. In addition, the elevated location made it difficult to make maintenance to whatever was installed there.

In the IA-58CIII version, however, while it was not possible to convert it back to a two-seater without structural changes, the forward space was considered ideal for installing armament or avionics, due to its easy accessibility. While this version would require some additional tooling, it could be produced along the same lines

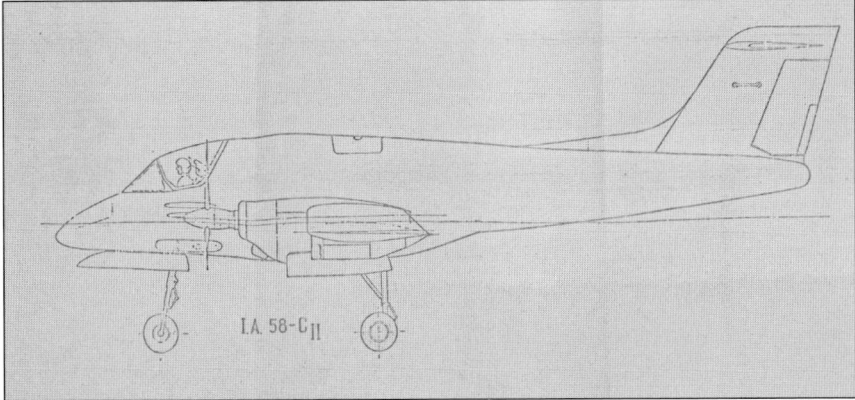

Proposal design of the IA-58CII, with one pilot in the forward position.

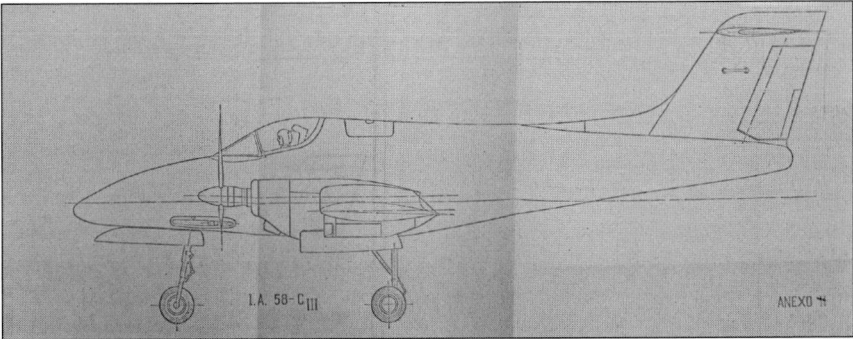

IA-58CIII configuration, finally chosen for the IA-58C but retaining the 20mm guns and adding a 30mm one.

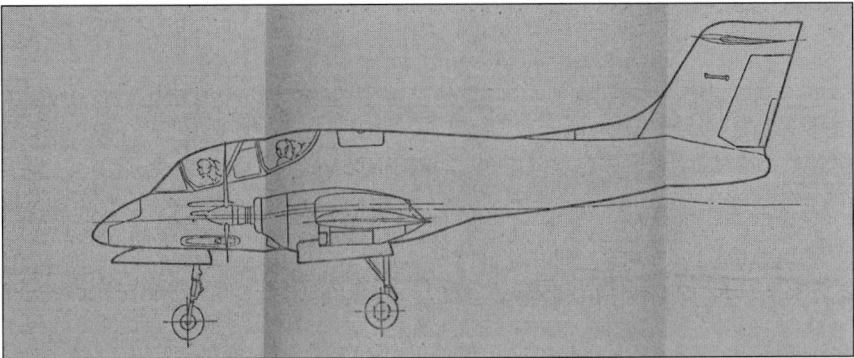

IA-58CI configuration, with a new canopy. The idea was that the second seat could be easily removed. The proposal also includes 30mm guns.

A-577 as the first IA-58D Pucará, seen at the 30th anniversary ceremony of the type, 2005. (Photo Santiago Rivas)

as the two-seaters. In addition, pressurization was considered feasible without structural changes, given the small size of the cabin.

Although the downward forward visibility angle was reduced with respect to the two-seater, it was maintained at 15°, which allowed the firing of all the intended weapons. The position of the propellers in front of the cockpit was considered not to significantly affect vision, although it could be a nuisance on night landings due to the reflection of the landing lights on the blades. This could be solved by painting the blades black or changing the position of the lights. For both this version and the IA-58CII, it was considered possible to redesign the fuselage fuel tank to increase its capacity.

An interesting aspect is that they were all planned with similar armament to the IA-58B, with two 30mm guns instead of the 20mm, although in the diagrams presented, the IA-58CIII is not shown with the machine guns.

Although the idea was not taken forward at that time, the South Atlantic war experience led to it being taken up again in 1983, when the AMC carried out preliminary feasibility studies for three versions of the Pucará, which appear in the factory's memoirs of that year as IA-58B rear single-seater, IA-58C rear single-seat with 30mm guns (basically the original IA-58CIII) and IA-58 Malvinas, front single-seat with cabin redesign and 30mm guns (based on the other two ideas from 1979).

The IA-58D serial A-524 seen on its base during the pre-*Cruzex* exercise in 2008, in preparation for the *Cruzex* exercise in Brazil. In the end, participation in that exercise was cancelled. (Photo Santiago Rivas)

From these ideas, the single-seat rear IA-58C was chosen, although it was decided to keep the 20mm guns, due to the problems encountered on the IA-58B, and adding a 30mm DEFA 553 gun above the nose, the ability to launch Matra Magic air-to-air and Martin Pescador radio-guided air-to-surface missiles. Airframe 043, originally to be built as IA-58B, was modified and publicly presented on 10 October 1984 as a mock-up of the IA-58C, known as Pucará Charlie.

In 1985 the aircraft was completed as the prototype of that model and re-serialled AX-06. A new installation was made for the French DEFA 30mm gun with 270 rounds, the two upper machine guns were removed, although the idea was to keep them, a Saab RGS2/A sight, coded altimeter, accelerometer and variometer were installed, and the first flight was made under the command of Major Horacio Oréfice on 30 December 1985.

During 1986 the AX-06 received Collins equipment such as an Electronic Horizontal Situation Indicator (EHSI), VHF (AM/FM) AN/ARC-186(V), VOR/ILS/MK VIR-32, ADF, DME, gyro unit and Photo Sonics camera. In addition, extra Kevlar armour was added to the cockpit sides, Garrett air conditioning, APU and cockpit instruments and commands were redistributed. It was planned to lengthen the exhausts to reduce the infrared signature and to fit the Pampa avionics. In addition, it was to receive Omega, HUD, chaff and flare launchers, radar warning receiver (RWR), IFF and radio altimeter, of which the wiring was laid, but never the equipment.

Up to 12 November 1986, 16 flights were completed, all under the command of Major Oréfice, of which the first five were for qualitative evaluation, from the

A-539, now as AX-06, with the original Garrett engine nacelles.

6th to the 9th for calibration, and the remaining flights were for air-to-air and air-to-ground firing in Río IV (Córdoba).

However, due to budget cuts, the programme was relegated in the following years and the aircraft flew a few more times, until in 1995 the AX-06 was finally retired, since the IA-58C programme had been cancelled and because it was not compatible with the rest of the aircraft in several aspects. After being completely cannibalized and remaining outdoors in the factory facilities until 2002, it was restored and transferred to the Aerospace Technology Museum of the Area de Material Río IV.

IA-58D

After the cancellation of the Pucará 2000 project, the Air Force decided in 2002 to move forward with the simpler IA-58D project, called 'Pucará Delta'. This consisted only of changing some cockpit instruments and radio navigation equipment, such as Collins VHF 22B, Marker CTL 22 and 32, VIR 32, RMI 30, Garmin 150 XL GPS and a Litton HSI. The plan was implemented during 2003, with the first aircraft being officially launched on 27 October 2003. A-590 was used to test the installation of the components, while A-577 was the first of the modernized series, which had some of its components changed at the request of the Air Force and was delivered on 2 June 2005, after a period of testing. The second IA-58D was A-524, followed by A-534, A-504, A-582 and A-580, although, due to the fact that the programme did not fully satisfy the force, and budget cuts, only A-577 received the complete instrumentation of the new version and the others received only the GPS, while the structure was prepared to receive the other equipment, which was never installed. In addition, the paint scheme was changed to air superiority grey, with no serials or insignia. Given the criticism of the programme, it was cancelled shortly afterwards.

IA-58G and IA-66

At the request of Venezuela, which was interested in purchasing 24 units, in 1981 the IA-58G project was developed, consisting of a Pucará with 1,000shp Garrett TPE-331-11-601W engines and Dowty Rotol R 316/4-82-F/6 four-blade propellers, on which the FMA, AeroFalcon of Argentina and Volpar Inc. of the United States worked together. Although it was initially planned to install these engines on the AX-05, in order not to slow down the trials with the 30mm guns, it was decided to modify A-539 after its tour in Iraq. The central wing was changed and the engine cowlings were redesigned to install the Garrett engines and the heating of the same brand. This work was carried out by Volpar and A-539 wing assembly had to be sent to the United States, where engineers Frank A. Nixon and A. Chana worked on it. On 20 August 1980, the wing assembly was delivered in the United States and sent back to Córdoba in an FAA Hercules. The installation of the wing with the new spars was carried out between 6 and 9 October and on the 13th the aircraft flew for the first time with Vice-Commodore José Videla at the controls. Shortly afterwards, on the 28th of that month, the aircraft was re-serialled AX-06 and received the new designation IA-66. Early trials indicated the need for some major changes to the wing, so the wing assembly of the aircraft c/n 042, in the process of manufacture, was sent to Volpar in 1981. There, a new engine mount and cowlings were made, returning to the country on 8 July 1981. At that time, after 37 test flights, the aircraft entered the workshop to receive the new wing, returning to testing on 29 September.

The original plan was to build 200 units in 1982 to be sold abroad as training and attack aircraft. The IA-66 had a minimum take-off run of 240 metres or 490 metres with a 15-metre obstacle, 86 metres assisted by JATOs and 155 metres with obstacles. Two pre-series aircraft began production and it was envisaged that four would be delivered to the Instituto Nacional de Aviación Civil (INAC, National Institute of Civil Aviation), based in Morón, Buenos Aires province, for advanced training, equipped with full instrumentation in the rear seat. Although the results were satisfactory, as the aircraft vibrated less (in 1981 they had received McCauley propellers), had lower noise levels and had autonomous starting, the performance was inferior in terms of fuel consumption and take-off and landing performance;

The IA-66 at the factory.

The IA-66 preparing to taxi from the factory tarmac. (Photo FMA)

The definitive fairings installed on the IA-66, with a more streamlined area on the lower part. (Archive Eduardo Ruiz)

there were some vibration problems and no fuel system for inverted flight, as well as the engines being heavier and the nacelles reducing the view to the sides. Added to this, the country's economic situation and the cancellation of the contract with Venezuela led to the project being abandoned and the AX-06 was retired in 1984, after flying for the last time in April of that year after 170 hours of testing, while the pre-series aircraft were completed as IA-58A.

The engines were sold to Lapa Airline for use in their Fairchild Metro, while the aircraft went to the FMA to return to its original configuration with a new wing, receiving the serial A-607, although it was never delivered back to the FAA. The engine nacelles remain abandoned at the factory.

IA-58E

Since the beginning of the new millennium, when Safran (formerly Turbomeca) stopped producing spare parts for the Astazou engines, various alternatives began to be analyzed. Initially, Safran's proposal to sell the rights and tooling to build the engines and their parts in Argentina was analyzed, but poor management by the Ministry of Defence led to the decision not to accept the offer.

Later, when in 2009 the factory returned to Argentine state ownership, now under the name Fábrica Argentina de Aviones Brigadier San Martín (FAdeA), a new plan was being developed to modernize the aircraft and install new engines, along the lines of the FAS 1160 programme developed since the beginning of the new millennium on the basis of the Pucará 2000 concept. The aim was to modernize a dozen aircraft to serve for up to 30 more years. This was possible because, despite their age, many airframes did not reach 1,000 hours flown and the biggest problem was the need to replace obsolescences.

Thus, the IA-58E version was born, starting with stage 1, which was communications, in which the UHF and HF were changed, two VHFs and a latest generation IFF were added, and the communications console in the cockpit was changed. The aircraft serialled A-568 was the prototype of this modification and carried out test flights from the end of 2009 and during 2010.

After the certification of this stage, A-568 returned to the factory workshop for the second stage, where the IA-58E project included the replacement of the navigation equipment (ADF, VOR, ILS, DME, etc.) by a Honeywell HG-764 EGIR (Embedded GPS/INS and Radar Altimeter) equipment for both inertial and GPS navigation plus radio altimeter (the same used in the Pampa II) installed in the aircraft, plus a Garmin 150 GPS.

To view the information from such equipment, the Centro de Investigación y Desarrollo de Tecnologías Aeronáuticas (CITeA, Centre for Research and Development of Aeronautical Technologies) of the FAA's Dirección General de Investigación y Desarrollo (General Directorate for Research and Development) and the National University of Río Cuarto developed a multifunction panel that allowed the representation of a mission generated in the Ground Mission Planning System, showing the aircraft's position in real time, as well as its height, speed and heading.

At that time, Captain Arturo Medici, from the Argentine Navy, had developed a mission planning and navigation software called CALNAV and worked with CITeA to solve some of the problems of this software, which was adopted by the FAA. Thus, they studied installing the CALNAV software on the Pucará, which ran on Windows, and which would work with the EGIR information.

The information was displayed superimposed on maps or charts. The system had a data input consisting of a USB port where the mission to be flown could be uploaded, then the crew could manipulate and represent the information coming from the aircraft's inertial control unit in different ways by interacting with the touch screen.

The equipment with the multifunction display was built in the Area de Material Río Cuarto, using aeronautical standards, and had, in addition to the screen, a computer and a Garmin GPS inside, a connector to communicate with the EGIR.

To evaluate the multifunction panel, a prototype was installed in the front seat of A-568, under the sight, for which the instrument panel was modified, with the

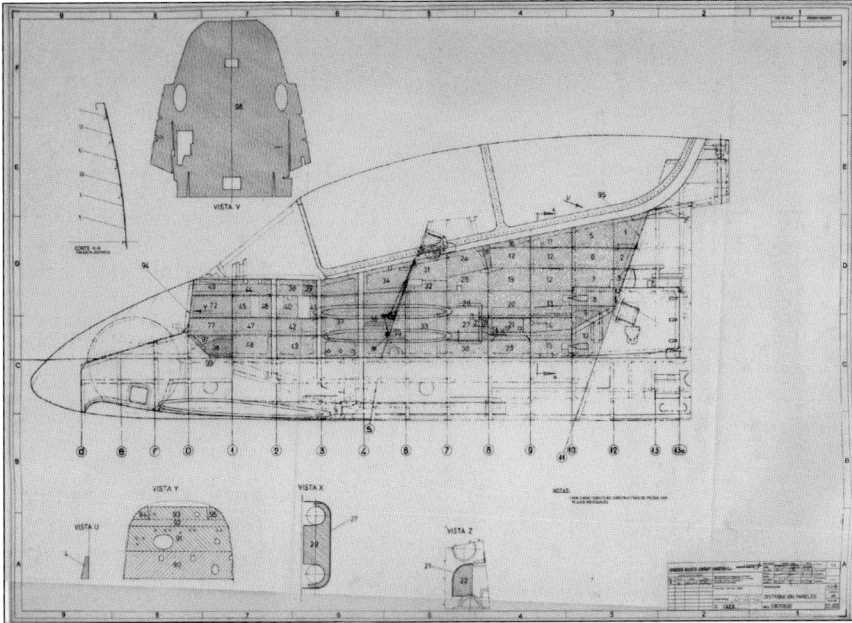

Blueprint with Kevlar plates planned as armour for the IA-58E version, to replace the original metal armour. This was not adopted on the modified planes.

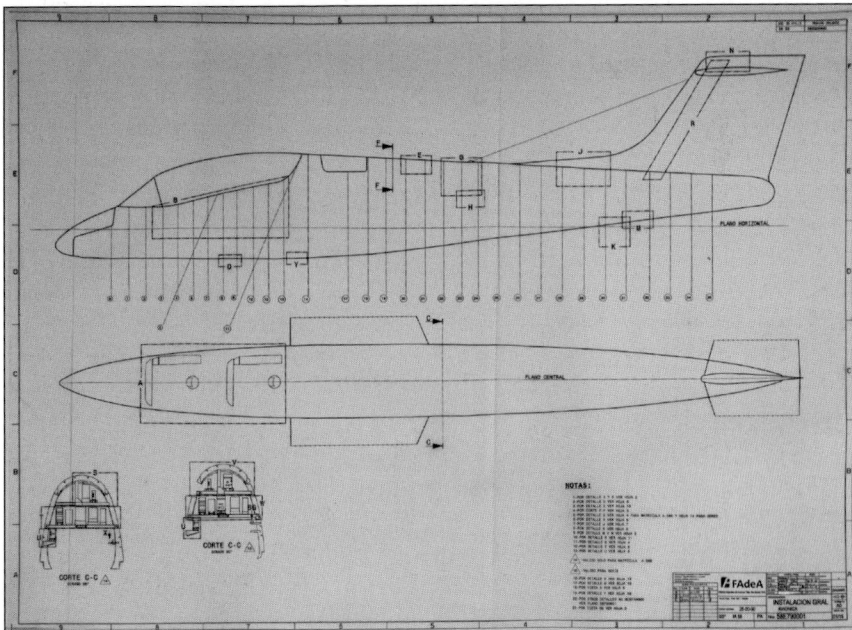

Avionics installation on the IA-58E.

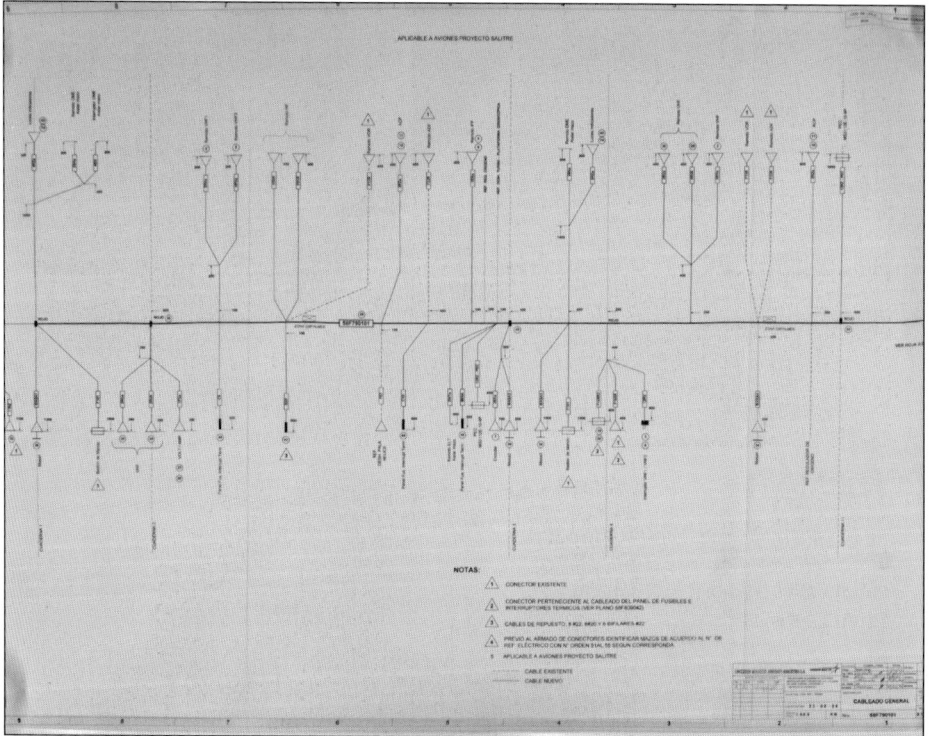

Above and below: Electrical layout for the proposed IA-58F version.

upper frame raised to allow the display to enter, modifying the faults light panel, which went from being in two parts to one, with all the lights together and in a different position from other aircraft, which caused concern to the pilots, as the aircraft was different from others.

The aircraft also received new camouflage in 2012 in three tones of green, with a grey belly, which set it apart from the rest. A-568 was also fitted with an Electronic Attitude Director Indicator (EADI) and Electronic Horizontal Situation Indicator (EHSI) in the central part of the panel, while the speedometer, altimeter and variometer remained analogue. In addition, the fuel quantity and flow indicators

Above: A-568 flying on 17 July 2010, during tests of the IA-58E modification. (Photo Santiago Rivas)

Right: View of the A-568 cockpit with the multifunction display. Below are the EADI (above) and the EHSI (below). (Photo FAA)

A-568 seen on August 2017 at the taxiway of the Military Aviation School in Córdoba that links the school with the FAdeA factory, shortly before the plane was returned to III Brigada Aérea. (Photo Santiago Rivas)

were changed to digital, but were cumbersome to use; it received a new oxygen system. The aircraft returned to flight in June 2015 after also receiving the new instrument panel with the multifunction display.

A first flight was made, in which the equipment performed well, including a climb to 20,000 feet to see if the capacitors of the multifunction display withstood the low pressure and there were no problems.

Subsequently, in 2016, it was decided to change the LCD screen for an LED screen, with lower power consumption, less weight and size and better performance, which allowed a saving in space in the box containing all the equipment.

The results were satisfactory and it was decided to build a pre-series of eight; however, when the system was operationally evaluated it was discarded after a few flights, as it did not meet the operational requirements, the software had problems and the visual interface was rather primitive. It was considered that it needed to evolve before it could be considered for operational use.

This project also contemplated a third stage, in which it was planned to change the engine and a HUD with a multifunction display similar to those used in the Pampa II. Although it was not planned to install equipment such as RWR, all-weather capability, chaff and flares, it was planned to add Kevlar and high-impact ceramic armour in the cockpit area, replacing the original 4130 aeronautical steel, as well as adding it to the engine nacelles, but this idea was abandoned.

For the engines, the Honeywell TPE-331 and versions of the Pratt & Whitney PT-6 with the same power as the Astazou were evaluated to minimize modification to the aircraft. The plan was for all three stages to be completed in 2012 and to begin re-engining the aircraft in service in 2013.

Thus, although A-524, A-571, A-575, A-580, A-582, A-583, A-585 and A-588 aircraft were modified with new communications equipment, they did not receive the modifications of the second stage, so A-568 remained different from the rest, returning to III Air Brigade at the end of 2017. A-551, -567, -584, -592 and -595 aircraft were to be modified but their work was cancelled.

IA-58F

For the Argentine Air Force's participation in Exercise *Salitre 2009* in Chile, for which the force raised the possibility of deploying Pucarás with some communications equipment upgrades, and given that there was neither time nor funds to quickly upgrade the aircraft with the scheme proposed for the IA-58E version, in 2009, before the factory was returned to the state, a simplified communications modernization version was proposed, which was called IA-58F. However, since it would not be in time to have the aircraft ready for the exercise, only A-4AR Fightinghawks were sent, the project was cancelled and it was decided to go ahead with the IA-58E.

The Pucará Fénix seen over the Dique del Molino dam during the first air-to-air photo shoot. The bigger engine nacelles are evident. (Photo Santiago Rivas)

New modernizations planned

At FIDAE 2010, the manager of FAdeA's Pampa line, Gualberto Natali, when asked whether the possibility of remanufacturing the Pucará was being considered, replied that yes, but only after the modernization was completed,

> because today there is no aircraft of this type and there is a need for it. There is talk of a Super Pucará, which would mean reopening the production of the Pucará, but with techniques that are 40 years more advanced. The Pucará has a lot of welding, both spot and cord welding, all the welded parts would be redesigned; we are already redesigning many parts and making them by numerical control. Some of this is being applied to modernization.

At the time, the aim with the modernization was to recover 30 aircraft to fly until around 2040, although initially only 16 were to be re-engined, due to the limited budget. In addition, an offer was made to modernize the Uruguayan aircraft, but this was not successful.

With the development of the IA-63 Pampa III, during 2015 and 2016 it was proposed to modernize the Pucará cockpits by installing the systems of that version, provided by Elbit Systems, with a full glass cockpit with three 5 x 7-inch screens, mission computer, INS, datalink, upfront control panel and HUD, but after some discussions with Elbit this was also dropped. A mock-up of the HUD and upfront control panel was obtained, but one of the problems was that the instrument panels of the Pucará were too small for the displays and the HUD did not permit appropriate ergonomics for a comfortable and safe cockpit, so a total redesign of the panels was necessary. Another HUD was considered, but it implied a higher cost and the fact that there was no compatibility between the Pampa and the Pucará.

IA-58H Pucará Fénix

In 2012, the selection of the new engines that would equip the aircraft was made, firstly prioritizing the Honeywell TPE-33 (returning to something similar to the IA-66 project) but the company's management decided to opt for the Pratt & Whitney PT-6A-62, despite the fact that the technical department had recommended going for the Honeywell. The reason given was that the PT-6A was a more widespread engine in Argentina, which made it easier to obtain spare parts.

A-561 aircraft, which was still in service with the Flight Test Centre, was modified to fit the new engines. Its wing was sent to Israel in December 2013, where IAI carried out the design and the new nacelles, and the work was completed in March 2015. Once sent back to Argentina, the wing was installed and on 24 November 2015, the aircraft, now serialled AX-561, made its first flight with the new designation IA-58H Pucará 2. In addition, some obsolete systems were replaced, such as the fuel, hydraulic, oxygen and pneumatic systems, among others.

The installation of these engines entailed a few problems, because the aircraft was not built in series and each one had some differences, making the modification very complicated. In addition, the nacelles were larger, reducing the view to the sides, the side exhausts caused problems to the fuselage due to heat, and the four-bladed Hartzell propellers had no reversible pitch for braking.

These criticisms and the high cost of the project (some $45 million was spent on the modification) led to the decision in 2016 to halt work, although in June of that year the AX-561 received an air data probe in its nose, with which it resumed test flights. After a few flights, it took off again in early 2017, and flew for a short time before the programme was cancelled.

In any case, flights with the prototype were resumed in July 2018, with a plan for some additional testing for 35 flight hours, but were suspended shortly thereafter without achieving those hours.

A-568 after being modified as the prototype of the IA-58H, initially called Pucará II. (Photo Santiago Rivas)

The IA-58H, christened Pucará Fénix in 2019, with new paint and serial, now as OV-X-501. A mock-up of the FixView POA observation pod was shown on 10 August 2019 at the Military Aviation School, during the Argentine Air Force Day ceremony. (Photo Santiago Rivas)

Meanwhile, a group of retired Argentine Air Force officers were looking at alternatives to modernize the Pucará, including the possibility of returning to the Honeywell engine installation, but their proposal, submitted in late April 2019, was rejected due to the time delay in having the new modification certified, while the original aircraft were to be retired in six months thereafter.

At the same time, the force's UAV programme was making slow progress on the development of the MALE Vigía UAV, but one of its payloads, the FixView FV-300 gyro-stabilized multi-sensor turret, had already been developed and was operational on civil helicopters; the company had already developed some years ago the idea of installing the turret on a pod to be used by aircraft such as the Pucará. As the force had already contracted FixView for the UAV programme, there was a pressing need for increased border control, and as the IA-58H was available, the idea arose to use the work already done for the UAV and the FixView concept with the pod to modify the aircraft for the surveillance role. The Pucará's endurance of up to eight hours made it a good platform for such a mission.

The Argentine Air Force requested the development of the reversible pitch of the propellers, which became available in early August 2019 and during 2020 certification work began, although it was delayed by the COVID-19 pandemic: in early 2022 FAdeA was still awaiting a visit from Hartzell personnel to complete the work. Although the engines are less powerful than the Astazou, the four-bladed propellers compensate for this and the aircraft performs similarly to the originals, although it has certain limitations in high-altitude flight and a slower response, as it is not a direct turbine.

The Argentine Air Force decided to convert four additional aircraft, with the possibility of adding more if the budget allows. Although there had been plans to remove their internal armament, it was finally decided to keep it and for the aircraft to maintain their attack capability. In November 2020, the Chief of the General Staff of the FAA, Brigadier Xavier Isaac, explained that he aimed to modify a second series of Pucará Fénix to be based on BAM Mar del Plata and to be used for maritime patrol missions.

On the other hand, in order to modernize the cockpit, it was decided to incorporate Garmin avionics for a full glass cockpit only in the front cockpit, which was expected to be certified in 2022, while the rear cockpit would have the pod screen instead of the instruments and a joystick to control the pod sensors. For now, the aircraft assigned to be converted into Pucará Fénix, in addition to the prototype, are the 571, 582 and 585. A-568 was sent to the factory but, as is different from the others, was not as yet included on the plans.

Pod de Observación Aérea

In June 2019, FixView began work on the production of what they called the Pod de Observación Aérea (POA), which includes an FV-300 turret, batteries for seven hours of operation and a wireless connection, weighing 50 kilograms. This means

The FixView POA pod developed for observation with a 360° ginball, batteries and wireless connection with the console on the cockpit, to facilitate installation. (Photo Santiago Rivas)

that the only modifications to the aircraft are the fittings to attach the display and the joystick to operate the turret from the rear cockpit. The display has a wireless connection to the pod and both the display and joystick can be easily installed, as they only need a 14-volt connection to the aircraft.

After the aircraft was displayed on 8 August 2019 during Air Force anniversary celebrations, with a mock-up of the pod, it was officially unveiled on 4 October with the pod operational, and with the new designation IA-58H Pucará Fénix and serial OVX-501 (received in June).

INVAP pods

Two new projects to increase the aircraft's capability were announced at the same ceremony in October 2019. One was a new pod developed by local company INVAP, with all the equipment of the POA but adding a synthetic aperture SLAR (Side Looking Airborne Radar), which was christened POD Inteligencia, Vigilancia y Reconocimiento – Radar Aerotransportado Banda X Argentino (ISR – RAXA, Intelligence, Surveillance and Reconnaissance – Argentine X-Band Airborne

Radar). As part of this project, the Pucará Fénix aircraft will receive a data link to send the information to the ground or another aircraft.

Thus, it was decided to integrate the FV-300 turret into the new pod, which would initially use a 318-litre fuel tank, to which the turret, radar antennas and equipment would be fitted. With the FAA's approval of the project, the company produced the MET-1 (Technology Evaluation Model), which only carries the radar antenna on one side. Evaluation flights began on 6 May 2021, using A-582 aircraft. The flights continued until the end of that month and then additional flights were carried out at the beginning of July, thus completing the first stage of the project. With these results, INVAP planned to produce the MET-2 in 2022, which would no longer use a 318-litre tank, since it was found that it was not easy to install the equipment in it, but a specific structure would be designed for the pod. The MET-2 would have the antennas on both sides and the FV-300, which would define the final configuration, to be evaluated in the MET-3, expected in 2023, would be the final product.

The concept of a communications intelligence pod, using the container of an LAU-60 rocket launcher, was also unveiled, but is at a very early stage of development by INVAP.

Pucará A-582 seen on 18 May 2021 during a test flight of the MET-1 version of the INVAP pod.

PART 2

OPERATIONAL HISTORY IN ARGENTINA

Chapter 8

Entry Into Service and Baptism of Fire

On 20 August 1975, A-501 and A-502, completed in July, were officially delivered. Their completion, although scheduled for January of that year, was delayed because the brake assemblies were not delivered in time. As soon as they were received, they were taken to BAM Reconquista by Major Ignes Rosset and Captain Igarzábal, where they were to form Escuadrón I de Ataque. Two days earlier, Ignes Rosset had already visited the unit with A-501, and then returned to Córdoba, in what was the first operation of a Pucará in Reconquista, which was repeated on the 18th by First Lieutenant Hugo Palaver. On 26 August the operational evaluation of the model by the pilots who had been trained the previous year began, with Lieutenants Carlos Filippi, Ricardo Grünert, Carlos Varela, José Vacarezza and Roberto Vila being received at the unit to train on the model, although the lack of available aircraft and the actions against the guerrillas carried out between November and December, described below, meant that it was not until January 1976 that they began their training in the Pucará. Meanwhile, serial construction of the other

Production of the IA-58A Pucará in FMA Hangar 90. This hangar is dedicated to the main production and final assembly of aircraft. (Photo FMA)

The AX-03 and A-505 flying together near the FMA in 1976. A-505 was used briefly to support the tests programme, between June and November 1976, before being delivered to the Argentine Air Force. (Photo FMA)

The first planes were delivered with the wingtips and stabilizers painted in red. A-502 was delivered in 1975 but destroyed by the SAS on 15 May 1982 at Borbón/Pebble Island, during the South Atlantic War. (Photo FMA)

aircraft continued, with A-503 being received on 15 October 1975 and A-504 being completed in November of the same year.

As the current Commodore (Retd.) Carlos Horacio Argente, then part of the unit's technical team, explains, the delivery of the first two aircraft

> did not come with spare parts, equipment, etc. The tools provided by Turbomeca's French consultant seconded to provide technical assistance to the unit were used to carry out even the smallest of interventions on the engines. The toolboxes purchased by the Air Force logistics took more than two years to arrive at their destination. The technical documentation for the Martin Baker ejection seat was not received either. At Reconquista, the only thing that was done was to periodically ventilate the parachutes and reassemble them.

For his part, Commodore (Retd.) Roberto Vila explains:

> the plane was new, everything was checked through the computers, but the real test had to be done. The plane flies, it has such endurance with so many bombs, everything, we were the ones who placed the bombs, how it behaved, we did everything ourselves with all kinds of weapons. That's how we started, then we got better and better at it and started to get the most out of it.

When the Pucará arrived at Reconquista, the unit had no firing range, so they had to use an island owned by the Air Force on the Paraná River until 1977 when the Garabato firing range was opened a few kilometres from the base. As Argente explained, in the first test firings with the 20mm guns, they observed that the planes returned with marks from the ammunition casings and also from friction from the projectiles from the left-hand gun. While they initially assumed that this was caused by firing while turning, a test sortie was conducted in which one round damaged the front landing gear cover, which in turn damaged the wheel, which burst on landing. While adjusting the guns to resolve this point, the problem was encountered that, when the casings were ejected, they hit the aircraft and caused damage to the antennae and other parts, which was resolved by installing a duct for each gun that allowed the casings to be diverted from the fuselage as they were ejected.

Baptism of fire

Meanwhile, in 1974, one of the most important guerrilla groups operating in Argentina, the Ejército Revolucionario del Pueblo (ERP, People's Revolutionary Army), began preparing guerrilla activities in the southwestern part of the province of Tucumán, a mountainous and jungle-like area ideal for guerrilla warfare, creating

Flight line at Reconquista in the 1970s, including A-501, -502 and -505. The planes are armed with AN-M57 bombs, which were used briefly during early operations.

the Ramón Rosa Giménez Bush Company as a front. Their plan was to take control of the northwest of the country and thus try to obtain international recognition as a belligerent force, to gain parliamentary representation and to contest the constitutional government for total control of the country. When President Perón died on 1 July of that year, his wife and vice-president, María Estela Martínez, took power in the midst of deep economic and political crisis, with countless attacks and terrorist acts by the ERP which was gaining strength in Tucumán.

Fully aware of the guerrilla activity in that province, which was in the first phase of guerrilla warfare, i.e. the reconnaissance of the terrain and the organization of its forces, it was decided that swift action had to be taken before the aforementioned bush company could gain a foothold. This situation led the president to sign secret decree no. 261 on 5 February 1975 ordering the security forces to 'neutralize and/or annihilate the actions of subversive elements operating in the province of Tucumán' through Operation *Independencia*.

At first, the Air Force limited itself to logistical support tasks, while Operation *Orion* was planned for December of that year, which consisted of close air support missions by the force's various fighter planes, with the aim of evaluating them and determining the form of operation during Phase IV Consolidation of Operation *Independencia*, to be carried out during 1976. The first three phases of the action against the guerrillas had consisted of reconnoitring the area, assessing the guerrillas' capabilities and forces, and beginning the encirclement of the guerrillas to prevent them from expanding their area of operations, which had been limited to an area southwest of the city of Tucumán, in the heart of a mountainous and wooded

A-505 operating on the highway between the cities of Córdoba and Villa Carlos Paz, which was under construction when the tests were done by this plane and the AX-03 in 1976. (Photos FMA)

area. The plan was now to prepare the ground to take the fight to the guerrillas in the area where they operated and put an end to their activities, which was expected to take place during the course of 1976.

In early November, the armament of the Pucará was evaluated to determine the feasibility of its operation in that theatre of operations, which is why A-501, -502 and -503 were deployed to operate alongside the AX-03 from the Escuela de Aviación Militar (EAM), next to the FMA, to be supported by the latter during attack

A-502, -504, -508 and -510 flying low near Reconquista in October 1977. A-504 and A-510 had a mid-air collision on 8 March 1978 and the former was lost.

missions. According to Bam Reconquista's memoirs, the aircraft were deployed to the EAM on 18 November and over the following days until 10 December they carried out target practice with locally manufactured PG-125 125kg fragmentation bombs, 70mm rockets and internal armament, with satisfactory results, and the system was considered ready to enter combat. On the 11th the four aircraft had their baptism of fire, attacking in sections with fragmentation bombs targets previously marked with smoke rockets by an FMA/ Beech B-45 Mentor of the EAM's Grupo Aéreo Escuela (planes serialled E-060 and -062 were used), at the request of the Army ground forces that were engaged in combat with the guerrillas. Along with the Pucará, the BAC Canberra from II Air Brigade, A-4Bs from V Brigade and FMA/Morane Saulnier MS-760 Paris from the EAM, as well as an F-86F Sabre from IV Brigade also took part. The operational activities by the Pucará were repeated on the 12th and every day 14 to 17 December, when they withdrew to their base after completing their mission. In this way, the Pucará's first operation for the FAA was in real combat, without having previously carried out any exercises. As Commodore Argente recalls:

> it was operated from the runway side, with a 250lb bomb at each wing station. Ground attack missions were carried out in a sector of the Tucuman bush. A Mentor aircraft in flight served as a forward air controller, indicating the correct drop zone. At that time, the unit did not have triple ejector racks [TERs] or multiple ejector racks [MERs].

Finally, the weakening of the guerrilla groups during Phase III *Progressive Harassment*, mainly due to the continual combat failures of the ERP's bush company in large-scale encounters such as Acheral and Famaillá, where they were defeated by inferior forces, meant that no further use of attack aviation

A-516 in front of Hangar 90. The plane was delivered on 31 December 1978 but was destroyed during the Malvinas/Falklands War.

was necessary. Also, the performance of the Air Force was a decisive element, as the guerrillas were given a demonstration of the firepower that could be used against them. After the coup d'état that overthrew the constitutional government on 24 March 1976, the subversives' actions gradually diminished until they were finally extinguished in 1980; but by 1976 guerrilla operations in Tucumán had been reduced to a minimum and by the end of that year the bush company had been destroyed.

On 18 December 1975, due to the political crisis the country was going through, a sector of the Air Force revolted at VII Air Brigade of Morón, in the suburbs of Buenos Aires, and the military sector of Jorge Newbery Airport, in the city of Buenos Aires, under the command of Brigadier Major Jesús Orlando Cappellini. While one of the objectives of the rebels, the replacement of the Commander-in-Chief of the Air Force, Brigadier-General Héctor Fautario, was achieved – he was replaced by Brigadier Orlando Ramón Agosti – they also demanded the resignation of the president. As negotiations continued with the intransigent rebels, on the 20th the three Pucará of the Escuadrón I de Ataque were deployed to II Air Brigade in Paraná, Entre Ríos, while Douglas A-4B Skyhawks were also deployed from V Air Brigade in Villa Reynolds. To force the rebels to surrender, an attack on the base was ordered on the 22nd, with orders to inflict minimal damage to intimidate them. While an A-4B dropped its bombs between the runway and taxiway, the Pucarás made passes firing their machine guns over the same area. After this, the rebels surrendered and the Pucarás returned to their base.

In January 1976, A-504, the first out of a total of nine planned for the year, was delivered, although it was not until 23 November that A-505 arrived due to budget cuts that slowed production. January also saw the start of the first training course for new pilots, with the four lieutenants assigned in August of the previous year.

A-529 before the war. The plane was deployed to BAM Malvinas and was damaged by the SAS at EAN Calderón on 15 May 1982.

A-530 at the FMA. The plane was finished in 1979 and used for tests at the CEV. It received a Garrett heating system in 1982 and was delivered to III Brigada Aérea in 1984. It had an accident in 1997 and was written off.

This year was also the first to see a serious accident, on 23 September, when A-503 crashed at VIII Air Brigade in Moreno, on the outskirts of Buenos Aires, while performing aerobatics at low altitude; it was completely destroyed, although its pilot, Captain Igarzábal, was unhurt. The aircraft had been deployed together with another to present it to various foreign attachés, for which it was replaced by the other aircraft, while another aircraft was displayed in one of the hangars with a full armament display. The Reconquista mechanics cannibalized A-503, and this lot (instruments, accessories, etc.) became the first stock available in the depot.

Also, shortly after its delivery, A-505 suffered an accident, although it was repaired. This last aircraft, before its delivery to the FAA, together with the AX-03, was used for the evaluation of its operational routes, on the highway from Córdoba to Villa Carlos Paz.

In 1977 the production line started up again thanks to a reorganization, delivering eight aircraft out of nine planned, up to A-512. However, only A-506, A-508 and A-510 were delivered to BAM Reconquista, the rest having to wait until 1978. By then the unit, with seven operational Pucarás, was structured into the Air Squadron with the 1° Escuadrilla Operativa, 2° Escuadrilla Instrucción, 3° Escuadrilla Instrucción and the Escuadrilla de Servicio with a Douglas C-47 and an Aerocommander 500U.

Between 30 March and 11 April, A-501, -502, -504 and -505 aircraft were deployed to the Military Aviation School to carry out their first firing exercise at La Cruz range, in the province of Córdoba, repeated between 9 and 19 June with the same aircraft. At the same time, A-506 was delivered by the FMA on the 10th.

Meanwhile, on 15 August, the first flypast outside the country was held when they flew over Asunción del Paraguay on the occasion of that city's anniversary.

A-518 was originally built for Mauritania and received their colours, serials and markings, but the contract was cancelled and the plane was delivered to the Argentine Air Force, wearing the desert camouflage for some time. It was used for a photo shoot armed with 125kg bombs and INC-220 napalm bombs.

A-518 with 125kg bombs and LAU-60 rocket launchers.

On 10 October, after participating in the 50th anniversary of the FMA in Córdoba, and until 19 October, the Pucará A-501, -502, -505, -506 and -508 flew to IV Air Brigade in Mendoza to perform air-to-ground firing at the Las Lajas range near the brigade, using bombs, rockets and guns. In these operations, the pilots would normally dive in from 6,500 to 10,000 feet above sea level, putting in a lot of g's on the way out, which caused structural damage to some aircraft, especially A-508, to which reinforcing had to be added.

From 3 to 9 November, the first deployment was made to the south of the country with aircraft A-501, -502, -504, -505, -506, -508 and -510, to the city of San Julián, in Santa Cruz, to train in Patagonia in the event of a possible conflict with Chile, due to the existing tension with that country over various border disputes, especially in the area of the Beagle Channel in Tierra del Fuego. The deployment was under command of Captain Kettle, and as Argente recalls:

> as a preliminary task, the engine oil was changed in all the aircraft. The flight took place between Reconquista, Comandante Espora Naval Air Base and San Julián. A French advisor accompanied the flight to verify the behaviour of the Astazou engines, which were experiencing some problems.

That year, First Lieutenant Ricardo Grünert, on a training flight, had to land in a field 80 kilometres from the base because he had run out of fuel. A board of inquiry determined that the aircraft's fuel quantity indicators were unreliable.

On 8 March 1978, A-504 and A-510 suffered a collision in flight over the Garabato Shooting Range, Santa Fe province, when the number 4, pilot First Lieutenant Carlos Fillipi hit the belly of the leader, Captain Kettle, with his propeller and had to eject. Kettle, in A-510, made an emergency landing, resulting in minor damage to the aircraft, which was later repaired.

A-542 was never delivered to the Argentine Force as it was sold to Uruguay to become FAU-220. Here it is seen with an array of weapons including 50kg and 125kg bombs, INC-50, INC-100 and INC-220 napalm bombs, 1.36kg training bombs, T-10, SCAR and 70mm rockets, two JATOs, two extra 318-litre tanks, a 30mm gun, internal 20mm guns and 7.62mm machine guns.

A-534 and -541 escorting the Hercules that supported them on their tour across South America.

During the year, at the factory, the aircraft left over from the previous year (A-507, -509, -511 and -512) were delivered and 11 of the 13 planned were produced, up to A-524 (A-521 serial was not used). Of these, originally, those with construction numbers 013, 014, 017 and 018 were produced for a contract with

Mauritania for four aircraft, which were to be the first to be exported. However, the contract was cancelled when the first aircraft had already received the colours and 5T-MAB serial. Thus, aircraft 017 and 018 were delivered to the FAA with serial numbers A-514 and -515, and 013 and 014 as A-518 and -517 respectively. This led to a change in serial numbers of those aircraft originally assigned A-517 to -519 (c/n 021, 022 and 023), which became A-520, A-522 and A-523 respectively. The aircraft with c/n 019 became the new A-519. A-518 entered FAA service with the camouflage originally painted for Mauritania, which it retained for a time and distinguished it from all other Pucará aircraft.

In addition, during that year a liquid oxygen system was received at the base and crews began flying with appropriate masks.

Crisis with Chile

Due to the border conflict with Chile at the end of 1978 in the Beagle Channel area in the extreme south of Argentina – the dispute was over the Lennox, Nueva and Picton islands and the surrounding sea – the Argentine government ordered the mobilization and deployment of all its armed forces, with the support of the security forces and many other state bodies, as well as some civilian organizations, foreseeing the possibility that the crisis could lead to war between the two nations.

In order to evaluate the operation of the aircraft, Vice-Commodore Ignes Rosset flew to San Julián on 7 November, making stops at Comandante Espora Naval Air Base and IX Air Brigade in Comodoro Rivadavia, returning to his base two days later.

Faced with the increasingly imminent possibility of war, and in order to learn more about the area of operations, the Pucará Airmobile Squadron was organized and deployed on 19 November to BAM Río Gallegos under the command of Ignes Rosset, from where on the 21st they deployed to the city of Gobernador Gregores, returning the same day, and to Puerto Santa Cruz the following day, returning to Río Gallegos the same day, before returning to Reconquista on 22 November.

A Pucará deployed on a road near Fuerte General Roca, Río Negro province, during the crisis with Chile in late 1978.

A Pucará at a dispersal site near Fuerte General Roca during the crisis with Chile in 1978.

A-540 was tested with this special paint scheme and used briefly by the CEV in 1980 and 1981, until it was delivered to Escuadrón IV de Ataque in December 1981. The plane disappeared on 24 May 1982 while performing a reconnaissance near the coast.

While the crisis continued to escalate during December, on the 21st of that month Ignes Rosset's airmobile squadron was deployed to BAM Santa Cruz, organized for the occasion at the airfield in the town of Puerto Santa Cruz (planes A-511, -512, -514, -516, -518, -520 and -522) with pilots Captain Kettle, First Lieutenants Palaver, Varela and Filippi and Lieutenants Carlos Ballesteros, Héctor Cáceres, Francisco Navarro, Ernesto Raffaini, Manuel Bustos and Augusto Brunacci and Ensigns Alfredo Gismondi and Raúl Cordini. They were joined by First Lieutenant Spika who belonged to the CEV.

The Pucarás arrived at Puerto Santa Cruz at night and the aircraft were prepared in the bombs/guns weapons configuration. At dawn on 22 December the crews completed the pre-meeting with the assigned targets.

A ground column moved much of the material and contracted trucks were in charge of transporting 125 and 130kg bombs. On arrival in Santa Cruz, the trucks were not unloaded, as they would be used as mobile magazines to accompany the successive planned deployments of the aircraft. Shelters for the nine aircraft were improvised at the airfield.

Another squadron was deployed to BAM Fuerte General Roca, also organized for the occasion in the town of General Roca, in the north of the province of Río Negro, near the city of Neuquén, under the command of Vice-Commodore Carbó Bernard (aircraft AX-04, A-507, -509, -510, -513, -515, -517 and -523), with Captain Igarzábal as second in command, plus Captain Juan Carlos Bonavía, First Lieutenants Jorge Benítez, Eduardo Rodino, José Vacarezza, Roberto Vila and Ricardo Grünert, Lieutenants Ricardo Fasani and Raúl Federici, Ensigns Tadeo Russo, Jorge Hernández and Jorge Braun, who were joined from the CEV by Major Carlos Digier, Captain Carlos Tomba and First Lieutenant Rogelio Marzialetti.

Both air bases had been specially constituted to allow better deployment of Air Force aircraft in the Patagonian territory, both locations being chosen at a distance of about 300 kilometres from the border, which, while allowing the Pucará to reach their targets in less than an hour, provided greater security against the possibility of an enemy attack. Given the two-base deployment and the small size of the squadron at the time, logistical support was provided by the FMA and the EAM. Roberto Vila recalls:

> It was all improvised. We started by living in the prison, then in a hotel. The day of the attack arrived and we were the first ones. We set the ball rolling, we went to the head of the runway, we had everything ready to attack and the commander of the base appeared and asked us to open the cockpits and wait a bit, he said, 'I made this base badge and they just gave it to me, I didn't have time to sew it on, put it in your pocket,' and he gave each of us the badge. When we were about to close the canopies, a Fokker F28 landed. The plan was that, once we took off, we left the frequency. The F28 was coming to withdraw everyone because the war had stopped. If they hadn't given us the badge, we would have taken off, we would have gone to attack and we would have started the war ourselves. We were going with bombs, I think the target was a base, we had done a lot of pre-computed navigations, because depending on the weather we would either attack directly or go all the way to the sea and head east. That day we were going to cross the mountains; if the weather was good, we would attack from below; the good thing was that we had so much endurance that we would go in low through the canyons.

On 22 December, the attack against the Chilean forces would be carried out and it was planned that on returning from the mission, the Pucarás would land on ranch airstrips in the area near each base. Maintenance and logistical support would accompany them.

Finally, the intervention of the Vatican enabled a peaceful solution to be found. Once the conflict was over, the withdrawal from General Roca began on 24 December, followed on 13 January 1979 by the withdrawal from Puerto Santa Cruz, although some technical staff remained for longer, in case it was necessary to redeploy the planes.

By the end of 1978 BAM Reconquista had 19 Pucarás in service, in addition to the C-47 and the Aerocommander. During 1979 the FMA delivered A-524, A-526, A-528, A-529, A-531, A-532, A-533, A-534, A-535 and A-536, completing the manufacture up to A-538.

Despite the end of the dispute with Chile, on 25 May 1979, the anniversary of the May Revolution of 1810, three Pucarás conducted flypasts over the cities of Comodoro Rivadavia, Puerto Santa Cruz and Río Gallegos. Then, between 24 and 30 June, several aircraft were deployed to the town of Merlo (San Luis) to take part in the *Lenga* exercise. On 10 August they moved to Calilegua, Jujuy province, to celebrate the anniversary of the Air Force, and between 3 and 7 December they were deployed again to form the deactivated BAM Santa Cruz to carry out Operation *Fortaleza II*, as a show of force in the face of the conflict with Chile the previous year.

In III Air Brigade

On 7 December 1979, BAM Reconquista became III Air Brigade, demonstrating that the unit had reached full combat capability. The unit was organized with the Grupo 3 de Ataque formed by the Escuadrón I Operativo, Escuadrón II de Instrucción, the Escuadrilla de Servicios (with the C-47 and the IA-50 G II serialled T-119, which replaced the Aerocommander) and the CEPAC Course which was responsible for providing combat instruction to pilots who had graduated from the CAM (Military Aviators' Course) at the Military Aviation School. Until then, CEPAC was only taught at IV Air Brigade in Mendoza, with the FMA/Morane Saulnier MS-760 Paris, but the force realized, after the crisis with Chile that it needed to speed up training of its combat-ready pilots. That year, the first such training was carried out in Pucarás, using the resources of II Squadron, starting on 27 August (in addition to continuing the training already being carried out in Mendoza); the unit ended up with 30 Pucarás in service.

In addition, the brigade was organized with Grupo Técnico 3, in charge of aircraft maintenance, and Grupo Base 3, in charge of base security and maintenance.

In March 1980, A-539 that was under evaluation at the CEV was taken under the command of Captain Carlos Tomba to participate in the FIDA show in Santiago de Chile, flying Chilean Air Force personnel during the exhibitions. This aircraft also participated during the year in an evaluation in Iraq, for which it was transported aboard the C-130 serialled TC-61. There, among other demonstrations, a combat exercise against helicopters was conducted by Major José Ignacio Igarzábal. At the time, the Iraqi government was very interested in the Pucará. This visit took place before the start of the Iraqi invasion of Iran in September of that year. On its return, the aircraft was sent to the factory to be converted into the IA-66.

On 16 March 1980, a flight with the callsign 'Huayra' was flown to Montevideo, Uruguay, to participate in the Uruguayan Air Force Day, the first time the Pucará had visited that country.

Shortly afterwards, on 31 May, a tour of South America began using A-534 and -541 aircraft under evaluation by the CEV, with Captains Carlos Tomba, Jorge Benítez and Fillipi, supported by the C-130 TC-67. The first display was carried out at Palanquero Base (Bogotá, Colombia), followed by another at El Libertador Base (Maracay, Venezuela), Las Palmas (Lima, Peru), Nhu Guazú (Asunción, Paraguay) and São José dos Campos (São Paulo state, Brazil). On 3 July, the aircraft returned having successfully completed the demonstrations, in which they used real weapons equipped with an MER (multiple ejector rack) with six 125kg bombs and two TERs (triple ejector racks) with two LAU-61 rocket launchers for 19 FFAR 70mm (2.75-inch) rockets.

During that year, the FMA completed 12 of the 21 aircraft planned. At the end of the year III Air Brigade had 32 Pucará, the C-47, the G II and the recently arrived Hughes 369HS, serialled H-20. The armament in the unit consisted of TER and MER racks, conventional bombs of different weights, LAU-61, FMA-1, LAU-60-A, LAU 68 and Aspid Yarará rocket launchers.

Throughout 1981 the 19 aircraft planned were completed, up to A-569, c/n 070, and the final assembly of the 072 began, with the delivery to III Brigade of A-549, A-550, A-552, A-553, A-555 and A-556 aircraft. The unit consisted of Grupo Aéreo III de Ataque, made up of Escuadrones Aéreos I and II and the Escuadrilla Servicios, and had 29 Pucará aircraft, as A-507, A-508, A-535 and A-554 had been lost in accidents during 1980 and 1981. The aircraft originally serialled as A-542 to -544 and -546 to -548 were sold to the Uruguayan Air Force, so those serials were never used in the FAA.

At that time, the possibility of incorporating night vision goggles was studied to increase the all-weather capacity of the aircraft. For this purpose, two different goggles were purchased that, according to Commodore (Retd.) Raúl Páez:

> One was similar to today's goggles, with two lenses. The infrared vision was very good. The other, which the co-pilot used, was like a long-range sight: it showed you the distance of what you were seeing. The co-pilot passed information to the pilot, but it was a mess, because if the pilot didn't have his visor on, which was complicated with the helmet, the co-pilot passed the information verbally. [In 1984 the idea of using them for night shooting was taken up again] but they advised against it, because to use the visor you had to turn off the dashboard lights and without the visor you couldn't see any instruments – you were flying in total darkness. The one that looked

like a scope was primitive, heavy – you had to focus well – but the other one was attached to the head and was very good.

In addition, in order to form a combat unit in Patagonia, in December 1981, Escuadrón IV de Ataque was created in IX Air Brigade in Comodoro Rivadavia, a unit equipped until then only with Twin Otter and Fokker F27 transport aircraft. Escuadrón IV was commanded by Major Manuel Navarro, plus First Lieutenant Raúl Federici and Ensigns Miguel Filipanics and Raúl Colla, with aircraft A-540, -551, -557, -558 and -559, delivered by the FMA without the backseat.

On 22 February 1982, at 0930, the Hughes 369HS H-20 that III Air Brigade had on its inventory crashed and three days later A-553 was lost, causing the death of Ensign Daniel Sabella and injuries to Ensign Puga. Meanwhile, on 26 February, A-570 was delivered from the FMA workshops.

At the time, III Air Brigade had aircraft A-501, -502, -505, -506, -509, -510, -511, -512, -513, -514, -515, -516, -517, -518, -520, -522, -523, -524, -526, -527, -528, -529, -531, -532, -533, -534, -536, -537, -538, -545, -549, -550, -552, -555 and -556. The aircraft serialled A-540, -551, -557, -558 and -559 were allocated to IX Air Brigade, while A-530 and -541 were stationed at the Flight Test Centre.

On 11 November 1979 the first of two exhibitions at Buenos Aires racetrack took place, in this case the XXX Semana Aeronáutica. Pucará A-532 is seen here taxiing on the track. (Photo Alberto Martín)

Chapter 9

The Pucará in the Malvinas

Due to Argentina's unsuccessful attempts to find a peaceful solution to the sovereignty dispute over the Malvinas /Falkland Islands, despite the fact that since 1962 the United Nations had recognized that sovereignty of the territory was in dispute and urged Argentina and the United Kingdom to negotiate, in January 1982 the Argentine government decided to occupy the islands to force the British to negotiate.

While the original plan was to occupy the islands in July when winter had set in, giving an opportunity to fortify them in case of a British armed response, an incident on the Georgias* forced the occupation to be brought forward to 1 April; the operation was then delayed to 2 April. In order for the Air Force to have a presence in the operations and to provide close air support, if necessary, on 31 March the Air Operations Command ordered the deployment of III Brigade to the south to cross to Port Stanley, Malvinas, by 1700 hours on 2 April.

On 31 March, Major Miguel Navarro, head of Escuadrón I Operativo, received the order to prepare four aircraft to cross to the islands on 2 April.

Captain Roberto Vila, who was preparing for a deployment to Salta in the northwest of the country on 1 April, was ordered to change destination and prepare for a flight to Rio Gallegos at the southern end of Patagonia and was given an envelope to open when instructed to do so.

Thus, at 1235 on 1 April, A-556 under the command of Captain Vila, A-529 with Lieutenant Héctor Furios, A-552 with Lieutenant Miguel Giménez and A-523 with Lieutenant Roberto Címbaro left Reconquista. Vila recalls:

> what surprised me most was that the brigade commander was a very strict guy; when I started to give the briefing, which, for us, who always went south, was easy, I said, 'Let's go from here to Comandante Espora Naval Air Base and from Espora to Gallegos'

---

* A group of workers from a private company contracted to disassemble a whale factory raised an Argentine flag which led to protests from the British government and an increase in the tensions between the two countries. The UK sent the HMS *Endurance* to expel the workers and Argentina sent the ARA *Bahía Paraíso* to protect them.

and he told me, 'I don't want you to go through Espora, go to a place that belongs to the Air Force' and I said I was going to Tandil.

They landed at VI Air Brigade in Tandil to refuel, while repairing a fuel transfer problem in one aircraft and another that had a tyre with little air, with the intention of staying overnight there due to the bad weather, but at 1945 they received the order to continue the flight south to Río Gallegos, while Vila was instructed to open the envelope and read his orders, which indicated that the following day they were to cross to the islands to support the landing operations, which he did not communicate to the rest of the pilots. Vila relates:

> We hadn't slept a wink and we set off. I had already been given the new frequencies and new callsigns when we left Reconquista. We were about to leave for Gallegos when the flight officer stopped me and wouldn't let me leave, because the aerodrome was closed. I said I was going to go anyway. One of the pilots, Giménez, said to me, 'Sir, they are all alerted that we are going to fly there.' But in reality, nobody knew anything. We set off and the four of us stuck together and took off because it was all stormy. I tried to contact the different airfields we were passing and everything was closed. So, dealing with the storm, we flew as far as Gallegos, but couldn't go

Helicopter crews of VII Brigada Aérea of the Argentine Air Force, which deployed with Bell 212 and Chinook helicopters to the islands, standing in front of Pucará A-529 in early April, before the plane was painted. The plane deployed to the islands on 2 April but was damaged during the SAS attack of 15 May.

any further. The only one who answered me was Címbaro, an ensign, who said, 'Four' while the rest didn't say anything. I turned on the headlights so that they would have a chance to form up, because the lights on the Pucará are small. I couldn't see anything and that's how we arrived. I told them to split up and we went straight in. Rodoni, who was commander of the base, was waiting for me and he asked me if I had the Malvinas charts but I had nothing. He told me that he had one and to send the squadron to bed: 'We are going to prepare the navigation to the Malvinas and you leave in a couple of hours.' At that moment a Boeing 707 came in with a flight. Benítez was there and he said, 'We're coming to replace you.' I said no, that if he wanted to come, he should come on the first plane.

Címbaro recalls: 'I was struck by the movement, but we were so tired that we went to sleep. It was 4 or 5 o'clock in the morning. I woke up around 10 a.m. and found out what had happened.' That day the Pucará Airmobile Squadron was created under the command of Major Navarro. A-529 suffered problems with the liquidometer (fuel gauge) in Tandil and after taking off in the rain at 2330, arrived in Rio Gallegos at 0430 on 2 April. The mechanics, together with pilots Captain Jorge Benitez, First Lieutenant Francisco Navarro and Lieutenants Daniel Jukic and Hernan Calderon, arrived at Rio Gallegos on a Boeing 707.

At 0930 that day, the order was received to take off at 1400 to the islands. Supported by the KC-130H Hercules serialled TC-70, they landed at the recently created BAM Malvinas at 1600 with Captain Jorge Benítez and Lance-Corporal Piaggi in A-532, Vila and Giménez in -556, Lieutenant Daniel Jukic with Lance Corporal Toloza in -529 and Hernán Calderón with Lance-Corporal Ramos in -523, flying with the callsign 'Nahuel'. The other pilots were in the Hercules along with the mechanics.

A-515 on the mainland, before flying to the islands. The plane was camouflaged at Santa Cruz using gloss paint from a Fiat workshop, the colours being those available for cars.

Loading INC-220 napalm bombs at BAM Cóndor. They were only used once in combat.

Pucará A-516 flying very low over Stanley Harbour on 23 May. (Photo Graham Bound)

A-552 at BAM Malvinas with an Argentine Army Aviation pilot standing in front.

A-515 and A-555 at Comodoro Rivadavia, before the flight to the islands.

Since the islands were secured that day with the surrender of the British forces, no sorties were flown, although the following day cover flights and the first armed reconnaissance flights were made with A-523 piloted by Benítez and First Lieutenant Navarro, followed by A-556 with Vila and Jukic searching for possible British troops on the rest of the islands together with a Sea King helicopter of the Argentine Navy; at the same time they began to reconnoitre the terrain for possible future operations. These flights continued over the following days: 38 armed reconnaissance missions were completed and target practice conducted over a small islet off Goose Green; the pilots acquired an intimate knowledge of the Falklands/Malvinas.

Due to the British response, which consisted of sending a task force to reconquer the islands, it was decided to reinforce the Escuadrón Aeromóvil Pucará Malvinas to 12 aircraft. This was mainly because it was impossible to deploy other fighter aircraft to the islands, as the short runway, small apron and lack of major facilities prevented the operation of the Skyhawks, Mirages or Canberras.

For this reason, on 8 April, A-528 left Reconquista under command of Major Miguel Navarro (who had been appointed head of the Escuadrón Aeromóvil Pucará Malvinas), alongside A-502 with Lieutenant Cruzado, A-520 with Lieutenant Hernández, A-506 with Lieutenant Néstor Brest, A-527 with Captain Ricardo Grünert, A-513 with Lieutenant Alsogaray, A-509 with Lieutenant Alcides Russo and A-517 with Lieutenant Túñez, which all arrived at Comodoro Rivadavia at 2030.

Navarro recalls that he decided to make the direct flight from Reconquista to Comodoro Rivadavia, passing over Comandante Espora Naval Air Base, which meant covering a distance of 2,000 kilometres:

> When you go straight, you partly go over the sea; it is not a good
> idea to go over the sea with the Pucará, but in this case you go more

117

A-522 before flying to the islands on 29 May, armed with three INC-220 napalm bombs and two LAU-60 rocket launchers. The plane was captured and taken to the UK.

directly, so we were flying at almost 20,000 feet. We all had extra tanks, with very little margin, but we made it. The last check we did was in Trelew (400 kilometres before arriving), where we had to descend 5,000 feet due to cloud cover. One of the wingmen, Cruzado, said he had minimal fuel in one engine. As number one I went to get him to line me up. After 10 minutes the engine stopped. He said to me, 'Boss, let's go a little further up the road.' It was already dark. The other six planes were orbiting overhead and I was with Cruzado descending almost to touchdown on the runway. I told him, 'Visualize and land.' He ran out of fuel on the runway. All had their lights on with minimum fuel.

Cruzado recalls:

The Pucará had a problem with the liquidometer, it kept jumping and you didn't know the number of litres it had left. We arrived in Trelew, we checked, it was flickering, it was quite windy, it was already dark. The wind was blowing us towards the sea. I was with a non-commissioned officer, Miguel Morsillo, and he told me, 'The inverted light is coming on' – the pump for inverted flight. The ones on the tanks below had not come on, so I went to the most serious emergency. I had an engine stop due to lack of fuel. We continued.

On 29 May A-549, A-522 and A-514 flew to the islands supported by a civil Mitsubishi MU-2. All Pucarás carried a weapons load of INC-220 napalm bombs, as well as ammunition for their guns. (Photo Alférez Carlos Miranda)

Grünert told me, 'Don't pass cross instructions to avoid the fuel going to the other tank or you will consume the little fuel you have left.' And that's how it was. I was aiming at the lights of the port of Comodoro Rivadavia; there was the hill and past that was the runway. I was aiming at the lights and then I had to go to the runway. The squadron leader was marking the way for me in front. It was very tricky, because we all started having fuel problems. I would go in with one engine stopped. I told Morsillo, 'When I tell you, you are going to eject.' There were Mirages flying over Comodoro Rivadavia and they were sent to 40,000 feet to save fuel as the eight Pucará were facing an emergency; they gave us priority to land. I was the first one, then I saw the port, I was coming in with a lot of altitude, then I saw the lights of the other engine that I still had working starting to come on. Then it stopped altogether and with both engines stopped I went for the runway. I was already coming in with altitude and the Comodoro runway was long. I feathered the propeller and landed. We stopped. I went to the side of the runway where they were carrying out works on the airport taxiways, and the plane stopped right at the side of a big hole. The other seven planes started to land. I lit everything up – the plane was a little Christmas tree – so they could see me.

On 10 April the Technical Squadron arrived at the Malvinas/Falkland Islands, together with Major Navarro, who flew in a Fokker F28. The aircraft were ordered to be painted in a camouflage scheme appropriate to the terrain of the islands, a task carried out both at Comodoro Rivadavia and in the islands, including the Escuadrón IV aircraft. In Comodoro Rivadavia, since paint was not available, car paint was purchased in the city and different lots were used, which resulted in all the aircraft having different paint schemes.

The armament deployed to BAM Malvinas consisted of 211,000 rounds of 7.62mm, 31,120 rounds of 20mm war and 8,850 exercise ammunition, 5,440 70mm rockets with 12 LAU-61 7-tube rockets, 60 LAU-60 19-tube rockets and 30 IIAE-238s (locally produced LAU-60). In addition, 131 INC-220 220kg napalm tanks and 142 INC-100 100kg tanks, 87 ARM B-J 125kg bombs and 18 Mk.1 130kg bombs were sent.

After his arrival in the islands, Navarro says that he presented himself

> to the air commander, who was Brigadier Castellano, and he told me to try to find a redeployment site for the airmobile squadron between the two islands. What hindered us was the sleeping bag: wherever we went we took the bag with us because we always slept on the ground. An Islander [aircraft] was found, and a vice-commodore explained how to start it. I went out to reconnoitre the places according to the mapping. The only one that really had a runway shape was Elephant Bay on Borbón/Pebble Island. The Navy was there, but their Aermacchi had landed in Puerto Argentino/Stanley. The other runway was at Goose Green, as well as a rectangle and a kind of small construction, 2x2 metres; you could see that a very small plane was operating there. I tried to land on the diagonal because it was longer, but it had an undulation. It was only 250 metres long, so I asked for a wire to be lowered and I ran 250 metres more. I gave it as semi-suitable.

This was done on 12 April in order to be able to deploy the aircraft out of Stanley, as that runway would be the main target of any air attack; it was also saturated with aircraft. This task was carried out in the Britten Norman Islander serialled VP-FAY captured from FIGAS (Falkland Islands Government Air Service). At Fox Bay they found that the runway was only usable to 350 metres. At Port San Carlos and San Carlos settlement no runway was usable.

Reconnaissance flights were made but with limitations due to a shortage of fuel, as the helicopters had priority. On these missions they flew with full internal armament and two 70mm rocket launchers under each wing, at an altitude of 50 feet and a speed of 220 knots. Cruzado recalls:

> We would go out on reconnaissance at different levels of alert because there was information that some commandos had landed. We would go out to look for possible places where they might have landed, which, in fact, they later did. We knew the islands beforehand without a chart; we flew over the two islands, around and between the islands, especially the part of Gran Malvina/West Falkland Island where there is a series of high cliffs.

On 14 April, at IX Air Brigade, the weapons systems of all the aircraft waiting to cross were inspected and all were found to have issues; the aileron of A-506 was sent to the FMA because it had a crack. That same day A-526 and A-534 were

A-515
after being
captured.

deployed to the city of La Plata, 50 kilometres from Buenos Aires, for possible
interceptions over the Rio de la Plata. A-526 crash-landed on 9 June in the town
of Atalaya, on a reconnaissance flight, and its pilot ejected. This aircraft had been
informally given the registration I-26, due to its interceptor mission, which was
painted on the aircraft nose landing gear door shortly before its crash.

Meanwhile, on 15 April, the Base Aérea Militar 'Cóndor' was established
at Goose Green with the deployment of a Bell 212 helicopter. In addition, at
Comodoro Rivadavia the technical staff worked day and night in conjunction with
people from the FMA to fix the aircraft problems and, on the 18th, they finished
their work, leaving all planes fully operational. Recalls Címbaro:

> The runway had no facilities, it was a square and we used the
> diagonals to take off. It was undulated, which led to some planes
> breaking their nosewheels. The ground was very soft and light
> aircraft had no problems, but with armament and fuel it would break.

The following day, a joint flight with Mirage IIIs, IAI M5 Daggers, A-4B/C
Skyhawks and Pucarás was coordinated with the Argentine Navy to make a
simulated attack on the Argentine fleet formed by the aircraft carrier ARA *25 de
Mayo*, the type 42 destroyer ARA *Santísima Trinidad* and the three A-69 corvettes
ARA *Drummond*, *Granville* and *Guerrico*, which were off Trelew and 170 miles
offshore, to be carried out on 17 April. Miguel Navarro says:

> they called me urgently from Comodoro Rivadavia to do a practice
> run with two missile frigates, the *Hercules* and the *Santísima
> Trinidad*, to see how they move when they are attacked. I went out
> with a squadron; I was two or three metres high; we flew about 150
> kilometres from the coast, and we couldn't see anything. I asked the
> Mirages, the Daggers, the A-4s – nobody could see anything. We

came back indignant; we asked the Navy and the position they had given us at 3 p.m. was for 6 a.m., a difference of nine hours.

The simulated attack was carried out with four planes that left at 1200 and met up with a Learjet; the fleet was 120 miles from the indicated position.

On 23 April it was reported that the eight aircraft at Comodoro Rivadavia were ready to be deployed to the islands. Meanwhile, that same day, Major Navarro and Captain Vila landed for the first time on BAM Condor in A-529. After take-off, they fired their IIAE-238 rocket launchers on an islet off Darwin to check weapons. Navarro says:

> I went back to the islands because I wanted to test the runway with the plane loaded: three rocket launchers in the central pylon, each rocket carries 19 rockets and two on each wing pylons – that's seven rocket launchers, which makes 133 rockets. We went with Vila, and as was common in the Malvinas winds were 40 to 50 knots and as the plane always lands against the wind, the runway was reduced. We tried it and it worked well: it practically stopped by itself, we had 150 metres left and we were loaded with weapons and fuel. We searched for a small island far out and there we fired the 133 rockets in salvo. The peat was smoking for more than a month.

This firing exercise was followed by others, including gun fire, in different parts of the archipelago, where all the pilots were trained. In addition, offensive reconnaissance, shooting and bombing flights were carried out.

As Navarro recounts, immediately afterwards he had to return to Comodoro Rivadavia:

> They called me back from the mainland to test the eight planes because there were faults in the weapons system. They prepared the range for me at Comodoro Rivadavia but the easiest thing to do was to go to the sea to fire the weapons; it worked perfectly. All eight were ready.

On 25 April, at 1300, the planes from Comodoro Rivadavia left for Río Gallegos, arriving at 1400, where they were dispersed in anticipation of a possible air attack, as the British fleet was close by. After spending the night, at 1400 the following day, they left supported by a Fokker F27. Major Navarro in A-528 was unable to leave, remaining with Lieutenant Giménez in A-517. Adds Navarro:

> The plan was for us to spend the night in Río Gallegos. Of the eight of us, four planes stayed inside a hangar and the others outside because there was no room; among them was my escadrille. The first plane they always start is the squadron leader's. When I went to start up, the canopy didn't close and the cockpit specialists were on the islands. I always flew

with a chief corporal but he had little knowledge and it never locked. I sent six planes and I stayed behind with my wingman, Giménez.

Two hours after leaving, the six aircraft arrived in the Falklands/Malvinas (A-502, -506, -509, -513, -520 and -527). The planes at BAM Malvinas were on 10-minute alert with the pilots sitting in the cockpit. The next day Navarro and Giménez arrived with A-517 and -528. Navarro says:

> We drilled a hole [in the cockpit], put a screw in and I left with Giménez. I was already about 15 miles out to sea when a vibration started: the screw had come out. I slowed down and we got there without a problem, and then the specialists fixed the cockpit.

Major Carlos Tomba also arrived on the islands; he had volunteered despite serving in the Flight Test Centre.

In the meantime, Vila asked the Construction Group to dig a shelter, with a roof made from the spare aluminium sheeting used to extend the runway, for all the squadron personnel, so that they would be close to their aircraft. However, due to the intense activity in BAM Malvinas with the transport planes and helicopters and the fact that this would be the main British target in the first attack, it was decided to deploy the 12 Pucarás to Goose Green, a task carried out on 28 April. Says Vila:

> They ordered us to redeploy to Darwin. The flight is 55 miles; it was time to deploy but nothing could be seen. I had in my head where each plane was with the callsigns and I started with, 'Let Bagre Four take off ... get on the runway and when you are in the air let me know.' So I was taking them off and the last one to take off was me.

Some of the ensigns of Grupo 3 de Ataque, who had joined between the end of 1981 and the beginning of 1982, had not been deployed, but they insisted on being able to participate. As one of them, Rubén Sassone, recounted:

> We went to Comodoro Rivadavia on the 28th, slept there and on the morning of the 29th a Fokker F28 with no seats was leaving, full of Zanella enduro motorbikes for the commandos and four seats in the back. We were four pilots, Fassani, Pontecorvo and Carlos Morales. On the morning of the 30th we went to Goose Green in a Chinook with the remaining pilots and mechanics; the Pucarás were already there.

Miguel Cruzado says that at Goose Green they stayed in a sheep-shearers' dormitory:

> it was like a U; in the middle there was a kitchen and on the sides the rooms. We went with our sleeping bags, that's all. There was a place

that was used as a food storage area, and those who knew how to cook cooked, and those who didn't washed dishes.

On 30 April, Vila and Furios were sent to look for the British fleet. Vila:

> I was sent to fly above the fleet the day before the attack. I went with Furios. I knew I was above but I couldn't see them. It was an illogical order; they told me, 'If they don't shoot at you, don't shoot at them.' Thank goodness, because if they shot at me we had nothing, neither a life vest nor an anti-exposure suit.

On his return, he landed at BAM Malvinas where the nosewheel retracted and was put out of service. Although it was repaired, it would not fly again.

Deployments and new weapons

Meanwhile, aircraft A-501, -511, -512, -513, -514, -515, -516, -518, -522, -524, -531, -532, -533, -536, -537, -538, -549 and -555 were progressively sent to BAM Santa Cruz to carry out offensive reconnaissance flights in the coastal area, in support of the aircraft at Comodoro Rivadavia to prevent attacks by British troops on the mainland bases. Only A-505, -510 and -550 remained at Reconquista, while A-545 was sent to Comandante Espora Naval Air Base to test launch the Martin Pescador air-to-surface missile.

With the intention of expanding the anti-ship combat capability, the use of torpedoes was proposed, which, although it had been foreseen in the original

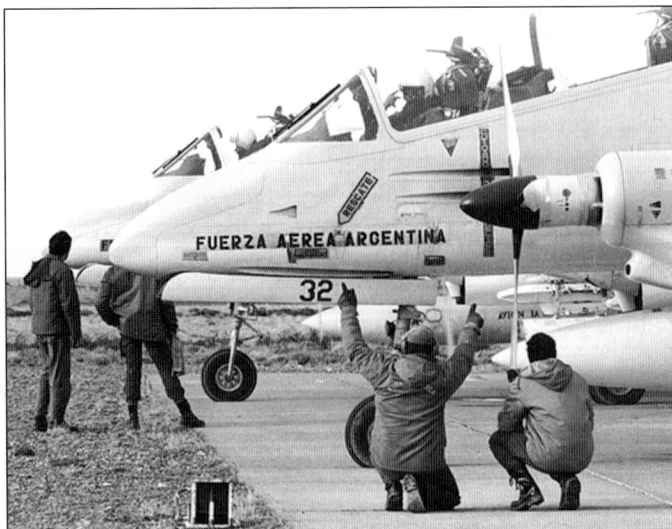

A-532 at Puerto Santa Cruz before flying to the islands.

design of the aircraft, was never intended to be implemented. When the Navy was consulted about this possibility, it responded in the affirmative, with the provision of the World War II-era Mk.13 torpedo of US origin. These torpedoes had been fitted to the 10 Higgins-class torpedo boats that had been in service until 1966, and more than 40 units were available. With the provision of these torpedoes, they were used to test the launching from the Aero 20A-1 ventral pylon of the Pucará, serialled AX-04, belonging to the CEV, which had been equipped with a camera to follow the launching. This work began on 21 May at Comandante Espora Naval Air Base, with the first launch the following day, which was unsuccessful, as was the second, carried out on the same day. In both launches, the exercise torpedo was used and in all cases the device was destroyed on impact with the water due to the high launch speed. This situation was due to the fact that the model of torpedo used had been designed to be launched from the four cradles on the deck of the torpedo boats at a speed of about 50 knots; in the Navy they had also been used from the Martin Mariner seaplanes and Catalina amphibians, in straight and level flight and whose speed for a successful launch was at the time of launching approximately 95 knots and 20 metres high.

In the case of the Pucará, the launch speed was much higher and the correct angle of release was not set, which is why the first attempts failed. The aircraft was then transferred to Trelew to continue testing alongside A-566. On 24 May, the first successful launch was made in the San José Gulf, using the flight profile of a PBY-5A Catalina as an example. On 10 June, the first successful launch was made with a torpedo equipped with a warhead, against a cliff in the Puerto Santa Cruz area at a speed of 120 knots. Although another launch was planned four days later, it was cancelled due to the end of the war. Another idea was to adapt Mk.12 anti-ship mines, but the end of the war also put a stop to the project after the first trials.

A Pucará taking off from BAM Santa Cruz.

The technical characteristics of the torpedoes were: a range of 5,000 metres, a speed of 30 knots, a weight of 970 kilograms with a warhead of 272 kilograms, a length of 4.10 metres and a diameter of 0.57 metres. The directional control system was by means of a gyroscope and the propulsion was a 103hp engine driving two counter-rotating propellers. The maximum operating depth was 15 metres.

The war begins

At 0130 on 1 May, a communication was received from the Comando de la Fuerza Aérea Sur (South Air Force Command, in charge of all air operations in the South Atlantic Theatre of Operations, TOAS) informing that the enemy was 150 miles away and that an attack was imminent, so at 0445 the 11 Pucará were ordered to take off towards the grass airstrip of the Calderón Naval Air Station in Elephant Bay (Borbón /Pebble Island) as soon as dawn broke. At 0645 the 'Bagre' flight began to start up, at a slow pace because there was only one APU to start the engines.

Because the leader had problems with the start-up, at 0705 Bagre 3 (Lieutenant Russo in A-529) and 4 (Lieutenant Címbaro in A-523) took off. As the other two were taking off, number 1 (A-506, Captain Grünert), which was on the edge of the runway, broke its nose landing gear after taxiing for 150 metres. The plane was immediately removed and abandoned at the side of the airfield and would not fly again, while Lieutenant Calderón's plane joined the other two with A-509. At 0810 the 'Tigre' flight formed up under Captain Benítez, while Lieutenants Brest, Hernández and Daniel Jukic made ready.

Just as Jukic began to get underway, at 0823 there was a surprise attack by Sea Harriers with Hunting BL755 bombs with submunitions. One of them hit A-527, killing Jukic, mechanics Lance-Corporal José Maldonado and Agustín Montaño,

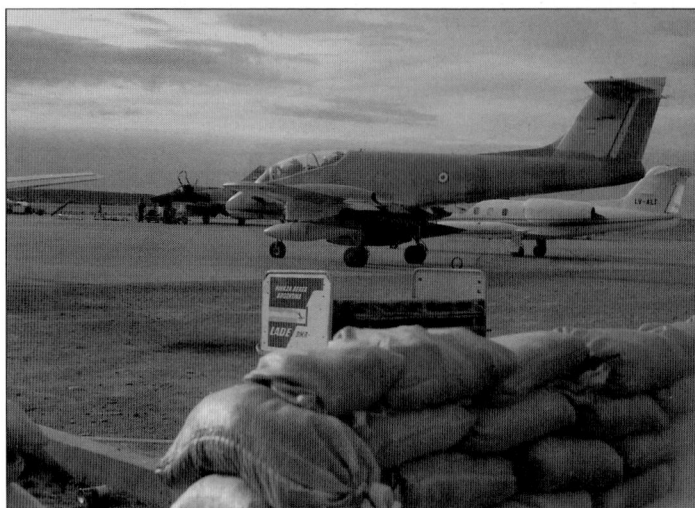

A-536 at BAM San Julián before flying to the islands on 28 May. It was captured on 14 June.

armourers Auxiliary Warrant Officer Mario Duarte and Lance-Corporals Luis Peralta and Andrés Brasich, instrument specialist Lance-Corporal Juan Rodríguez and electronics specialist Lance-Corporal Miguel Carrizo, as well as wounding seven others. A-502 was left with a broken cockpit and holes in the rudder and fuselage, A-517 suffered some damage and would not fly again, and the maintenance tent containing tools, spare parts and armament was destroyed. Címbaro recounts:

> On 1 May we were resting in a hut about 500 metres from the runway and they told us to go to the planes urgently, allocating the sorties to evacuate the runway because they [the enemy] had attacked Puerto Argentino and they assumed that the next target was us. The idea was to get the Pucarás out quickly; a couple of planes started up, one of them was delayed and then they told Russo and me to take off. Lieutenant Alcides Russo took off, I took off second, and behind came Grünert, I think, who went down on the runway and the other take-offs were delayed. We took off and stayed at half height waiting for the others to come. At that moment Russo said to me, 'Look to the left.' I saw the runway and the columns of smoke – the Harriers had just attacked. Right there we pointed our noses to Borbón, thinking the worst; we didn't know what had happened. We had taken off a few minutes before the Harriers attacked. I don't know how they didn't see us. We didn't fly any more that day. Later, more planes came from BAM Condor and we found out what a disaster they [the Harriers] had caused, with the death of the mechanics and Daniel Jukic.

The planes that had taken off observed the British attack from their aircraft, fearing they would be attacked by the Sea Harriers; but they were kept in the air for offensive reconnaissance and to attack a possible British helicopter landing near Puerto Argentino/Stanley. When they returned, they were ordered to proceed to the alternative at Calderon Naval Air Station (Elephant Bay, Borbon/Pebble Island), as the red alert continued.

Sassone explains that after the attack, they devoted themselves to

> setting up the paddock, because we were flying the Pucarás full of fuel, with a 318-litre central tank and four rocket launchers with 19 rockets each, 250 20mm shells, and each machine gun at full capacity. The weight was not the maximum take-off weight, but the runway was too short. The Kelpers used the diagonal of the paddock, but as we went along it, we realized that it had a lot of undulations. Grünert's wheel got buried in the peat, which is like a waterbed, and the wheel went in and broke off. When we started to go over it so that the same thing wouldn't happen again, we realized that one of the sides was much shorter than the diagonal, but it was smoother. It was decided to use that section, but it was 450 metres, but with

that configuration it was enough. We operated without problems: as soon as we felt that there was lift, we just had to go out a little and put the landing gear in to clean it and it would take off. The engines performed well with the low temperature.

Sassone adds that in the days that followed, the four ensigns, among their tasks, had to fill in the tracks left by the Pucarás on the runway

> With the tractor that later became the missile tractor, one drove and the other with a shovel filled in the gullies left by the aircraft and two others, one at each door of the tractor, watched at 180 degrees in case the Harriers appeared.

In the afternoon two aircraft left Darwin to attack two frigates shelling Puerto Argentino/Stanley; however, before arriving, the ships were bombed by M5 Daggers of Torno Flight and withdrew, so the two Pucarás flew to the Puerto Argentino/Stanley area. On arrival they were alerted to the presence of two Sea Harriers, so they escaped to Elephant Bay. Meanwhile Lieutenant Brest's A-513 flew to BAM Malvinas, where it landed with a blown engine and was put out of action. When Lieutenant Címbaro's A-529 landed at Elephant Bay, it buried itself in the soft soil that served as a runway, although it was recovered shortly afterwards. A-523 suffered the same fate and was not repaired. Meanwhile, at 10 o'clock, Captain Benítez left BAM Condor in A-552 for Elephant Bay, but was unable to land

A-526 on a patrol over the city of La Plata. The plane was lost during a mission on 9 June.

because both Pucarás were still on the runway, so he returned to Goose Green to fly back to Elephant Bay at 1300 in A-520, together with Lieutenant Hernández in A-552. Thus ended the first day of combat for the Pucarás, which had had a very negative outcome, with only five aircraft remaining in service.

The next day Major Carlos Tomba directed the repair of A-502, which was the only one of the damaged aircraft that could be salvaged using the few materials they had available. Using the plexiglass from A-506, the cockpit was repaired (it was installed under the damaged plexiglass) and the holes were patched up and riveted.

Jukic's death had a big effect on the pilots, as he was strapped into the seat at the time of the bombing and could not escape from the plane. Sassone says it led to a discussion among the pilots as to whether it was preferable to waste time strapping in:

> In engine start-up there's time on the ground that you're exposed. Everyone had their own technique: mine was to start up very quickly, I would go to the head of the runway and if I had to take off, I would take off first – there was that freedom, the issue being: minimum time on the runway and I would not go out strapped in. I was very scared of being killed by a Harrier bomb. It wasn't fear, but anger. How can it happen that a pilot dies on the ground? If an engine fails and you have to eject, or you crash into the water – we didn't have an anti-exposure suit and the whole perimeter of BAM Cóndor was mined by the Army – why would you strap yourself in if you fell into a minefield?

As a British landing and further attacks were expected, to meet the objectives that had not been achieved the previous day, a large number of fighter sections were planned to depart from the mainland, including two sections of six IA-58s from BAM Santa Cruz with guns and bombs, to attack land and naval targets in the Malvinas/Falklands area. It is quite possible that the planes were scheduled to land on the islands to refuel. In the end, this mission was not carried out.

In any case, the British did not show up and the only IA-58 flight was the one made by Lieutenant Furios from Calderón Naval Air Station to BAM Cóndor.

On 3 May, coastal reconnaissance flights began at BAM Santa Cruz by Pucará aircraft, flying alone or in sections, patrolling the coastline to detect British movements on the mainland, as it was known that there might be commandos operating near the air bases and there was fear of an attack on the fighter planes stationed on the ground.

Meanwhile, on the islands, a Bell 212 helicopter was sent to Borbón/Pebble Island with personnel to repair A-529 and recover it, while two aircraft made a coastal reconnaissance flight from BAM Cóndor. Miguel Cruzado explains:

> They had given us information about what had happened to Ardiles [shot down on 1 May in an IAI M5 Dagger] and there was a version

that a life raft had been seen; we went out to look for it and saw it but when they went there it was no longer there.

On 4 May the Sea Harrier attack was repeated, this time with three aircraft and a different outcome, as Lieutenant Taylor's Sea Harrier XZ450 was shot down by anti-aircraft fire, falling on the perimeter of the base, killing its pilot. In this attack, A-517, which had broken its landing gear in a take-off attempt the previous day and had been positioned as a decoy alongside A-506, received damage to one wing and the side of the fuselage.

The following day only the Santa Cruz aircraft flew. On the 6th, a section of two aircraft and a flight of three flew offensive reconnaissance from Goose Green. That same day, Majors Navarro and Tomba made the test flight of A-502 after repairs, and Navarro took the opportunity to rehabilitate Tomba in the aircraft.

On 7 May there was a single reconnaissance flight carried out by Lieutenant Miguel Cruzado in A-509. Captain Grünert took another of the aircraft that was at EAN Calderón to BAM Cóndor to receive instructions as there were still four Pucarás in operation there.

The offensive reconnaissance continued on the 8th with the departure of First Lieutenant Ricardo Fasani's A-502 and Lieutenant Rubén Sassone's A-509. Sassone recounts:

> We went out to look for some helicopters that the Army had seen in Gran Malvina [West Falkland], as there could be a landing of commandos and as one of our most important tasks was to hunt helicopters, we felt very good about doing that. I took off and with no problems, I strapped myself in. I never wore the leg straps. I put myself next to Fasani, about 300 metres away, which was the technique we used to be able to see each other's tails. We were watching sheep, very low, until we came out of the San Carlos Strait/Falkland Sound. In front of the strait there was a layer of mist over the water; we started to go in and when we were in the middle of the strait, I saw a ship ahead and to the left. I was on Fasani's right and I shouted to him that there was a ship: for me it was a frigate. I turned very close to the water. We went to the right and started to pull, Fasani tried to communicate, nobody answered, the fog started to get thicker and we lost sight of the ship and Fasani told us to go back because of the fog. We saw the runway and we went in sideways, the landing gear came down and the fog behind us came in. Fasani landed but as I was on approach, the fog came overhead and stayed over the runway. I couldn't see it. I broke radio silence and I told Goose Green that I was going to Puerto Argentino, because at some point I had to land; they told me, 'Negative, Puerto Argentino is under Harrier attack.' Then I heard someone tell me that he was going to help me and it was Vila. He told me to keep turning 'then reduce power, lower the gear',

all in the fog. I lowered the flap, 120 knots; there wasn't much wind or turbulence. I turned on the headlights. 'A bit to the left, a bit to the right, keep going down,' he said; he could hear me over the noise. I was going down slowly and I saw things next to the plane: they were the roofs of the houses in Goose Green. I kept going, I reduced all power without seeing anything and I went down smoothly. Vila had brought me to the runway like a radar. Navarro came to pick me up in the Land Rover. I saw Vila and hugged him: he gave me peace of mind. It was a pity we couldn't complete the mission.

This flight was repeated the next day with the same planes, this time flown by Captain Vila and Lieutenant Giménez, with the objective of flying over Port Howard. The leader had to turn back due to radio problems and A-502's wheel sank in the mud on the Elephant Bay airstrip; due to this incident it did not fly again. Similarly, the other aircraft at this base would remain on the ground because the ground was too soft, until a British Special Air Service (SAS) attack on 15 May.

Vila narrates that

there was a generator that was turned off at 7 p.m. but that night the owner of the generator (who had made friends with the Navy and had given him things) left the generator on so we could watch a film. We watched the film and went to bed, just as a mechanic appeared and said, 'I've been watching red flares for two nights and tonight I saw a green flare.' Shortly after, the attack began. First a frigate [actually it was the destroyer HMS *Glamorgan*] dropped flares that lit up everything. It seemed strange to me and then suddenly they came in and shot at us. It was the SAS who were attacking us; we were outside and I told the Navy officer to call Puerto Argentino and inform them that we were under attack and he replied, 'Sir, we have communication from 8 a.m. to 8 p.m., when the service is cut off.' I told a lieutenant to connect up our very sophisticated communications equipment and inform Puerto Argentino that we were under attack. A sailor came up and told us that they had a raft on which we could escape. I asked him where the raft was and he told me that it was eight kilometres away; there was no way we were going there. Then the airfield was blown up and time stopped: Navy personnel had put explosives in the middle of the runway and had blown it up. When it started to clear up there were bloodstains and ammunition all over the place. We found that each plane had a plastic bomb in a turbine.

As a result, A-520 was destroyed by a hand grenade in the cockpit, A-556 by explosives in a wing that caused a fire, A-502 was set on fire by explosives, A-529 had its fuselage and fuel tanks shot through by rifles, A-523 by explosives and gunfire and A-552 by a rocket strike. In addition, four T-34C Turbo Mentors from the Naval Aviation Command and a Shorts Skyvan from the Coast Guard were destroyed or damaged; none of the aircraft would fly again. Címbaro recalls:

> We were woken up by the explosions, we were sleeping near the runway; we woke up and saw the planes burning. We tried to get close to the runway, but they shot at us with machine guns with tracer ammunition. We threw ourselves to the ground. The Marines detonated the two strips of explosives they had to disable the runway. One didn't work, but the other one did, so they [the enemy] decided to end the attack and left, abandoning a lot of equipment. They disabled all the planes. A Chinook came for us and took us to Puerto Argentino.

From that moment on, the planes were assigned individual custody, mines were installed in the perimeter of BAM Condor, the planes were dispersed and a constant patrol began.

This left only A-509 operational, so it was decided to immediately reinforce the Pucará force, sending four aircraft from Santa Cruz with the callsign 'Póker', armed with LAU-61 rockets and a full complement of ammunition for the internal weapons. These aircraft were A-511 of Vice-Commodore Saul Costa, A-516 of Ensign Gustavo Lema, A-531 of First Lieutenant Juan Micheloud and A-533 of Ensign Carlos Diaz and were guided by a civilian Mitsubishi MU-2, a member of the Phoenix Squadron, which accompanied them to the area of

A-536 on the mainland, before going to the islands.

Gran Malvina /West Falkland Island. Although Costa was Navarro's superior, the latter remained in charge of the squadron.

The following day Captain Vila and Lieutenant Cruzado flew A-509 and -516 to make an offensive reconnaissance over the western end of the islands, searching for possible troop movements, followed later by Lieutenants Giménez and Carlos Morales in the same planes but without finding anything.

Faced with the imminence of a British landing on the islands, the defence of BAM Condor was organized on 17 May, using the machine guns and guns of the aircraft that were out of service. On that day flares were seen north of the runway and explosions were heard at Port Howard and Fox Bay. In addition, two Sea Harriers attacked the base, while five aircraft went out to patrol for possible landings in the San Carlos Strait/Falkland Sound off Port Salvador. First were Captain Grünert's A-516 and Lieutenant Hernán Calderón's A-533, which flew between 1000 and 1200 without finding anything. During that flight, Ensign Sassone was Calderón's co-pilot. Says Sassone:

> They had seen boats over Gran Malvina [West Falkland]. The flight was over the sea, two and a half to three hours of offensive reconnaissance over the coast, looking for boats. I was helping Calderon with his charts and a captain told me to go and fly as co-pilot, which was a sin, because you're losing two pilots if you get shot down. In combat there was always only one. So, four eyes see more than two. The co-pilot's ejection seats had the straps tied down so they wouldn't get in the way, everything had to be loosened and, in the rush, I not only didn't put on the anti-exposure

A-549 at Puerto Santa Cruz, some days before flying to the islands.

suit, I didn't put on a life vest either. We took off, we couldn't find anything, but always over the water, not too low, we looked to see if we could see the boats. At one point we were over the coast. I was looking and I heard a noise, I thought it was a Harrier and Calderón told me it was him firing guns. Some Kelpers [native Falklanders] were throwing stones so he made another pass at them and when he was over them, fired a burst to scare them. We didn't find anything on that flight.

The AX-04 performing the first successful launch of a torpedo on 24 May 1982 at Golfo San José. (Archive José Martínez)

That sortie was followed by Lieutenant Russo on A-531 between 1100 and 1330, which then departed again with Lieutenant Morales on A-516 between 1600 and 1730 with the same result.

On 18 May, Lieutenant Benitez on A-516 and Lieutenant Brest on A-531 conducted an offensive reconnaissance over Howard Bay between 0800 and 0830, while two RAF Harrier Gr.Mk.3s bombed the anti-aircraft positions at BAM Condor with Hunting BL755 cluster bombs without success, as they failed to explode.

At the Army's insistence on enemy presence near Port Howard, Captain Vila's A-531 and Lieutenant Cruzado's A-509 flew out the following day between 0830 and 1000 without finding anything. They were followed by First Lieutenant Fasani and Lieutenant Gimenez between 1000 and 1130 and between 1200 and 1300 by Major Tomba and First Lieutenant Micheloud in the same planes and with the same results.

On 20 May, reconnaissance continued despite bad weather, with a flight by A-531 with Grünert and A-509 with Lieutenant Calderón, as the British landing was still considered imminent. In addition, there were attacks on BAM Condor's anti-aircraft artillery with light weapons by heliborne forces and naval gunfire. That night the crew slept in their flight suits and were ready to go.

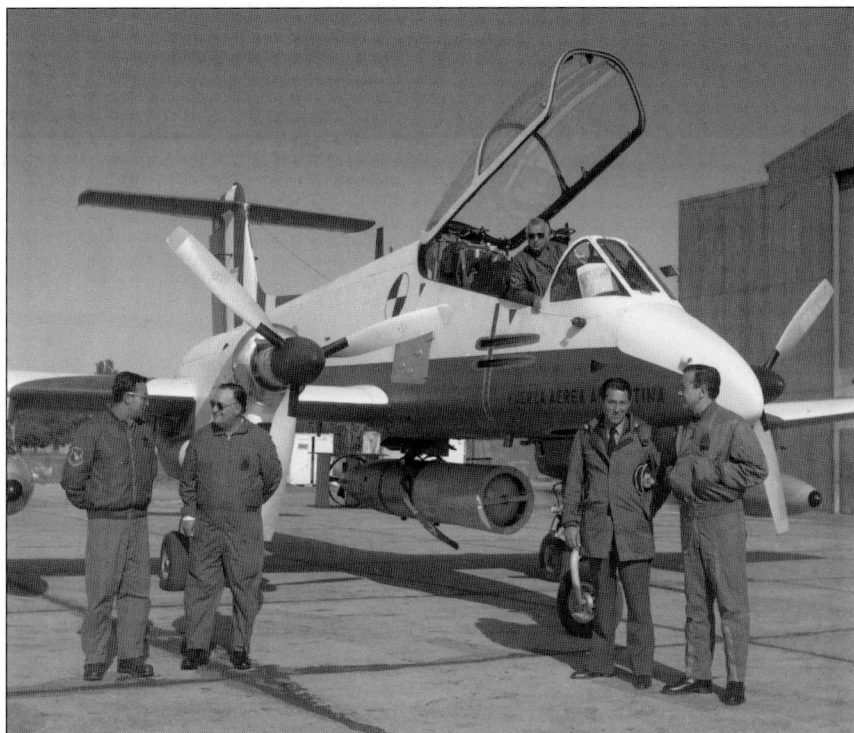

The AX-04 at Base Aeronaval Comandante Espora during the initial tests of the torpedo on the Pucará.

The Pucarás in action

At 0330 on 21 May, the pilots of the Pucará Squadron were informed that as soon as dawn broke, two sections would leave to patrol the area near Air Observer's Network post No. 5, which had been attacked by commandos and had reported the start of a landing operation in the area of Port San Carlos. Two and a half hours later, the Type 21 frigate HMS *Ardent* began shelling BAM Condor, which lasted most of the day until Air Force and Navy aircraft sank it. In any case, the shelling had only a psychological effect on the Argentine forces, as there were no casualties or damage.

At 0700 Captain Benítez (in A-531) and Lieutenant Brest (A-509), who were to leave first, went to the command post to prepare for the flight and then to their respective aircraft. Captain Benítez recalls their mission:

> The red alert found us on board our planes, engaged in the task of getting them underway. We taxied to the runway in use. I secured the ejector seat, proceeding immediately to take off and receiving the information that I was doing it alone, as my wingman, further behind in the operation, aborted [take-off] and left the aircraft, seeking shelter.
>
> For an hour I flew over the southern part of Soledad Island (East Falkland), scouring its coasts and channels without being able to see the enemy. When I received radio information that the alarm over the area I was to reconnoitre had ended, I headed for it anyway to carry out my mission.
>
> The first overflight was made without locating any British. I began a second reconnaissance by widening the turn radius and taking a little more height – 50 metres – to cover more ground in the observation.
>
> It was at that moment that over the hills I observed a British frigate in the San Carlos Strait [Falkland Sound]. Its presence at the time of take-off was unknown, so I suspended my turn and, sticking to the slope of Alberdi Hill (Mount Usborne), I began to approach, protected by it from radar detection. As I climbed at the same time, I was in a better position to observe his activity.
>
> Absorbed by this unexpected variant of my mission and regretting more and more that I was armed only with guns and machine guns, I continued my approach, when suddenly I felt a strong vibration in the airframe.
>
> Once it was under control, I managed to make out the trail left by a British missile in its trajectory, which indicated to me the position occupied by those who were probably members of the commando group I was to locate and who had travelled to this place some five kilometres away during the night.

The missile [a Stinger] had been fired at me head-on and from below, at a distance of about 150 metres, so being so close did not give me the opportunity to use my weapons against them. As I did not know the extent of the damage I had received, I decided to slip into the ravine that opened up to my right and over the enemy position, in order to prevent them from firing another missile at me when they saw me continuing my flight. After about a minute's flight I appeared in the valley between the mountain ranges located to the north and south respectively of San Carlos settlement, some 15 kilometres from there.

I was proceeding to carry out a more thorough check of my aircraft when the right engine stopped. Almost simultaneously the flight commands slackened and there was no further response to my actions; the aircraft began to adopt a 40° pitch and about 30° of bank to the left, in the classic pre-spin position.

From there my stay in the aircraft must have lasted about five or six seconds, time which I used to feather the operational engine, push the rudder with my right foot and actuate the electric depth compensator forward. These actions together resulted in lowering the nose of the aircraft towards the horizon. Having achieved my purpose, I operated the lower ejection handle with my left hand, beginning my abandonment of the aircraft far from home and with enemies close by.

I immediately felt the effect of the force exerted on me by the initiator cartridges and the impact of the air in my face. I looked at the black opening of the cockpit of the plane I had just left and which was lost below me. I saw the pieces of plexiglass from the cockpit, which floated close to me for a long time. I felt the explosion that occurs when the seat separates and I had the sensation of floating in the air as I hung from the parachute. It was 0930.

Shortly after Benítez's departure, the other section planned for that morning took off, made up of Major Tomba in A-511 and First Lieutenant Micheloud (A-533), who recalls that

in an interval of enemy fire I found myself strapping in as fast as I could and began to start up; no sooner had I finished the starting cycle of the second engine than I saw some of the ground personnel running for cover. There was no doubt that the naval guns were looking for us again and I had no alternative but to get out of the area. I pushed the throttle lever looking for the runway end while making a quick last check. As soon as I felt the runway, I put full throttle and felt my Pucará vibrate at the demand for power. The 500 metres of runway seemed endless at times and scarce at others.

A glance at the speedometer was enough to realize the reality, so I ignored it; I made sure that the engines were working well and at full throttle; when I reached the end of the runway I simply pulled out, I had 75 knots of speed.

My mission now was to search for enemy helicopters on Bombilla Hill, near San Carlos harbour, and destroy them.

Meeting again with a pleasant and also familiar sound restored confidence and serenity; I was in my 'zone'. We headed off at a very low altitude, making a detour to Alberdi Hill (Mount Usborne). We did not find anything at the point indicated, nor in the area either, and widening our search with the same result, we went back over the Alberdi Hill, 'leaning' on it towards San Carlos. At that moment we received heavy anti-aircraft fire and two missiles passed very close to us, leaving their bluish trail. They came from behind, from seven o'clock.

We began to circle the area where they came from to locate the firing position, but to no avail. We would later learn that our flight leader had been shot down in the same place and that we almost met the same fate. A few minutes after we were ordered to head for Puerto Argentino, our coveted prey appeared: the helicopters.

We were unable to enter Puerto Argentino and when we communicated again with the Condor Base we were told to attack an establishment where the enemy had been detected and from where naval fire was being directed. We were guided directly onto the target where we engaged with rockets, which scored a direct hit, leaving only smouldering ruins.

We were instructed to continue southeast to reconnoitre a similar position when we noticed three Sea Harriers heading towards us: they had evidently seen us. We came across on the opposite course, descending steeply. By the time the enemy section came in over us they had already overrun, so we managed to turn 90° left towards them. We noticed that they were unable to shoot and sought height; at that moment the third appeared, surprising us and continuing the action of the section that had preceded it.

As I reached his gun range, I saw in front of me a deep canyon in a transverse shape. Following the attacker's manoeuvre, I continued to turn 90° to the left and disappeared between its walls with minimum speed. The manoeuvre was not so fortunate for my wingman, who did not make it inside. I glimpsed for an instant as the attacker opened fire with his guns before our radio communication went silent. A kilometre further on, my protective cover ended and I saw my attacker climbing over the area, perhaps looking for me, so I had to return to base alone.

Major Tomba's aircraft was attacked at 1030 by Sea Harrier Frs.Mk.1 serialled XZ451 commanded by Lieutenant Commander Nigel 'Sharkey' Ward (commander of 801st Naval Air Squadron), who recalls the combat:

Initially it was a quiet mission with no traffic until we began our climb after 45 minutes of low flying. When we were at 10,000 feet, the Antrim controller reports, 'I have two low-speed contacts on the ground south of you. Possibly helicopters or ground-attack aircraft. Can you investigate?' As soon as the controller said the word 'south' I initiated the turn to starboard and down. Steve Thomas and Alasdair Craig [Ward's wingmen] followed me. 'Affirmative, descending heading 160°. Do you still have the contacts?' I asked. 'Affirmative, 10 miles, very low.' Steve saw them first; they were a good picture against the indistinct colours of the undulating terrain. 'We've got them Sharkey! Looks like two Pucarás, 15° off the nose.' 'I don't see them, you attack first,' I said. Then as I spoke, I saw one of the Pucarás. Steve was approaching it from his right, up at his 4 o'clock. I decided to attack the same plane because I couldn't see the second plane. 'I have one on visual, the same as you, I'm attacking on your six.' My wingmen opened fire together, the bullets from their guns hitting the ground around the Pucará. I had very little more time to aim and came up behind the enemy aircraft, which was flying very low and manoeuvring almost touching the ground. I centred the Pucará in the HUD sight and squeezed the trigger. The plane jerked as the two 30mm guns opened fire. They hit the target, the Pucará's right engine started to catch fire and then the ammunition hit the left wing. It was very close, so I climbed up. Meanwhile, Steve was getting into position for a second pass. I reduced power and prepared for a second pass from port. As the ground around the enemy took gunfire from Steve and Alasdair, I lowered the flaps halfway. I wanted to come in as slowly as possible. Aiming ... on target ... firing! The left engine of the Pucará burst into flames and a chunk of the rear of the cockpit broke off. My radio altimeter indicated on the HUD that I was firing at a height between 10 and 60 feet above the ground. I climbed back up, fully considering that the pilot had ejected. I thought, 'There must be a very brave pilot in there' because he was still trying to escape the fighters. Steve's section again attacked from the right, but it wasn't their day, with their shots hitting the ground again. I was surprised that the Pucará was still flying and prepared for my third and final pass. 'On target and this time you'll go down,' I thought. Pieces of its fuselage, wing and cockpit surrounded the plane. The fuselage began to catch fire. I stopped firing at the last instant and when I pulled the stick to climb, the pilot ejected. The plane hit the ground at the same time as the pilot. All three of us climbed and returned to the carrier short of fuel.

Once ejected and having landed normally, Tomba walked for a while and was rescued by Bell 212 serialled H-85 commanded by Major Longar of VII Air Brigade. It was the only Pucará shot down in air combat and the difficulty its three attackers had in shooting it down proves the aircraft's endurance and the courage of its pilot.

Faced with this situation, in which they had lost two other planes, Navarro says that he met with the command post and the chief officers 'to see what we were going to do; I said I was going to Puerto Argentino. All the pilots and mechanics went up in helicopters and an escadrille was left at the Condor Base'. Later, at 1600 that day, A-533 commanded by Lieutenant Giménez and A-516 with Lieutenant Cruzado were sent to BAM Malvinas, joining A-509 that had flown earlier with Lieutenant Brest, so that there were no operational aircraft left at Darwin.

Although most personnel went to BAM Malvinas, First Lieutenant Fasani, Lieutenant Calderon and Ensign Sassone remained at Goose Green with a few mechanics and armourers, to support the defence of the base.

Darwin's defence

The day after the landing, Sea Harriers unsuccessfully attacked BAM Condor, while British troops were advancing towards the site, eight kilometres away. Meanwhile, at 2130, the Comodoro Rivadavia Information and Control Centre reported that it had three echoes to the south of IX Air Brigade, presuming that they were helicopters. For this reason, at 2203, Pucará A-558 under the command of Lieutenant Miguel Filipanics was sent to spot the helicopters, which turned off their navigation lights when they detected the Pucará. The Argentine pilot lost them and returned to his base at 2237, leaving again at 2341 and returning at 0026, with negative results.

On 23 May, Lieutenants Brest, Cruzado and Giménez carried out an armed reconnaissance over the islands, without success. Meanwhile, on the mainland two planes left Santa Cruz armed with guns to intercept three echoes of possible helicopters approaching the coast, probably a fresh attempt to infiltrate commandos. Another section of Pucarás remained on the ground ready to scramble, although the helicopters remained elusive.

Offensive reconnaissance flights on the islands continued the following day with Lieutenant Brest's A-533 and Lieutenant Címbaro's A-516, which flew over Beaucheme Island, to the south of the archipelago, between 1400 and 1600, in view of the possibility that there might be British troops there. Címbaro says:

> We went to patrol all the islands one morning to see if there were
> abandoned boats, signs of a night landing. At one point we were told

that we had two Harriers coming down on us, although they were not going below 15,000 feet. When we were about to land, the tower wouldn't let us because they said they [the Harriers] were going to drop bombs on us when we landed. So, we stayed for almost an hour flying low in front of Puerto Argentino waiting for them to withdraw. The Harriers eventually dropped the bombs near the airport and left, so we were able to land.

In addition, at Comodoro Rivadavia, during a coastal reconnaissance flight, A-540 disappeared without trace, causing the death of Ensign Mario Valko, presumed to have fallen into the sea in the San Jorge Gulf. Another action carried out by the Pucarás based on the mainland was the transfer to BAM San Julián of six 1,100-litre Aero 10 extra tanks for use on the A-4Cs, as these aircraft were short of them. For this purpose, three aircraft were used with an empty tank on each wing pylon, which had not been done until then, since these pylons did not have the capacity to carry them full and these were only used on the belly pylon.

On 25 May at 1324, A-516 left with Címbaro at the controls to search for a detected British helicopter but the appearance of a Sea Harrier CAP forced him to return. At 1435 Lieutenant Giménez took off in the same plane and Címbaro in another to reconnoitre the San Luis peninsula (without a British name, the forms the land north of Port Louis, from Rincon Grande to Volunteer Point), without results, and while they were flying, BAM Malvinas was attacked for the second time that day.

The British continued to try different methods to destroy the Puerto Argentino/ Stanley runway, such as toss bombing, high-altitude drops or low-flying attacks preceded by aircraft that served as decoys at high altitude, all of which failed. Nor had the Vulcan strategic bombers been successful in their *Black Back* missions, flying direct from Ascension Island, or naval gunfire. However, a projectile from a ship hit A-516 at 0100 on the morning of the 26th.

During that day almost all the remaining personnel on BAM Condor were evacuated to BAM Malvinas by helicopter, while those who remained joined the ground forces defending the town. Sassone recalls:

We helped with the mechanics to make the tractor *misilístico* [missile tractor], set up a rocket launcher on top of a chicken coop and on top of a slide. Some Pucarás that were broken had had their machine guns removed, so we made some mobile shafts for the 7.62mm machine guns and cut off the rocket launchers that were no longer useful. As we had more than 250 rockets, which had not gone to Puerto Argentino, they were made into Stalin's organs. Some peat bricks were laid and each tube was laid on peat, and the mechanics connected them to an old telephone battery with two terminals.

In addition, 20mm and 35mm anti-aircraft artillery fired over open sights at ground level would cause casualties among the British troops, although they also shot down a Harrier Gr.Mk.3. In this regard, Warrant Officer Mansilla of Grupo Técnico 3 recalls:

> Between 27 and 28 May, we engaged in combat with the British, defending BAM Condor. The idea of making a rocket launcher came one day when the casing of an IIAE-238 rocket launcher cracked and the tubes came loose. Then someone suggested that the tubes might be useful for something. Lieutenant Lombardi led the construction. We pulled out all the tubes, using three of them, an apple crate, two iron profiles, wire and some other items. The aiming system for graduating the range by angle of fire was also improvised and was effective.
>
> During the British attack, I was firing the FFAR rockets from the Pucará that had been left with the improvised missile launcher and Vice-Commodore Costa was in charge of the fire control. We aimed at the advancing British troops and that was where the rockets hit. Our position was close to the coast and very close to one side where there was a two-storey house.

A 19-tube rocket launcher from a Pucará mounted on a slide at Goose Green.

The British fired five Milan missiles at them to neutralize them without success and kept firing. 'They sent three Harriers to silence us because we were making a mess of them. The British asked us afterwards what weapons we had been firing,' recalls Sassone, who added that the 35mm guns were wreaking havoc among the British infantry and

> you could see how they swept through the British ranks. This was not told to me; I saw it myself. Although the British do not acknowledge many casualties, later, after the action, our medics went to assist the British medics and told us that they had had more than 250 casualties that day. You could see in the distance, 500 metres away, on one of the hills, that they would appear in a small group and there the cannon would fire, the ammunition would come out, hit, explode, and the soldiers would fall like dummies, and after a while in another sector another group, until they were closer and came under our FAL fire.

The rocket launcher was one of the most sought-after artefacts for the British after the surrender and when they saw that it was only three rocket tubes and not a ground-to-ground missile launcher, they could not believe it. More than 170 rockets had been fired at them. Sassone also adds:

> We were shooting with FALs [7.62mm FN rifles]; we had a lot of ammunition from the Pucarás, the guns turned red and the soldiers filled our magazines, we had two soldiers, two NCOs, Lema and me. I got to have the British 50 or 100 metres away, who were firing Milan missiles at us; the noise of the rounds passing over our heads was intense – it was really a land battle where we ended up in the front line.

For his part, Fasani remained at the command post to lead the Pucará and Aermacchi MB-339 on their support missions. 'Sometimes when they were coming in, there was such a mess of troops facing each other on the ground that they couldn't tell who was British and who wasn't,' explains Sassone, adding:

> Then came the night, the ceasefire, and the five of us officers who were there decided not to surrender; we prepared a bag, rifle, ammunition, combat rations, to go to Puerto Argentino. Commodore Pedrozo grabbed us and said, 'What you are doing makes no sense, because anyone who moves here will be killed, either by our troops or by the British.'

While this was happening on the ground, the Pucará would go out on critical missions.

Before the battle for Darwin and Goose Green began, on 26 May, A-533 and A-509* with Lieutenants Cruzado and Giménez carried out an offensive reconnaissance to the north of Darwin, determining that the British had at least five Blowpipe anti-aircraft missile launchers, mortars, machine guns and rocket launchers, advancing in groups of 20 to 30 men. To reinforce the two aircraft remaining in service, on 27 May, A-537 with First Lieutenant Hugo Argañaráz and A-532 with Ensign Luis Blanchet were deployed from Río Gallegos, arriving at BAM Malvinas at 1724 covered by two Mirage IIIEAs and guided by the civilian Mitsubishi MU-2, serialled LV-ODZ.

Close air support

At dawn on 28 May the assault on Darwin and Goose Green began and despite the bad weather, with very low clouds and rain, the first close air support mission to the ground troops was carried out. At 0800 the 'Nahuel' flight left, formed by Captain Vila's A-537, Lieutenant Címbaro's A-532 and First Lieutenant Argañaráz's A-533, which successfully attacked targets in Camilla Creek despite the intense fire of Blowpipe missiles and light weapons, returning at 0920 although A-537 was put out of service due to the large number of hits received. Címbaro recalls:

> On the 28th I flew two missions, the first one because the pilots who had to relieve us from the alert could not come because of the red alert, because during the alerts vehicles could not go to the airport. When we arrived, after 30 minutes we were ordered to make the first sortie. Vila was the leader, I was two and Argañaráz was three – it was his first flight on the islands, with no war experience; he had only arrived a few days before. We were guided onto the target to some houses where there were some British in position. Argañaráz saw a missile come out of the house and shouted at me. I didn't understand him, but I looked up and saw something above me, a red dot. The missile didn't engage because they were firing head-on. Another

---

* Although in some texts it is stated as seriously damaged by a bomb dropped by a Harrier GR.Mk.3 on 24 May, losing its tail, the official Air Force report states it taking part in this mission two days later. From this point on, all trace of this aircraft is lost. It is possible that the attack in which it was damaged took place after this date. Also, on the morning of 28 May, it is reported that there were four operational aircraft (A-509, -532, -533 and -537), two of which were out of service after the attack by the Nahuel flight, and the Bagre flight had to leave with two aircraft out of the four planned. During that day A-532 and -533 were also damaged. However, there was no sortie using A-509, which suggests that it was out of service, but was intended to be put back in good condition, and that the most serious damage was received later. At the end of the war the aircraft was captured with a split tail and severe damage caused by an explosion.

missile exploded in Argañaráz's belly and inverted the plane. He thought about ejecting, but he was inverted, so he followed the barrel and saw that the commands responded, then he came back, but he had lost us, so he did it alone. We didn't see the damage we did, but we shot up the houses and probably destroyed them. This attack was at 9 or 9:30 in the morning. I came back at 10 o'clock and at 11 o'clock I went out on the other mission. The weather was horrible.

As he explains, the entire flight was done at low level, visual, and when they reached the area, they were contacted by radio by the controller on the ground who told them where the enemy was.

We flew direct. In my case, I flew back along the coastline, especially because there was a low ceiling. The attack was at 220 knots, which is the maximum speed with rockets. The guns and machine guns were jammed up by the salt, which affected them a lot. As for the rockets, 15 or more were usually fired from each rocket launcher. In this attack we took a lot of hits from light weapons, and if they hit close by, you could feel the crack in the structure. In the second attack I was hit again. In the houses I could see the British troops, but at that moment you are concentrating on the height, the sight and following your leader. We lifted up to the cloud ceiling, we dived and fired the rockets, which took three to four seconds to come out, finished off and made our escape.

Vila says:

I was shot 47 times in the plane. Luckily the Pucará withstood it. I discovered this when I landed. Among the hits was one in the parachute package. Giménez then went out with that plane and fell. The enemy troops were advancing. I met two of them coming at me with missiles and it seemed illogical to shoot at two guys with one plane. One managed to shoot and hit my number 3, it exploded next to him to the point that I lost him. Argarañáz didn't fall, but I don't know where he went next, because we were in a tactical formation. I told Puerto Argentino that we had lost one but after a while Argarañáz came upon the radio and said, 'I'm still alive'. He came back when we had already landed. I hadn't wanted him to fly, because he had arrived the night before but he wanted to go. On the way in we attacked a position with a hut, which we blew up with rockets. I had the guns reserved in case I came across a Harrier.

The next sortie was by the 'Bagre' flight at 0920, which, although it had been planned with four aircraft, the existence of only two in service meant that only the first section of Captain Grünert (A-533) and Lieutenant Russo (A-532) armed with LAU-61 rockets and internal armament went out. Grünert attacked scattered troops near the runway with all rockets on the first pass, moving the pedals to cover more area and taking intense small-arms fire, which damaged his left engine. He kept firing with the guns. Russo was unable to fire his full load and after a turn made another pass, also taking heavy flak. The aircraft returned safely at 1015, although A-533 was put out of service due to engine damage.

The next sortie consisted of the 'Sombra' flight, which was formed by Lieutenant Giménez in A-537, repaired as best they could so that at least they could fly, and Lieutenant Címbaro in A-532, who were the ones who should have formed the second section of the 'Bagre'. Címbaro recalls:

> Giménez had not flown but the rest of us had, so I volunteered to go. I explained to him how we had attacked before. The mission was the same, to look for targets of opportunity. After 20 minutes we entered the area and communicated with BAM Condor, but at that moment we saw two helicopters coming almost head-on from the right, diagonally. Giménez asked me if I had seen them and I said yes, then he asked Cóndor if they were ours; it seemed to me that they were Bell 212s, but we were told they were British. At that moment the helicopters saw us and separated. I went for the one on the right and Giménez went for the one on the left. While I was manoeuvring, I saw Giménez firing and I heard, 'I've shot him down! I've shot him down!' I didn't hear him again as I continued with my target. I put it in my sights but the helicopter changed course, and after doing this twice I decided to shoot at it anyway. I aimed further ahead, with the three rockets, as it took a long time for the rockets to come out. I got very close and as the rockets hit the ground the helicopter lost stability and the blades touched the ground, the helicopter sprawled stricken on the ground. I was swallowing mud from the explosions. I got away from the scene and started the turn to set an escape course, but I realized that I was aiming for San Carlos, I reversed the turn, passed close to the helicopter and they threw everything at me. I saw that it was being evacuated. When I landed I had more than 50 bullet holes in the aircraft.

Meanwhile, Giménez had returned on his own. Címbaro called him on his way back and said, 'I'm on a climb, inside the clouds, on such a course,' to which Giménez replied, 'I'm below you in visual, below the clouds.' When Cimbaro started to fly over the sea, he called him to tell him to set a left course towards Puerto Argentino, but he had no answer.

> I asked the radar operator, but he said he had an echo at one position, but had lost it. I went back and when they asked me what had happened, I said, 'Relax, we split; he's inside the clouds, but he's coming.' I think he wanted to fly for a while and when

he thought he was over the water he started to descend, but he miscalculated and crashed into Rivadavia Hill [Blue Mountain], the highest on the islands. At no time did he say he had any problems in the plane.

As for Giménez's attack, some say he attacked with guns, but Címbaro maintains it was with rockets because he saw a glare similar to that of rockets being launched. Both helicopters were on their way to the front to evacuate wounded, each manned by a pilot and a crewman acting as a paramedic. The Scout shot down by Gimenez was XT629, in which its pilot, Sergeant Richard Nunn, was killed and his wingman, Bill Belcher, lost his left leg. According to his account, the Pucará attacked them first with guns and then with rockets, making two passes. In the case of the helicopter shot down by Cimbaro, it was Scout XP902 and he says that he made three passes to attack it, 'but I didn't shoot at it in the first two. With guns I didn't shoot at it at any time. The guns jammed on the second shot when I tried them on the way back. The machine guns jammed after 10 or 15 rounds.'

On his return, because he was one of the pilots who had been in combat from the beginning, he was ordered by his boss to return to the mainland.

> I left on the night of the 29th/30th in a C-130. I went to Reconquista and from there to Resistencia to go home, but they immediately sent for me to go to Santa Cruz and be on alert. There I was given a mission to go to the islands, attack with napalm or bombs and return. I thought it was impossible to return. We were only two or three planes. We were going with extra tanks so we could get back. It was 11 or 12 June, over Dos Hermanas [Two Sisters]. In the end the mission was cancelled. It was the first time I was going up in a plane with fear, it was very difficult to escape.

Giménez's remains were found by chance, several years later. Regarding the attack on the helicopters, Brigadier Julian Thompson, in his book *No Picnic* (Editorial Atlántida, Buenos Aires, 1987) stated that 'The Pucará could slow down and become a reflection of the helicopters' manoeuvres, they were a lethal enemy'.

At midday of 28 May, A-536 aircraft arrived from the mainland under the command of First Lieutenant Luis Martínez Chávez, A-515 with Ensign Rubén Omar Mansur and A-555 with Ensign Rubén Galván, flying with full internal armament, three bombs in the central station and two 318-litre tanks; on this occasion they were guided by the MU-2 serialled LV-ODZ. This increased the number of aircraft to five, as A-533 was out of service.

The last sortie of the day was by the 'Fénix' flight, with First Lieutenant Micheloud in A-536 and Lieutenant Cruzado in A-555, who left in the afternoon. Micheloud remembers their mission in this way:

> We were ordered to leave at dusk and by the light we must have been the last ones that day. The sky was grey, almost totally overcast and

the ceiling was 500 feet, although we would not reach it; for us it was too much. Our mission was to provide direct fire support to our ground forces. The target was located very close to the Condor base and the latest indications were given to us at the time of our entry.

My armament consisted of bombs [napalm containers, the only time they were used in the war], rockets, guns and machine guns, and my numeral's [wingman] was the same, only without bombs.

Less than 20 minutes after take-off, the scene of our combat awaited us. We were flying so low that we even doubted at times the distance to this familiar ground, although we had a good reference: the smoking ruins of the school of Goose Green. Our final acceleration puzzled us because we did not find the bulk of the enemy; only dribs and drabs on the ground that did not constitute any profitable target. In reality, what had happened was that the front had moved inexorably.

We had more precise indications by VHF and after making a detour around the enemy rearguard we entered from the northwest, from their flank, close to the water from the end of the channel and with a headwind; we tried to hide the noise of our engines coming ahead of us, trying to increase our surprise. When the distance permitted, I began to open fire on the enemy positions, who were firing hellishly. I had to pass over them to drop my bombs, endless yards, grey afternoon mingled with smoke, smoking ruins, figures disappearing into the terrain, tracers coming from everywhere. I dropped my load where I remembered I had seen my target. I felt the impact on my plane and I stuck even more closely to the ground. I swerved a little to see my bombs: they were out and the plumes of smoke confirmed that they had exploded.

I started calling my wingman. I did it several times and the control answered that they had seen him eject over enemy lines. Alarm lights were flashing on my dashboard, the engine was spluttering. I let it do so but it kept running. I heard the friendly voice of one of our helicopters telling me it would cover my return, which gave me confidence. The engine ran until I arrived. Once again, my Pucará had not failed me.

Cruzado, for his part, recalls:

First, Navarro was going to go out, but in the end, it was Micheloud as flight leader and me as a wingman. When we started up, there was an air raid alarm, in the middle of which a section of Aermacchi MB-339s from the Navy took off, in which Lieutenant Daniel Miguel was killed. We left with Micheloud. We went out, we made a pass near what had been the little school in Darwin; everything was on fire as they [the enemy] had bombarded the area with artillery. They marked an area for us on the radio. We went in with Micheloud at a low angle, we couldn't see very well, the people couldn't be seen when they stood still on the ground. We came in again from another direction, then we started firing; someone on the ground on our frequency told us, 'Keep firing close to there.' I fired the first rockets in salvo. I climbed a little and bullets began striking the aircraft on the right side. I began to feel like when you walk on glass – that noise stayed with me. They told me later that Blowpipe missiles had been fired at me, but I didn't see them. I heard sputtering and smelled smoke; that didn't bother me so much as the bullet strikes. I wanted to turn to the left. I fired a rocket and I could see that something moved, then nothing. I was guided by what they had said – to keep on firing. I felt that the plane was not responding. I was already very close to the ground. I ejected at no more than 15 metres from the ground. I had been coming in from a low angle and would have lifted to 30 metres to look for a bit of angle and sweep. Some didn't see me eject and thought I had stayed in the plane. I didn't look at anything. All of a sudden, the cockpit opened. I remember, beyond all the adrenaline of that moment, the fear, and how everything comes into your head. I pulled the handle and saw that the seat came out through the dome. I could see the cockpit full of smoke and I saw tracers flying towards the plane. I don't know at what moment it stopped, because I was already on the ground; we are talking about seconds because the process of the parachute opening is a thousandth of a second and until the parachute opened completely, it must have been half a second. I calculated that I'd fallen very close to the airfield. I didn't know which way to run. It was twilight. I wanted to run away. I got tangled up and fell. I had fallen near a British soldier in the heat of battle. The man grabbed me. He was very upset; he must have been 19 or 20 years old. A non-commissioned officer appeared and ran him off and took charge of the situation; he took my weapon and told me that we were going to move to the rear. We were still in the middle of combat and had to dive to the ground every so often. We arrived at the rear where there was already a large group of Argentine prisoners.

Sassone recalls how he saw the shootdown from below:

He ejects, but the plane continues flying and that's when we started to see it, we saw it in one piece, level, it makes a very smooth turn, with the left plane hitting the ground, but it doesn't explode, at the moment it hits the plane and hits the nose, the right engine comes off the wing and flies away, the plane starts to spin. I'll never forget about the engine being ripped out of the wing root and flying out of the top of the plane.

Rick Strange, a British Royal Marines Blowpipe missile operator, was in the area and says:

> We could hear a plane but we were watching the battlefield to our front, I looked around and shouted, 'Plane!' and with one hand I indicated the threat. It was about 600 metres away, too close for a missile. My buddy beat me to the MAG machine gun, so I was relegated to feeding the gun and backing him up. My buddy (a big guy) hit the target on the first burst, firing the weapon the same way I would fire a rifle. I could see the stream of tracers hitting and bouncing off. I think Lieutenant Cruzado got the better of the 120 rounds of 7.62mm with his plane. Interestingly, the engine noise didn't change, but we could see it was coming down. We stopped and watched him all the way out of the place, and the next thing I could see is a black and red oily ball and we could see little men running away from the place. I said I didn't think we should claim the shootdown, as it landed very close to the 2 Para men.

Lieutenant Cruzado fell inside the British lines and was captured, while Micheloud landed at 1720 with the aircraft with many strike impacts on the ailerons, flaps, left side and the propeller pitch command disabled.

By the end of the day only A-515 was fully operational, with A-532 having strikes to the ailerons and left flap. The other two remaining aircraft were out of service. With few Pucará operations possible, that night the C-130H TC-66 evacuated nine pilots (Captains Grünert and Vila, First Lieutenants Martínez Chávez and Navarro, Lieutenants Címbaro and Russo, Ensigns Blanchet, Galván and Manzur) to Comodoro Rivadavia.

The next morning the position at Darwin and Goose Green fell and fighting ceased in that area, so the Pucarás had a respite.

The final days

On 29 May, A-549 commanded by First Lieutenant Marcelo Ayerdi, A-522 commanded by Ensign Rodolfo Hub and A-514 commanded by Ensign Eduardo La Torre were ordered to cross from the mainland. The planes, with the callsign 'Mayo', crossed again supported by an MU-2 until they saw the islands. There were now seven Pucarás on strength, although they would not leave again until 1 June.

On 1 June an Army Roland anti-aircraft missile shot down the Harrier GR.Mk.3 serialled ZX456, commanded by Lieutenant Ian Mortimer and FAA Chinook helicopter serialled H-93 was sent to rescue him, escorted by A-514 commanded by Benítez, followed by Micheloud in another Pucará. As they were leaving, the leader's plane lost steering control, went off course and crashed into A-532, disabling both aircraft, although the pilots were uninjured. Micheloud continued with the

Chinook, although they had to interrupt the search because of an approaching PAC escorting a British Sea King on the same task.

By this stage of the war, the lack of spare parts and the poor conditions in which the mechanics had to work made the operation of the aircraft very difficult. In addition, the weather was very bad for the aircraft, which were left outdoors on a runway by the sea. In particular, the electrical circuits were damaged.

For that reason, the Pucarás would only make a single combat mission before the end of the war, on 10 June, and it consisted of the departure of Micheloud's A-536, A-515 with Lieutenant Morales and A-522 with Ayerdi, to provide close air support to the Army forces, attacking artillery positions and troops on the northern slope of Mount Kent, to try to stop the British advance on Puerto Argentino/Stanley. At 0828 the 'Fierro' flight left and attacked British positions on Mount Kent and Murell Bridge with rockets (each carrying five 19-tube rocket launchers) and guns, although the third, which was to attack the bridge, had problems with the rockets and didn't fire. Nevertheless, they hit the target and returned safely at 0845, but as in almost all previous cases, the two wingmen were hit by small-arms fire.

By this time, it had been decided not to send any more aircraft to the islands, as the end of the war was anticipated over the next few days and they would not have much influence on the fighting; in the meantime, the aircraft that were on the islands did not fly again. On the 11th a mission was planned with A-522 and A-515 in the area near Mount Two Sisters where the 40th, 42nd and 45th Commando Battalions of the Royal Marines were preparing to attack the Army's 4th Infantry Regiment, which was to take place the following day, but the fall of the Argentine position and a failure of A-522's nose gear wheel led to the mission being cancelled. On 13 June, a final close air support sortie with the four operational aircraft was planned for the following day, to then return to Santa Cruz and avoid capture of the aircraft by the British, as the final assault on Puerto Argentino had begun. Navarro explains that there were

> four pilots and three and a half planes left. They told me that the war was still going on, and I asked for Vila and Grünnert to return if the war continued. We had prepared those planes with fuel, guns and machine guns to attack a ship, but they wouldn't let us.

An attack from the mainland was also planned, as Vila recalls:

> They took us to Puerto Santa Cruz to look for planes and leave the next day. At 8 a.m. the brigade commander woke us up and told us 'Take off your flight suit and go to sleep; the war is over.'

Thus, both planned sorties from the islands and from the mainland were cancelled and the aircraft and crews remaining in the Falklands were captured. During the two and a half months they were in the Malvinas/Falklands, the Pucarás flew 186 sorties from the islands, completing 317 flying hours, destroying at least one helicopter and causing numerous casualties among British ground personnel.

Chapter 10

Return With Glory

On 19 June, six of the Pucarás at BAM Santa Cruz withdrew to Reconquista, arriving three days later, followed on the 24th by A-501, which arrived on the 26th. They were joined by A-541 on the 28th, used until then by the CEV, in addition to A-563, -572 and -573 aircraft, new from the factory. This delivery was followed on 15 July by the planes A-564, -567 and -568 and on 12 August by A-560, -569 and -575, while on 9 September III Brigade officially dropped from the inventory the 24 aircraft lost in the war and IX Brigade did the same with A-540.

Deliveries continued in December 1982, with the arrival of A-570, -571, -574 and -577 on the 14th and A-578 on the 29th, already covering 15 of those lost in the war and the FMA ending the 14 planned aircraft, registering A-583 from the workshop on 29 October, starting the assembly of the serial 088 aircraft (A-588) and also building an airframe for fatigue tests with the example 087, delivered on 16 September.

Due to the fact that the Patagonian area was still 'hot', on 18 December 1982, the Pucarás carried out a deployment to BAM Río Gallegos, a task that was constantly conducted by the other weapons systems to maintain a presence in the area, until in 1983 the 10th Air Brigade was created at that base, equipped with the newly received Mirage IIICs.

III Air Brigade ended 1982 with 25 Pucarás, an IA-50 GII and the Hughes, although it was damaged; on 6 January 1983 A-570 crashed in Laguna del Bonete, Santa Fe, killing both pilots. By then, Comodoro Rivadavia's IV Squadron had six aircraft.

The fleet continued to increase with the arrival of A-579 and -576 aircraft on 16 February, A-580 and -582 on 16 March, and A-583 on 20 April, with the FMA completing nine of the 10 planned. In addition, on 21 January, the FMA Cessna 182J with serial PG-373 joined the Services Squadron.

In September A-541 was lost at the Garabato firing range, when the structure collapsed while the aircraft was exiting a firing run, killing the pilot. Due to this, flights in the Pucarás were suspended until October.

Earlier, on 22 April, the first solo flight of the CEPAC was carried out, with the participation of two officers from the Uruguayan Air Force (FAU). On 28 June, 10 Pucarás were deployed to the Avellaneda aeroclub, a few kilometres from the brigade, where they made nine day and night tactical sorties, returning the following

Above: A-538 received a special paint scheme during the war, which was kept for some years. The plane was destroyed in an accident in 1988.

Right: On May 1982 the FMA delivered 12 planes. They were A-541, used by the FMA on the Latin American tour in 1980 plus A-559, -561, -562, -563, -564, -565, -567, -568, -569, -570 and -571. (Archive José Martínez)

The planes delivered in May 1982 all received a paint scheme designed especially for operations in the Malvinas. A-561, which was destined for the CEV, kept the scheme, with minor variations, until 2019. (Archive José Martínez)

day. This deployment was followed by another between 18 and 22 December to BAM Río Gallegos of a squadron with 24 pilots and 14 specialists.

During 1984 and with the objective of increasing the combat capacity of IV Squadron of IX Air Brigade, it was planned to transfer to A-560, -569, -573 and -574 aircraft of III Air Brigade, which was carried out throughout the year, increasing the strength of the unit to 10 Pucarás. Likewise, the aircraft in service would be fewer because on 1 April A-566 suffered the breakage of the leading edge of the wing when colliding with a bird and on 18 July A-569 collided with telephone cables during a tactical navigation.

Meanwhile, the FMA planned to deliver the aircraft A-596 to A-608, but budget cuts that began with the inauguration of President Raúl Alfonsín on 10 December 1983 overturned these plans and none was delivered. At the end of the year the planes with serial numbers 096 to 100 were at 62 per cent and 101 at 5 per cent. The others had not started assembly. The main problem was the lack of engines and propellers which prevented completion. Furthermore, although there were 29 Pucarás at Reconquista at the end of the year, only 10 were in service.

III Air Brigade began 1984 with the incorporation on 13 February of the Hughes H-28 to replace the crashed H-20. Shortly after, on 12 March, the planes were

154

Pucarás of Escuadrón IV, including A-551, -557, -558, -565 and -566. A-557 is without camouflage, A-565 and -566 were delivered to the unit in December 1982, wearing the scheme applied at the FMA in May 1982, and A-551 and -558 were camouflaged during the war.

TA-560 had a nose with a small unknown air intake, which was seen on the planes modified with radar.

deployed to Córdoba to carry out a firepower demonstration in front of President Alfonsín on the 15th, returning that day.

That year Pucará A-591, which was delivered to the workshop but had not been delivered to the Air Force, was sent in March to participate in a new iteration of the FIDA fair, at the El Bosque Air Base, in Santiago de Chile.

Dissimilar combat exercises

The Malvinas/Falklands War left among its legacy the lack of training of most units in air combat against aircraft other than those of the unit itself. In the years before the war, combat exercises were carried out by each unit on their own, so the pilots only knew how to fight against the model in which they flew. Furthermore, the attack units, as was the case of the Pucarás, did not carry out air-to-air combat exercises. This led to the failure of attack aircraft pilots to generally apply effective techniques to escape, or contest, Sea Harriers when intercepted.

To remedy this situation, the Argentine Air Force decided to organize dissimilar combat exercises, where they would face, in different circumstances (one against one, two against one or two against two, mainly), the different models of combat aircraft of the force. Thus, in general, the Morane Saulnier Paris and F-86F Sabre of IV Air Brigade, A-4B and C Skyhawks of V Air Brigade, the IAI M5 Daggers of VI Air Brigade, the Mirage IIIEA of VIII Air Brigade and IA-58A Pucará of III Air Brigade. Commodore Raúl Páez, who joined Attack Group 3 after the war, explains that 'there was always a lot of resistance within the FAA for the Pucará crews to prepare on air-to-air manoeuvres'.

Thus, from 24 to 30 June 1984, Operation *Zonda 84* was carried out in Mendoza, deploying three Pucarás. In addition, Grupo II de Vigilancia y Control del Espacio Aéreo (Airspace Surveillance and Control Group II) participated with a mobile radar to guide the aircraft. According to Páez, the result was very poor, because the units were not ready. On this occasion, the Mirage III managed to film the Pucarás with their machine guns, simulating kills, which would not be repeated in the future. Páez explains that the pilots who were destined to fly Pucará, after doing the CEPAC

> did not learn anything more about air-air if you did not go to hunting units. So, with the other Pucareros [Pucará pilots] we were exchanging experiences, talking about how each one did before a manoeuvre, but then there was something that changed things a bit and we went to the front, someone stole information ... In the year '85, we were already fully preparing for the next exercise and not to be embarrassed, we were practising air-to-air themes. There was a French pilot, his name was Pierre, and before going to fly an air-to-air subject, he always sneaked in to fly, opened a briefcase, took

out a manual he had, looked at it, put it away and went flying. A pilot says, 'I saw that he had air-to-air manoeuvring drawings there, it must be an air-to-air combat manual.' So, one day we prepared everything and Pierre went off to fly with Rubén Sassone on an air-to-air exercise, as a co-pilot. He had an hour and a half or more to fly. As soon as they started up and left, the pilots got hold of Pierre's briefcase which had a combination that they deciphered and took out the manual that was for air-to-air manoeuvres for Mirages in the French Air Force. There were basic manoeuvres, about 20 pages, so they copied them, put the manual back inside his briefcase and left it where it was. The manual was in French and the wife of another officer, who knew French, translated it. After it was typed up, we drew the manoeuvres as they were in the original and distributed it. Then we practised the manoeuvres, two against one, two against two and we got to do simulated combat of four against four. It was a mess: instead of looking at the opponent you made sure no one else hit you, but it had good results. The Frenchman never knew that we had taken the manual from him; he spent about 30 days at Reconquista.

Páez adds that

in the manual it also said that if you have a lower-performance aircraft, you have to find the defensive manoeuvre that is most favourable for you: a horizontal manoeuvre. In Pucará, if they attacked us, we would turn as tightly as possible, with an 80- or 90° inclination, to make a circle as small as possible. As you are putting G, he cannot shoot you, because you are permanently leaving the shooting zone. And if he enters the horizontal plane to get in line, he loses, because it has a higher performance and it overshoots, then you reverse the turn, you get in line and you have about 30 seconds to film it. Against Mirage and A-4 it was the main manoeuvre.

Sassone adds:

There we learned that in the Pucará the best weapon is not what we had in mind in Malvinas, which was to look for a canyon, slow down and hide, but that the best defence is to face it [the enemy aircraft]. Tomba noted that when he saw the Harrier he tried to sneak away. In those fights I had to fly against M5 Dagger.

In 1984, II Air Squadron took part in another exercise, carried out in conjunction with II Army Corps at Laguna Blanca, the first time that they carried out exercises with that force. Operation *Nahuel* was also carried out at V Air Brigade from Villa Reynolds, San Luis province, between 9 and 14 September. Finally,

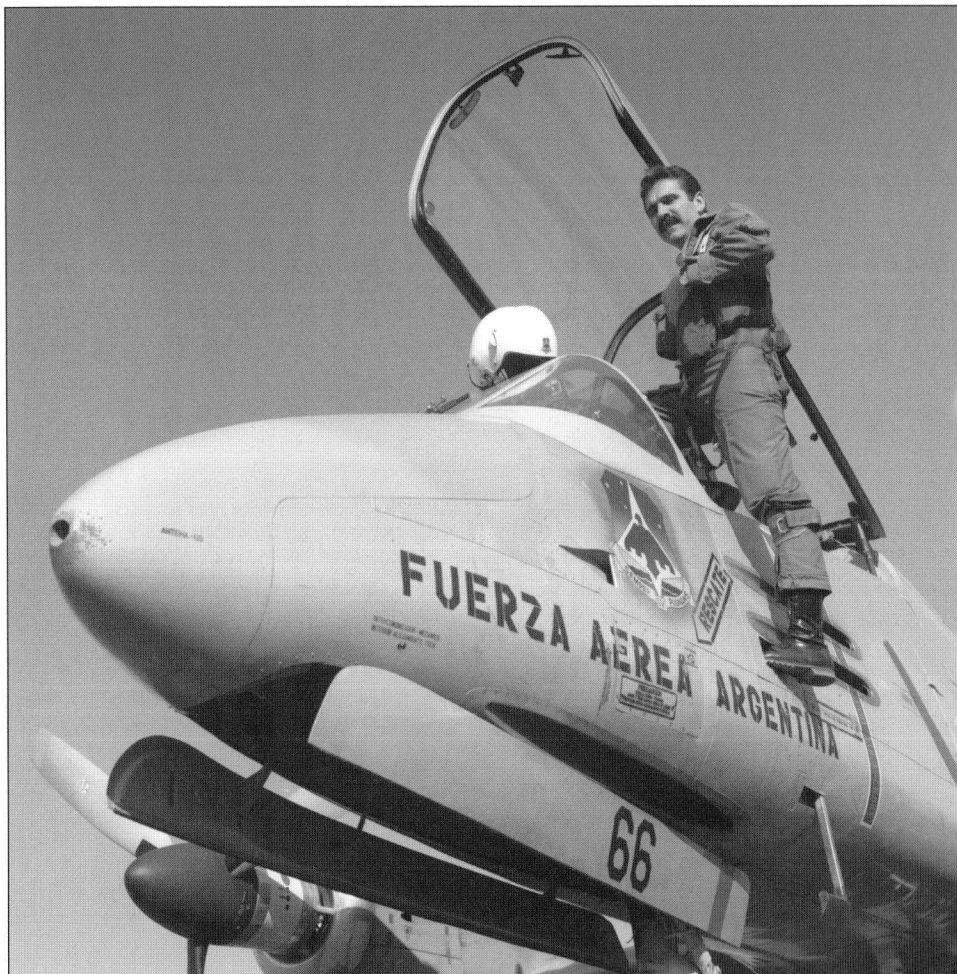

A pilot posing on A-566, which wears the Escuadrón IV badge.

between 23 and 28 September, eight Pucarás were deployed to the Mar del Plata BAM to carry out air-to-air firing over the Mar Chiquita shooting range, in order to put into practice the tactics they were developing based on what had been learned in Exercise *Zonda*.

While the FMA plan in 1985 was to finish seven aircraft, up to c/n 108 (A-608), the lack of engines and propellers again paralyzed production, leaving c/nos. 096 to 104 at 62 per cent, 105 at 3 per cent and the rest without starting to be assembled. Additionally, A-595 (c/n 095), which was 90 per cent from final assembly, had its engines removed for use in other aircraft that were in service.

In addition to constant budget cuts, which forced all funds to be diverted to the IA-63 Pampa trainer programme, which was starting flight tests, the

Pucará A-576 is seen at I Brigada Aérea, El Palomar, on 10 August 1984. (Photo Alberto Martín)

Argentine Air Force no longer had the need for an anti-guerrilla plane, as this type of threat had practically disappeared. Now the Pucará served only as a close air support, supporting combat rescue missions and patrolling the borders in search of illegal flights. For this reason, the assembly line was frozen as the FMA, through the recently created Tecnología Aeroespacial (TEA S.A.), a company owned by the factory to sell its products, began to negotiate the sale of the Pucará abroad.

Meanwhile, III Brigade had in 1985 been assigned A-501, -505, -510, -512, -518, -524, -530, -534, -538, -550, -562, -563, -564, -567, -568, -571, -572, -575, -576, -577, -578, -579, -580, -581, -582, -583, AX-04 and AX-06. IX Air Brigade, for its part, had the ones serialled A-551, -557, -558, -559, -560, -565, -566, -569, -573 and -574. The aircraft from A-584 to A-594 – except for A-586 and -587 whose serials were not used, although they had been delivered to the FMA workshop – had not as yet been delivered to the Air Force.

Due to the reduction in the number of pilots who were trained for the fighter units and before the next incorporation of the IA-63 Pampa, in 1985 the last CEPAC was made in Pucará, which left only IV Air Brigade to teach the course.

The main operation of the Pucará in 1985 was the participation in Exercise *Zonda 85* in Mendoza, the second round of the dissimilar combat training, which included the first participation of the Mirage IIICs from IV Air Brigade. What was learned in the previous year had led to the idea of installing an air-to-air sight on the Pucará, for which a sight taken from a Mirage IIIEA was tested. Roberto Vila says:

> my idea was to put missiles on the Pucará. The first hurdle I faced was from the engineers, who told me that to install missiles you had to put them on the tip of the wing, because of the propellers. My idea was that if we had had that in Malvinas we could have spent four hours flying overhead with the missiles while no one came near.

With the support of VIII Air Brigade, the sight was installed on an airplane, together with an Omera camera, and during the exercise it was evaluated by Vila in combat against an M5 Dagger under the command of Roberto Janett. Vila relates:

> It's all filmed, it was in super 8. We ran into each other. Janett and I head-on, and the moment we cross each other I turn and stay in shooting distance until he moves away, it's all filmed. What we were doing with the Mirage, we started together; he put on his afterburner and he went up, but I couldn't follow him. I was following him with my eyes until he was a little dot and from there he would turn back, but then I would go down, forcing him to get to 90° and he couldn't – he had to go back out with me running him.

Páez, on his side, adds that the Mirage

> would go down, try to pull and come up to make turns and search backwards, diving on the plane. When you saw that they were going up, you changed the turn; when they lowered their nose and looked for you, you turned again 90° to one side or the other. If it was outlined for one side, you turned for the other to make the turn more difficult and they had no choice but to get back up. They went crazy, because they tried several times and they couldn't. Some, due to the anger, would enter to level up and there you would do a couple of basic manoeuvres to get them to go forward, because the Mirage, even though it comes with brakes and everything reduced, passes forward and if it slows down it will not have the kinetic energy to get away. There you put yourself in the queue. The same was with the A-4s and the Sabres. One of the first riders to go was Rubén Lianza and for almost a minute and a half he followed a Sabre.

In addition, Páez explains that tests were carried out to try to capture the Pucará with the Mirage missiles

> but they were quite negative. The Pucará has a small exhaust nozzle; it blows air at a not so high temperature and the propeller that is

blowing makes it lose the temperature of the nozzle. What the missiles captured was more the metallic silhouette.

It was thought as a strategy before a missile firing that, if the pilot sees the shot, he makes a very sharp turn and reduces power, so that the missile does not capture the heat.

Over time, the Mirage pilots learned to face the Pucará, although they were not able to shoot them down. Páez says that

> undoubtedly the most difficult was the Mirage, because if the pilot was seasoned and did not allow himself to be tempted to go down to our terrain it was a draw, maybe he could film us in a crossing of less than three seconds, which for the accounting of the shot does not work.

For his part, Vila says that with the A-4 Skyhawk they were even:

> it has more power, but you always cut the turn inside and you force it until it is thrown, and your work is easier; on the other hand, with the Mirage they wanted to take you up and I couldn't. When the Mirage came to me, I started to itch, forcing it to turn to 90 degrees.

Páez adds that

> With the A-4 there was no problem because they tried to go down to the horizontal plane and they passed by; they could not shoot because one was in a defensive manoeuvre and when they passed by, you would go from defensive to offensive with a small turn and that was it.

Thus, the Pucará was shown to be a most difficult prey for combat aircraft such as the Mirage or the Skyhawk, since, due to its low speed, fighters could not engage in a dogfight, but had to launch themselves from great heights, usually with the sun at their back, which allowed the Pucará to escape. The problem was that with the great manoeuvrability of the IA-58 and since they operated in pairs, covering their tails, there was always one of them pointing at the attacking plane. Explains Páez:

> The operation of two to protect us began to be seen during the war. It was seen in theory, but not in practice. But there, already in the exercises, it was practically mandatory that one protects the other and is watching and the other protects you. On each flight they would put themselves in defensive formation, where you have the other plane in sight and you look forward and behind it.

In addition, the Pucará began to test-combat against helicopters. Vila describes that

> with a helicopter combat is difficult because the helicopter does not manoeuvre. Unless you catch it while standing … but if it saw you, it is going to throw you with whatever it has. I can slow down to fire to up to 120 knots. It could up to 80, but the Pucará is already hanging and does not manoeuvre.

Sassone adds:

> We also learned to work with helicopters. Although we had an idea, it was not in the plans to be hunting helicopters. With Grünert we made the Pucará combat manual against helicopters. One of the ideas, without having had that doctrine, was to go looking for helicopters; the most likely thing was to aim the sight at the helicopter; now we are studying how to hunt it. The helicopter was looking to go under you to get away, the angle becomes more vertical and you can hit the ground. In Pucará, against helicopters, the technique is to always have speed to be able to manoeuvre: the turning radius may be greater, but speed gives control.

On his side, Páez says that

> We fought against Hughes 500, which caused us grey hairs, because they made tight manoeuvres or stayed stationary and we had to escape and relocate to an offensive position again. With the helicopters we became the Mirage. It happened to me once that they were hiding behind the trees; I was going with a certain height, 150 metres, and we had to face a Hughes 500 and when we faced off, he made a turn and disappeared, he got between some trees. When I saw him, I could go in to shoot him and he was an easy target. If I didn't guess where he was, I lost it.
>
> In air-to-air you have to try to slow down as little as possible. For a helicopter you could lower it to about 100 knots, but no less than that. If you come in at 270 you can decrease to 200, 180, but not less than that. At 100 it would be crazy because you have no way to escape.
>
> We did something similar to that with airplanes; we agreed on a sector to meet, and saw each other, and after such a reference we would move away in the opposite direction and fly for about three minutes. If the course was reversed , you knew you'd find him – it was a matter of searching until you had each other visual.

In addition, on some occasions the IA-58s carried pilots of other weapons systems in the back seat while Pucará pilots flew in planes such as the two-seater Mirage so that they could check how that airplane fought.

A-534 using the JATOs for the last time on a Pucará, on 28 April 1986 at the hands of Lt Ayerdi.

A-588 at FIDAE 88 in Chile. While A-594 was on the static exhibition, this plane performed the flying one. (Photo Alberto Martín)

The *Zonda* exercise would also be repeated in 1986, but this time in the Área de Material Río IV, in the province of Córdoba.

In 1986 the assembly of the airplanes progressed marginally, reaching 62 per cent in airplanes from 095 to 105, 45 per cent the 107 and 15 per cent for the 108, without being able to receive the engines and propellers, therefore that could not be finished.

At that time, the use of the FAS 250 bomb was evaluated in Pucará; this was a local development based on the 250kg Expal general-purpose bomb, with a tail

163

Planes of Escuadrón IV de Ataque flying over the Patagonia. A-551 is still wearing the camouflage applied during the war. A-560 was delivered to the unit in 1984, wearing the same paint as A-565 and -566. A-558 has had the camouflage removed, while the A-574 had already been delivered by the factory without camouflage, in December 1982, and sent to Escuadrón IV in 1984.

braked by parachute. The unit already regularly used the Expal of that weight and one of 454 kilograms. The FAS 250 would ultimately not be mass-produced.

On 28 April 1986, President Raúl Alfonsín visited III Air Brigade and flew in the Pucará under the command of First Lieutenant Furios, being the first president to fly in the model, which was only repeated by Carlos Menem. That day, Lieutenant Ayerdi demonstrated take-off with JATOs with A-534, the last time this system would be used for take-off.

The only modification to the fleet that occurred in 1986 was the retirement of the first plane, A-501, which on 30 September 1987 was transferred to the Air Force NCO School for use as educational material.

Budget cuts

During 1987 the FMA continued without being able to finish the series, although it made some progress in the assembly of aircraft 106 to 108.

The Reconquista aircraft, the most active, conducted air-to-air training in Tandil on 4 May 1987, together with the Mirages and Daggers of that unit, where two Pucarás were deployed. On 6 and 7 July, they participated in the joint operation *Laguna Blanca III* with the Army in La Paz, Entre Ríos province. In addition, in

August, four crews carried out an exchange with the Brazilian Air Force, where they flew the Tucano and the Brazilians trained on the Pucará.

On 6 August 1987, seven Pucarás moved to VII Air Brigade in Morón, to participate in the Air Force Day event on 10 August and taking part until 16 August through the Aeronautical Week. Once this was finished, while being transported through the streets of Buenos Aires, A-568 was hit by a bus. Although it was damaged, it was repaired and flown to Reconquista shortly thereafter.

On 23 September 1987, A-518 (still painted in the colours of Mauritania) suffered a minor accident and was sent to the FMA for repair. Although it was expected to be sent to the CEV later, it was never recovered.

The following month, from the 4th to the 10th, the Aeromobile Squadron was deployed to Mendoza with eight aircraft to participate in the *Antuna III* shooting exercise, on the Antuna firing range, in the province of San Luis on its border with Mendoza. During the same period, Uruguayan Pucará pilots joined in the first exchange between local Pucará pilots.

The last important task in 1987 consisted of the deployment carried out on 3 December by eight IA-58s to IX Brigade to conduct air-to-air training until the 12th of that month.

On 5 August 1988, A-584 was finished by the FMA, which was delivered to III Brigade shortly after, while A-585 and A-588 to A-597 remained in the workshop with completion between 75 and 90 per cent. In May of that year, the missing engines and propellers arrived, and manufacturing continued, albeit slowly. However, A-588 received engines from an aircraft in service, to be presented that year at FIDA 88, in Santiago, Chile, then returned to the FMA to be readied.

On 23 June the Pucarás participated with the Army in a joint exercise called *La Paz* and from 19 to 25 October a close air support exercise was carried out with the 6th and 1st Tank Cavalry Regiments in Nogoyá and Villaguay, province of Entre Ríos.

Due to a military uprising against the government of President Alfonsín on 23 October 1988 in Monte Caseros, Corrientes province, the Pucará carried out support flights for the Army units deployed there to quell the insurrection, although it was not necessary for them to enter combat.

On 24 June, A-583 was damaged when it collided with a cable in a tactical navigation; it was later repaired. On 29 June the loss of A-538 was recorded, where its pilot, Ensign Horacio Caballero, had to eject.

Thanks to the arrival of the missing material, in 1989 the 108 series production airframes were completed and between June and October the production line was shut down, to make way for the Pampa. Similarly, the tail of the 108 aircraft was used to replace that of A-563. At that time a plan was made to deliver four in three months and then one per month with the assembly line in hall 36 of the factory. A-585 and -595 were ready, while A-588 was finished by the factory and ready for check flights by the Air Force, to be officially received.

That year, on 15 September, President Carlos Menem became the second and last head of state to fly the Pucará, flying on A-583 from Jorge Newbery Airport, with Major Juan Micheloud, to the town of Zárate, with the president at the controls of the plane for much of the flight, including take-off.

Chapter 11

The Nineties

The nineties began with the loss of A-560 of IV Squadron that crashed in Comodoro Rivadavia on 4 January 1990. In June, A-505 was also decommissioned (some time before it had suffered a minor accident). In August, A-568 and -580 were sent to IX Air Brigade to replace A-560 and A-573, which were out of service. After being cannibalized, in 1989 A-573 was sent to the FMA and discharged in June 1990.

In March 1990, the Pucará participated again in what was now called FIDAE, in Chile, with A-594 together with the first prototype of the IA-63 Pampa (EX-01).

In the event, in December, A-565 and A-566 were sent to III Brigada Aérea. On 10 August A-510 was lost in an accident. Towards the end of the year, aircraft A-585, -588, -589, -591, -592, -593, -596 and -598 were delivered by the factory, reaching by the end of 1991 a total of 38 examples on strength, including A-518 that was out of service in the FMA.

A-594 seen in Chile at FIDAE 90 in March 1990, together with the first prototype of the Pampa. (Photo Alberto Martín)

A-566 firing a salvo of 70mm rockets from a launcher on the belly.

A-578 approaching Mount Aconcagua, the world's highest mountain outside Asia, being more than 6,900 metres high and located in the Mendoza province.

A Pucará taxies on Route 98 near Reconquista while another lands behind. This photo is dated 1995, but they operated there regularly.

A-504 was originally A-604 and was delivered in 1996, being the last plane delivered to the Argentine Air Force. Here it is seen with a Morane Saulnier Paris flying over the sea near the city of Mar del Plata. The Pucará is carrying a towed target designed by the Air Force adapting the towed targets used on the Morane Saulnier Paris to a pod for the Pucará.

A-604 before delivery, re-serialled A-504 when it was finally delivered to the Argentine Air Force.

Since 1990 the Pucará began operating in the *Vigía* operations, with the first carried out on 24 September, together with three IA-63 Pampas of IV Air Brigade. These operations consisted of surveillance of the northern border of the country to stop the illegal flights by drug traffickers and smugglers that were increasing. This exercise was followed two days later and until 30 September by *Gavilán I*, with the same objective, although focused on the use of Westinghouse AN/TPS-43 surveillance radars. In any case, authorization by the National Congress could not be obtained to shoot down any illegal aircraft failing to obey an interceptor's orders, limiting themselves to identifying and following the aircraft to its landing place, so that local police might try to catch the criminals on the ground.

During the first phase of Operativo *Vigía* in 1990, an FLIR developed by the local company Barisa was tested in a Pucará, using systems from the

Above: A-584 at Los Cerrillos
Air Base, Santiago de Chile, for the
FIDAE 96 exhibition. (Photo Patrick
Laurau)

Right: A special pod using a towed
target pod was built for the F-86F
Sabre; an external arm was installed
as used by the Morane Saulnier
Paris. The target hung from the rear
extension of the pod, with the chord
inside the pod; it was extended for
use and then released before landing.

American company Kollmorgen Electro Optical (KEO), within the framework
of the FAS-570 programme of the General Directorate of Systems of the Air
Force, although the results were not what was expected and the programme was
cancelled.

At that time, President Carlos S. Menem began with a much more marked budget
cut for the Armed Forces, affecting the FMA again, while some units practically
stopped flying. The manufacture of the Pucará, which had been reactivated, was
again suspended, delivering aircraft up to A-604 at a very slow pace.

Due to the lack of budget and, as a direct consequence, the logistical problem,
it was decided in 1991 to deactivate IV Squadron and between 15 February and
15 June A-551, -557, -558, -568, -569, -574 and -580 (sent to Comodoro Rivadavia

A-608 at the factory. It was one of the three airframes that were never finished and is still at the factory. (Photo Santiago Rivas)

A-584 taxies at IX Brigada Aérea, Comodoro Rivadavia, on 1 May 1998, for the commemoration of the FAA baptism of fire. (Photo Santiago Rivas)

in 1990 to replace A-559) were transferred to Reconquista. A-561 was transferred that year to the CEV.

In 1992, the decrease in spending led to only 26 aircraft being on strength, a number that was reduced over the following years, like almost all the combat aircraft of the Argentine Armed Forces. Despite this, three more machines were delivered that year, A-594, -597 and -599.

On the other hand, that year A-561 was sent, in March, to participate at the FIDAE 92 fair in Chile, now held at Los Cerrillos Air Base, in a new presentation of the aircraft abroad.

On 31 December 1994, A-559 and A-564 were retired and stored at the FMA. In 1995, the FMA was handed over in concession to Lockheed Aircraft Argentina

A-558 taxies at I Brigada Aérea on 10 August 1998, preparing to return to its unit. (Photo Santiago Rivas)

A-584 at II Brigada Aérea, Paraná, early 2000. The Pucará is marked with the 'kill' of a Westland Scout shot down on 28 May 1982. (Photo Santiago Rivas)

On one occasion, when A-568 and A-594 visited VI Brigada Aérea during a trip around the bases after the promotion of new Pucará pilots, the Mirage pilots of VI Brigada made jokes by painting the aircraft.

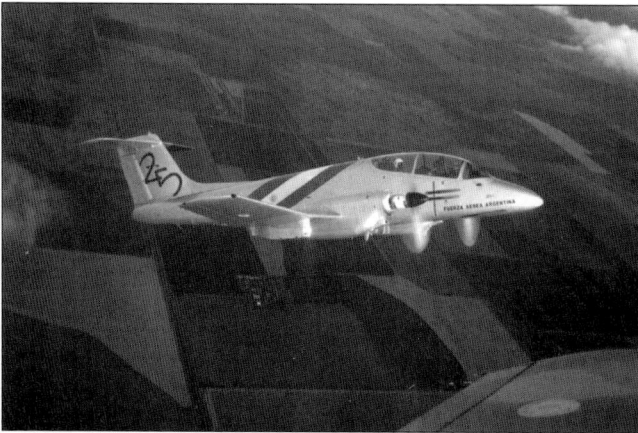

A-558 received a special paint scheme for the 25 years of the type in service, 2000. (Photo Guillermo Galmarini)

Flypast of 20 Pucarás for the 25th anniversary of the type in service, 2000. (Photo Santiago Rivas)

Sociedad Anónima (LAASA, later Lockheed Martin, LMAASA), which had obtained the privatization contract, although delivery of the pending aircraft remained delayed. In 1996 A-595 and -604 were delivered, the latter shortly after re-serialled A-504, and both were enlisted the following year at III Air Brigade.

Meanwhile, in 1995, the first *Pacú* exercise was conducted in the city of Resistencia, Chaco, which consisted of detecting illegal flights. A second phase was held in the city of Posadas, Misiones.

In 1996 Pucará participated again at the FIDAE fair in Chile, with A-584.

On 5 October 1997, A-530 was lost in an accident, reducing the available fleet to 35 examples. In that year, a reconstitution of the flight line began, although other aircraft were deprogrammed, such as A-550 and -581 in April 1999, while A-593 and -598 were returned to service after being progressively cannibalized over time.

Due to the forest fires that occurred in the vicinity of the city of Bariloche in January 1996, which destroyed several houses, with the evaluation of options for hydrant aircraft, the Argentine Air Force raised the idea of a Pucará Hydrant, using a modified ventral fuel tank to launch water, although the idea was eventually considered unsuitable and none was modified for this.

In 1997 the visit to the brigade of two Royal Air Force pilots was highlighted, who had the opportunity of flying the Pucará. This was part of an exchange through which two Argentine pilots were sent to RAF Cottesmore, in Great Britain, to fly the Harrier.

A fresh participation of Pucará at the Chilean FIDAE fair occurred in March 1998, when A-557 was displayed, in what was the last visit of the Pucará to Chile.

From that year until 2000, the Pucará participated with large numbers of planes in flypasts, both for the Argentine Air Force Day and for the anniversary of the force's baptism of fire, on 1 May. In this way, on 13 August 1997, 18 aircraft participated in the 85th anniversary of the force over I Air Brigade at El Palomar. The same number were deployed on 10 August 1998.

During the 1990s, for air-to-air target practice, it was decided to equip the Pucará with a towed target. As until then the only aircraft for this mission were the Morane Saulnier MS-760 Paris of IV Air Brigade and the Mirage of VI Air Brigade, this latter unit was asked to provide help. It was decided to use a pod initially produced for the already retired F-86F Sabre, to which an arm was adapted on the left side, to which the rollout firing target used in the Paris was installed. The pod was installed in the ventral pylon of the Pucará. Subsequently, the company Tecno Dinámica S.A. developed a new target with better performance, called Tecno Blanc, which was adopted over the following years.

Chapter 12

Into the New Millennium

Faced with the growing problem with illegal flights and drug trafficking on the northern border of the country, a new version of Operativo *Vigía* was held in 2000, based at the Resistencia International Airport (Chaco province), headquarters of the FAA Northeast Air Region, and in Posadas, Misiones province, with the support of Westinghouse AN/TPS-43 mobile radars. This was repeated regularly over the following years. As the National Radarization Plan, the installation of fixed radars, slowly advanced into the new millennium, the first example was installed in Resistencia; AN/TPS-43s were located in areas where fixed radars did not yet have coverage.

In addition, three iterations of the *Plata* exercise were carried out from Posadas Airport, which consisted of working together with the Brazilian Air Force in air control tasks in the northeast of Argentina and the border area of Brazil, in search

An Argentine Army Grumman OV-1D Mohawk escorted by two Pucarás over the Paraná River, near the city of Posadas, in the Argentine northeast.

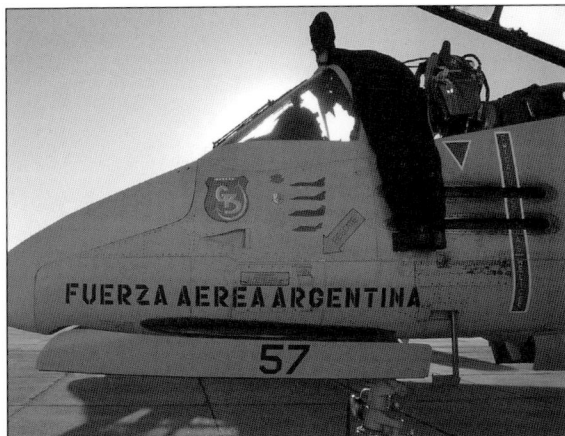

A-557 after an air-to-air exercise, displaying the 'kills' of other planes shot down during the training sorties: two Mirages, an A-4AR Fightinghawk and a Pampa. The Pucará was very hard to shoot down in a dogfight thanks to its manoeuvrability and slow speed.

In the early 2000s, some planes received special artwork on their tails for short periods, including this vulture on A-557, seen in 2004.

of irregular flights (those without flight plans) transporting drugs, contraband and, eventually, terrorists.

Both the *Vigía* operations and the *Plata* exercises were carried out in conjunction with the Brazilian Air Force, which used Neiva T-25 Universal, Embraer AT-27 Tucano and AT-26 Xavante aircraft, as well as Grand Caravans, Bandeirantes and Bell UH-1Hs. The Argentine Air Force, together with the Pucará, used the Morane Saulnier MS-760 Paris, Bell UH-1H, IA-63 Pampa, IA-50 G-II and

Two Pucarás take off for a sortie during the Ceibo 2005 multinational exercise in November 2005. It was the biggest ever international exercise in Argentina, with participation by the air forces of Brazil, Chile and Uruguay.

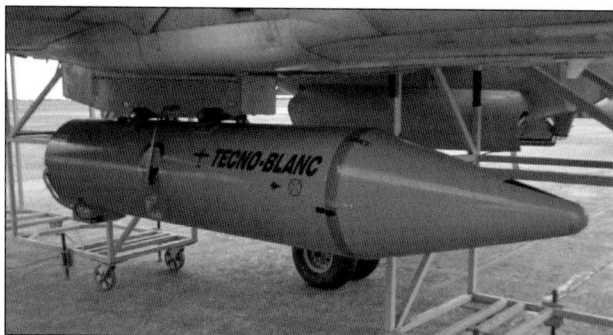

A Tecno-Blanc towed target on a Pucará. The pod was built locally by the company Tecnodinámica. (Photo Facundo Rovira)

Aerocommander 500U, although previously in the case of *Vigía*, it also used the Mirage IIIEAs from VI Brigada Aérea or the A-4ARs from V Brigada Aérea.

The *Plata I* exercise was carried out between 19 and 22 June 2001 and six Pucará participated, together with a Bell UH-1H and two IA-50 G-IIs on the Argentine side, while Brazil deployed four Tucanos, four Neiva T-25 Universals and a UH-1H.

In the case of *Plata II*, carried out between 17 and 21 May 2004, the exercise consisted of detection by means of Argentine radars or AN/TPS-270 of the Brazilian Aerospace Defense Command (CONDABRA) with headquarters in Brasilia, of aircraft on irregular flights heading towards the border between the two countries. The radars were deployed in Santa María and Santo Angelo, Rio Grande do Sul state.

A-557 with 125kg bombs built by the local company Tala S.A., 2007.

The *Cruzex* III exercise in 2006, held at Anápolis Air Base near Brasilia, in Brazil, was one of the few opportunities to see Argentine and Uruguayan Pucarás flying together.

During *Cruzex* 2006 the Pucarás also had the opportunity to operate together with the Embraer Super Tucanos.

A-568 seen from above, during a test flight of the IA-58E modifications. (Photo Santiago Rivas)

A-588 received a special paint scheme for the 40 years of the Pucará with the Argentine Air Force, 2015. (Photo Santiago Rivas)

Pucará A-568 after a night sortie in Reconquista, 2018. (Photo Santiago Rivas)

A-568 and the A-585 in flight near Reconquista, September 2018. (Photo Santiago Rivas)

The Control and Information Centre (CIC) positioned one in Posadas and the other in Curitiba (Brazil), and were to be immediately informed that they were trying to identify aircraft by radio. Information on flight plans would then be requested from the Air Traffic Control Centres to verify the irregularity of the flight. If identification was not achieved by these means, the Air Movement Information Table was set up, where the flights were marked on a chart, the regular ones in blue and the irregular ones in yellow. Then the interceptor planes (Pucará and Paris on the Argentine side or Tucano and Xavante in Brazil), on five-minute alert, were ordered to take off. The planes were guided by the radar until they intercepted the illegal airplane. Once this was done, the aircraft was visually identified in accordance with the international procedure for the interception of illegal aircraft and all the data was sent to the CIC.

A-568 flying low over a river near Reconquista, September 2018. (Photo Santiago Rivas)

Pucará A-568 showing its aerobatic capabilities at Reconquista in 2018, near the end of its career. (Photo Santiago Rivas)

A-568 and A-585 performed the last bombing missions of the type, over Antuna firing range, during the *Dédalo* exercise, on 12 September 2019. (Photo Santiago Rivas)

In 2005 the third iteration of this exercise was carried out. In the case of the *Plata* exercises, all the interceptions were simulated, while in the *Vigía* operations interceptions were real.

In addition to these exercises, in November 2005, the Pucará participated in Exercise *Ceibo*, carried out at IV Brigada Aérea in Mendoza and in which Argentina, Brazil, Chile and Uruguay took part. Argentina also participated with the A-4AR Fightinghawk, MS-760 Paris, IA-63 Pampa, Mirage IIIEA, Mirage 5A Mara, IAI M5 Finger, C-130H and KC-130H Hercules, SA-315B Lama and Bell 212. Brazil sent aircraft A-1A and B (AMX), Chile participated with Mirage 5 Elkan and Uruguay with Cessna A-37B.

Subsequently, between 21 August and 1 September 2006, the third iteration of Exercise *Cruzex* was carried out at Anápolis Air Base, Goiás state, in Brazil, about 50 kilometres from Brasilia, at which the Argentine Air Force sent its A-4AR Fightinghawk and IA-58 Pucará, Uruguay did the same with its Pucará and Cessna A-37B, Venezuela with the VF-5A Freedom Fighter, Mirage 50 and F-16C/D Fighting Falcon, Chile with the A-37B and France with the Mirage 2000. Although Peru was going to participate with the A-37, a fatal accident that occurred during the deployment prevented them from being present. Brazil participated with the A-1 AMX, A-29 Super Tucano, AT-26 Xavante, F-5E and F-5EM Tiger II, Bell UH-1H, H-34 Super Puma, H-50 Esquilo, Embraer R-99, SC-95 Bandeirante, T-27 Tucano, Boeing KC-137, KC-130/C-130 Hercules and Gates VU/R-35 Learjet.

During the Summit of the Americas, held in the city of Mar del Plata on 4 and 5 November 2005, in which almost all the American leaders met, including the president of the United States, George W. Bush, it proved necessary to mount a top-flight security operation and three Pucarás were deployed to BAM Mar del

Armed with 130kg bombs, A-585 departs on its last bombing mission. Night operations were uncommon as the Pucará lacked any night capability during most of its career; nor did it have any guided weapons. (Photo Santiago Rivas)

A-568 firing its machine guns for the last time during the Dédalo exercise on 12 September 2019 at V Brigada Aérea firing range. (Photo Santiago Rivas)

Plata to conduct patrol missions over the city, operating in conjunction with A-4AR Fightinghawks and coordinated by a USAF Boeing E-3D Sentry aircraft that operated from Comandante Espora Naval Air Base.

In 2007, *Vigía* operations were replaced by Operation *Fortín*, which in turn was replaced in 2011 by Operación *Escudo Norte*, which too was succeeded in 2017 by Operación *Fronteras*, although in general they maintained the same modus operandi. These tasks were also carried out with FMA IA-63 Pampas and A-4AR Fightinghawks, from 2018 by Embraer Tucanos and from February 2019 by T-6C Texan IIs. On several occasions, the planes deployed to the Santiago del Estero

Crews and mechanics posing with A-568 on the last day of the *Dédalo* exercise, 12 September 2019. They all signed the last bombs to be dropped by the plane. (Photo Santiago Rivas)

The failure of the compressors on both engines of A-568 during an airshow at III Brigada Aérea on 26 September 2018 accelerated the retirement of the type as an attack plane. The photo shows the fire in the engine exhausts. The pilot managed to land safely.

airport and Termas de Río Hondo, near Santiago del Estero, but currently they operate from Resistencia, Chaco province. The Pucarás operated on them until 2018.

From 27 June to 1 July 2011, Exercise *Río IV* was carried out with the Uruguayan Air Force, for which three Pucarás were deployed to II Brigada Aérea at Paraná and participated together with a Fokker F27, three Piper PA-28Ds and a Bell 212. The Uruguayan Air Force used three Pucarás from No. 1 Squadron, three Cessna A-37s, three Pilatus PC-7s, two Cessna 206s, a Beechcraft B58 Baron and a Bell 212, all operating from Durazno, plus a Casa C-212 operating from Carrasco, in Montevideo. During the exercise, irregular flights were simulated that were detected by the radars of both forces and intercepted by the Pucarás, A-37s and Pilatus PC-7s.

Meanwhile, in October 2011, a Pucará simulator developed by the Argentine Air Force was presented, using the modified X-Plane software to copy the aircraft's performance and installed in the cockpit of A-505, which had been decommissioned. The simulator was used by the new pilots to learn the basic concepts of the plane before making their first flights, as well as by the pilots to train in emergency procedures.

The Pucará also participated in Exercise *Arpa*, from 19 to 23 December, together with the Paraguayan Air Force, to improve operations in the control of illegal flights. Cessna 182, Piper Seneca and Dakota and Fokker F27 aircraft simulated as the irregular transits, while the radars from the cities of Resistencia and Posadas provided information to the control centres of both countries. Later, the IA-58 Pucará of the FAA and EMB-312 Tucano of the Paraguayan Air Force were used to intercept. In addition, Grupo 1 Comunicaciones Escuela and Grupo 3 Comunicaciones of the FAA participated.

Because of the visit of a large number of heads of state and personalities during the inauguration of President Mauricio Macri on 10 December 2015, three Pucarás, together with the A-4AR Fightinghawk, provided coverage over the city of Buenos Aires, conducting patrol flights. On the day, while the inauguration ceremony was taking place in the National Congress, the radar of the Air Surveillance and Control Centre in Merlo detected a Cessna 152 that had taken off from the Ezpeleta Aerodrome and was heading towards Buenos Aires. Two Pucarás immediately took off and intercepted the plane over the Quilmes area. As soon as the pilot realized that he had been intercepted, he obeyed the orders and landed at the Área de Material Quilmes, where he explained that he had not read the Notam (Notice to Airman) issued by the National Civil Aviation Administration (ANAC) about the 'no-fly zone'.

The problem of obtaining spare parts for the engines was compounded during that period by the difficulties in obtaining spare parts for the ejection seats, which also complicated the operational status of the unit, which only had six aircraft available for September 2018. This and the arrival of the first Beechcraft T-6C Texan II out of a total of 12 purchased for the Military Aviation School, led to the decision to transfer part of the Embraer Emb-312 Tucano fleet from the School to Grupo 3 de Ataque. Six aircraft flew from Córdoba to Reconquista on 26 June and formed Escuadrón Operativo II Tucano, with its first deployment to Resistencia on 4 September 2018, achieving a fleet of 12 Tucanos in the brigade in 2019.

The problems in the engines were aggravated when on 26 September, during an exhibition at Aeroclub Reconquista, A-568 had a loss in the compressors of both engines, having to stop one of them and make an emergency return to base with the other engine on reduced power. The damage caused to the engines involved their loss and A-568 being grounded. The problem was repeated on A-583 in October of that year during a deployment in V Air Brigade, when while taking off, loaded with bombs, the plane suffered a loss of power. The pilot had to eject the weapons and make an emergency landing, hitting the runway hard. Although the plane did not suffer any major damage, the landing gear was affected. A review of the deployed aircraft identified corrosion in the turbines of the other aircraft and A-575, -583 and -588 aircraft were unable to return to their base. This was because distilled water had not been used in the water injection system, but tap water. The failure led to the grounding of the other two operational aircraft at Reconquista, A-582 and -585, although they flew again in March 2019, while A-568 was put back into service in July 2019.

Meanwhile, between 15 and 23 November 2018, the Pucarás were deployed to VI Air Brigade at Tandil, together with the A-4AR Fightinghawk, IA-63 Pampa, Hercules and Bell 212 and 412 for the *Integrador 2018* exercise. The main activity was air-to-air combat against A-4ARs and Pampas.

After the exercise, five Pucarás were deployed to I Brigada Aérea, in the suburbs of Buenos Aires, along with five A-4ARs and four Pampas to face the challenge of providing air cover over the city during the two days of the G-20 summit, in which, on 30 November and 1 December, the leaders of the 20 most powerful countries in the world met in Buenos Aires. The USAF deployed two E-3D Sentries to aid in airborne early warning, operating in conjunction with the five Air Force ground radars, and the patrol tasks were carried out by Argentine fighter jets. The Pucarás carried out the cover at low altitude and against smaller aircraft, although there were no interceptions as no intruders were detected. Protecting the most important leaders of the world was one of the most important missions for the venerable Pucarás and, despite the fear that they could not provide air cover for the entire summit, they fulfilled the mission.

However, in view of the operational problems of the very small fleet of Pucarás, with only A-568, -582 and -585 operating, in 2018 it was decided that the model would be decommissioned in 2019.

The airspace protection missions continued to cover the Mercosur Presidents' Summit from 15 to 17 July 2019 in the city of Santa Fe. There, the Pucarás operated from their base, with two aircraft conducting low-level patrols, while the A-4ARs did the same at high altitude, operating from II Brigada Aérea of Paraná.

Shortly after, between 5 and 12 September 2019, the three aircraft were deployed to V Brigada Aérea in Villa Reynolds, for their last exercise, *Dédalo 2019*, where they carried out their last firing exercise with machine guns over the brigade range. In addition, bombing missions were carried out, the last in the aircraft's career. During this exercise, a night bombing run was also carried out at the Antuna range,

On the morning of 8 November 2021, A-568 and A-571 flew from III Brigada Aérea to FAdeA, ending Pucará operations at Reconquista; it was the last flight of a Pucará with Astazou engines. (Photo Jona Zorzón)

with nationally manufactured bombs of 130 kilograms, something that had not been done since the 1980s. On 11 September, they fired their last rounds.

On 6 October, an airshow was organized at the base in Reconquista, marking the final demonstration of the aircraft. The airshow also included the participation of Texans, A-4AR Fightinghawks, KC-130H Hercules, Pampa IIIs, a Learjet 35A, Cessna 182s, and a Bell 412 that performed a C-SAR (combat rescue) demonstration with the Tucanos in the presence of an Mi-171E.

Finally, on 19 December 2019, Captain Martín Liva made the last flight aboard A-568, lasting one hour, which was planned to mark the end of the original Pucará's career, while it was expected that the Pucará Fénix was finally certified to enter service in the Argentine Air Force.

However, due to the need to have aircraft to carry out the tests of the INVAP pod while the prototype of the Pucará Fénix progressed with the certification, the commissioning of A-568, -582 and -585 aircraft was ordered with 15 flight hours allocated for testing. Thus, on 22 March 2021, A-585 flew again, followed shortly after by A-582 and on 29 March both planes flew to FAdeA facilities at Córdoba. A-582 was used to test the INVAP pod during 2021 and the other was used for spare parts. Later, both are expected to be converted to Fénix. Meanwhile, A-568 and A-571 were recovered to be sent to FAdeA, also for conversion to Fénix, and both flew again on 30 June and 29 October, respectively.

Finally, on the morning of 8 November 2021, the two planes flew from Reconquista to FAdeA, in what was the last flight of a Pucará in III Air Brigade and the last flight of a Pucará with Astazou engines.

Chapter 13

Trials on A-561

Although it was not a prototype, A-561 served its entire operational career as a test aircraft and at the end of 2021, now with the serial OVX-501, as a prototype of the IA-58H Pucará Fénix version, it is the only Pucará that remains in service. The plane is one of those that was finished in the middle of the Malvinas/Falklands War, so it left the factory with a camouflage based on the one used by the planes in the islands, but neater. For a short period after delivery, the rear of the aircraft was painted with red, white and blue bands, both on the fuselage and on the tail and horizontal stabilizer. Also, for the tests, it received a roundel with markings in those three colours, on the side of the fuselage, but all this was put aside shortly after, when it was camouflaged in medium green, light green, sand and grey scheme which, with some variations, it maintained until 2019.

Although it was initially assigned to III Air Brigade, due to the needs of the Flight Test Centre, which only had the AX-04, it remained at the FMA, flying for the CEV. In 1986 the plane was administratively handed over by the FMA to III Air Brigade, but assigned in commission to the CEV. In 1991 it was again assigned to III Air Brigade in commission in the CEV, which was maintained until the new millennium, when it was administratively assigned to the CEV until today. Despite these administrative changes, the aircraft was always operated by the CEV, carrying out evaluation flights of different systems.

Project *Halcón del Sur*

At the beginning of 1985 the FAA signed a contract with the Italian company Meteor SpA, the Argentine Quimar S.A. and Pacific Aerosystems Inc. of the United States, which teamed up to develop a new high-performance airborne attack and reconnaissance system called the 'Halcón del Sur'. This system consisted of the integration of a mother plane (carrier/launcher), which was a Pucará, together with the MQ-2 'Biguá' multirole system, an RPV (remoted piloted vehicle) of high standard, based on the Italian Mirach 100, powered by a Meteor TRS-18-076 turbojet, manufactured at the FMA. The Biguá was a remote-controlled and/or automatic vehicle that could be launched both from the ground and in flight; in the

A-561 flying with the MQ-2 Biguá. This example has a different nose with a camera.

View of the Biguá under the central pylon of the Pucará. On the sides of the pylons are the camera pods to film the launch of the vehicle.

Right: Sensor installed on A-561 to indicate if the plane is flying straight and with any angle of attack. (Photo Santiago Rivas)

Below: A-561 with two locally developed FAS-250 bombs: 250kg bombs with a retarded tail with parachute. A small camera pod is on the front rack of the multiple ejector rack.

latter case, the Biguá was integrated into the carrier plane by a launcher pylon of reduced dimensions and weight.

The requirements for this vehicle were as follows: integrating a highly mobile system, composed of a mother plane capable of subsonic speeds such as the IA-58 Pucará and a controlled, unmanned, aero-launchable, transonic speed, long-range aircraft for use as a target for conventional weapons, surface-to-air missiles or air-to-air missiles, while simulating as an attacking supersonic aircraft. The Biguá measured 4.32 metres in length and had a wingspan of 1.8 metres, flew at 900 km/h, with an endurance of one hour, an empty weight of 220 kilograms and a maximum weight of 281 kilograms.

Mamboretá rocket launcher for 57mm rockets, installed on A-561.

INC-100 napalm bombs on a triple ejector rack on A-561.

FAS 250 bombs and a 125kg bomb on a multiple ejector rack on A-561. They were all built by the local company Tala S.A.

A-561 flying with the airborne system to start the engines.

A-561 landing at Buenos Aires domestic airport during the demonstration of the Biojet, May 2007. (Photo Santiago Rivas)

Nose of the AX-561 after it was modified with the PT-6A engines and called IA-58H Pucará II. The plane lacked ejection seats. (Photo Santiago Rivas)

The mother plane had to be able to transfer from its base of operations to a territory as vast as Patagonia, to be located at a distance no greater than 1,500 kilometres from its base, then to launch the Biguá programmed to simulate an attacking plane. After the launch, the mother plane would land near the point planned for the recovery of the target plane. As soon as the latter was recovered on the ground, it was taken back to the base of operations. In times of war, it could be used for reconnaissance, carrying out its operation in a similar manner. The Pucará would maintain control over the Biguá and would then be relieved by another machine until the RPV was sent to the landing zone, where it would parachute down. It could also be controlled from the ground by an Alamak mobile station. Another function was to saturate enemy defences, pretending to be attack aircraft. It was possible to modify them as a cruise missile.

The payload of the Biguá was 35 kilograms that could consist of a vertical camera for reconnaissance at high altitude or a panoramic one for low altitude, as well as infrared sensors, video cameras, electronic intelligence equipment and countermeasures.

The experiments began in Córdoba by the CEV, using A-561, between 23 July and 2 August 1985, with four launches over La Perla Firing Range in Córdoba, followed by those carried out on 13 and 28 August when six flights were made with a Biguá, followed on 23 July and on 2 August by four launches of the Biguá, to test the qualities of gliding and control, and recovering it without problems. In all cases, the Biguá had neither the engine nor the payload and only the aerodynamic behaviour was evaluated.

Subsequently, the propelled prototypes were fine-tuned and on 5 July 1988, the tests were restarted at Chamical Military Air Base (La Rioja province), beginning with 10 fine-tuning flights with the Biguá and the ground guidance systems. Then, on 20 July, the first test launch was carried out, which was unsuccessful when the Biguá was destroyed due to problems in the parachute. On 27 July, the system was publicly presented to the Minister of Defence, Horacio Jaunarena, using the Biguá serial number 00446, at an altitude of 6,500 feet and two kilometres from the base. After a first launch where the Biguá had to be recovered due to problems, another was carried out, where the image transmission systems were successfully tested and the RPV recovered at the same base. The system was tested with widely satisfactory results, both by the RPV and the carrier/launcher aircraft, the Pucará A-561.

Although around 1989 the Biguá was also mounted on A-585, there are no records that it was launched from it. Unfortunately, the budget cuts that followed led to the programme being postponed and finally cancelled in 1990.

Other tests

A-561 received a data acquisition system, which years later was replaced by a more modern one, which not only allowed it to record a large amount of information, but also to send it to a ground station. The most modern equipment sends in real time all the information collected, as well as the parameters of the engine and instruments and the position of the aircraft.

Roberto Quiroga, who from 1996 to 2004 and from 2007 to 2012 was assigned to the CEV and flew A-561, explains that the plane

> had many sensors and an electrical system designed to withstand the electrical load of the data recording system. In the lower hatch on the belly, in the standard Pucará there is a box where things are stored when the plane moves. We had a tray there and we put all kinds of sensors. So, if a new brake block had to be evaluated, for example, the train legs were instrumented with temperature, pressure sensors, etc., and the cables were routed to the recorder.

In addition to the data acquisition equipment, the aircraft received two VHFs (the Pucará had only one), a VOR, ILS, a transponder and an IFF (which was later withdrawn), the Pucará A-561 being the best equipped for many years. Then the other planes received a transponder and the idea of putting GPS on them came up, so A-561 was modified to receive it. 'If you look at the cockpit of A-561, at the top where there is a panel of annunciators and fault lights, in the middle there is a GPS and the annunciators are on one side,' Quiroga explains.

On the left side of the nose, a sensor that measures skidding, whether the plane is going across or going straight, was installed, along with an angle of attack sensor.

At that time, when seeing that the CEV was testing a real-time telemetry system in the Pampa prototype EX-03, the Air Force asked to make a similar system for all the force's airplanes, including the Pucará, so a board was tested on A-561 that transmitted the aircraft's GPS position in real time. The problem was that the VHF equipment had to transmit all the time, so it overheated and had to be cooled. In addition, because the VHF has visual range, it was not suitable for long flights, so it was finally put aside and only adopted for the planes of the Military Aviation School.

Weapons

Throughout the career of A-561 a large number of weapons were evaluated, including some already in use before, such as INC-100 napalm bombs, and others such as 105mm rocket-launcher tubes for Pampero rockets.

In bombs, those developed by the FAA were evaluated, such as the FAS 250 with tail braked by parachutes and 250 kilograms of weight or the 125 kilograms free fall, both produced by the company Tala S.A. on FAA designs.

In 1992 the aircraft participated at the FIDAE 92 fair in Chile, on its only departure from the country.

Start-up pod

The Pucará, due to the type of engine it has, a direct turbine, at the time of start-up has a very high battery consumption, in addition to the fact that it suffers a very large voltage spike, reaching 800 to 900 amperes. For this reason, if the battery is not in good condition, it is not possible to start the aircraft, in addition to premature wear of the nickel cadmium battery, which is very expensive. If it was possible to start an engine with a low battery, you had to wait a while to start the second one, since the generator does not directly assist the other engines, but charges the battery; only with an acceptable level of charge can the start-up of the other engine be started. This meant that on each deployment ground starter equipment needed to be transported to the airfields.

V Air Brigade had developed a ground starter for the A-4 Skyhawk using a supplementary tank, to which wheels were added, which could be mounted on one of the aircraft pylons, so that it could be deployed with the aircraft without any other support.

Copying the concept, it was decided to develop an external battery pod, but using gel batteries, which in the late 1990s were a novelty. Regular lead acid batteries could not be used in a plane that could make inverted flight, as the electrolyte leaked, but gel could be used. Roberto Quiroga, who participated in the pod test flights, explains that

> the problem was that these batteries needed a slightly more elaborate charger than what was commercially available. An electrical engineer at the CEV designed that charger. Tests were made, including the destruction of some batteries in the tests. And then we started doing tests in the Pucará. Trials were made to get the pod to start up 10 times before needing a recharge. Initially it was thought to put it in a 318-litre tank, but there weren't that many, and we found a napalm bomb in a tank – they put the legs on it, the entire structural part inside to charge the batteries and we did it.

After testing, it was shown on Air Force Day, 10 August 1999, and sent to III Air Brigade, along with a second pod that was made. Added Quiroga:

> There were no longer napalm containers of that model to make a third one. The tank had to be remanufactured – that changed the game a bit. Also, the batteries were expensive. And the problem was that when they got to Reconquista, people did more start-ups than they had to, they didn't charge the batteries well and they started having problems. They finally stopped using them. One of the prototypes was returned to us, the other was destroyed, and we continue to use it for maintenance in the hangar. It was good, but the budget to buy more batteries or make the containers was never obtained.

Fuel tests

During 2006 A-561 was used to evaluate the use of a biofuel for aviation, called Biojet, developed by the National Research and Development Directorate of the Argentine Air Force in collaboration with the Secretariat of Science, Technology and Productive Innovation, the Faculty of Chemical Sciences of the National University of Córdoba and the Aeronautical University Institute. On 9 May 2007, the official presentation of the plane was made flying with this fuel in one of its engines, at the Jorge Newbery Airport in Buenos Aires. The fuel used a high-quality biofuel mix with up to 20 per cent Jet A-1. Once the viability of the fuel had been demonstrated, tests in Pucará were completed.

Since then, A-561 flew for a short time, as it had to undergo a major inspection, but it was then decided to modify it as the prototype of the IA-58H Pucará 2 with Pratt & Whitney engines, which was done between 2012 and 2015 and was re-serialled AX-561.

PART 3

OPERATIONAL HISTORY ABROAD

Chapter 14

Frustrated Contracts

Poor sales management and the lack of security in the provision of spare parts after sales, added to the lack of credit from state banks, meant that exports were minimal, considering the benefits of the product offered. During most of its history, the FMA was oriented only to supply the Argentine Air Force, so more often than not there was never any intention to offer the products for export. When attempts were made to export or obtain clients outside of the Argentine Air Force, including within Argentina, the lack of experience and trained sales personnel frustrated almost all operations. In the cases where sales were made, the company was inefficient in after-sales support, especially as early as the 1990s, when the factory was non-operational until it was handed over to Lockheed. This complicated the operation of the three clients achieved – Uruguay, Colombia and Sri Lanka – and led to two of them having to decommission the planes after a short time in service.

As soon as the Pucará was developed, the FAA decided that it was a product that could be successful in sales abroad, given that there was a growing demand for anti-guerrilla aircraft, especially in small air forces in Latin America, Asia and Africa. Thus, a sales campaign began, frustrated in most cases by a lack of experience.

In 1978, the first export contract was signed with the Force Aerienne Islamique de Mauritanie for its Escadrille de Surveillance for $10.8 million for four aircraft, although it was cancelled shortly after due to financing problems. The original plan was to sell 12 airplanes and of the aircraft already built, one was painted with the colours of that country, with c/n 018 receiving the serial M1/5T MAB, the flag and the roundel. After the sale was frustrated and due to the fact that for the conflict with Chile it was considered that all the planes would be required, in December of that year the four planes were incorporated into the Argentine Air Force with the serials A-514, -515, -517 and -518. The latter (ex-M1/5T MAB) continued to be painted with the same scheme, albeit with the Argentine flag and roundel, until its retirement.

In March 1983, a pre-contract was signed with the Central African Republic for two planes for $9.5 million, with the intention of expanding the order to 12 examples, although the final contract was not signed.

At that time, the Venezuelan Air Force was interested in the plane, despite the fact that in 1973 they had received a batch of 16 Rockwell OV-10E Broncos. However, they preferred a power plant other than the Astazou, because the Pucará version was not used by any other aircraft. Thus, the FMA together with Volpar

One of the only known pictures of the 5T-MAB assembled, the only Pucará with Mauritanian colours. The plane was ultimately delivered to the Argentine Air Force as A-518. (Photo Jorge Figari via Carlos Ay)

Inc. proceeded with the IA-66 to satisfy the Venezuelan demand. Shortly after the Malvinas/Falklands War ended, a group of FAV officers visited Argentina and were able to study the Pucará, beginning negotiations for a batch of 24 IA-66s worth $110 million, with the intention of assembling them in Venezuela, using parts manufactured in Córdoba, although it was not possible to resolve the financing issues and the purchase was cancelled in February 1984.

Venezuela would regain interest in Pucará when, after the retirement of the last BAC Canberra B.Mk.82/B(I) Mk.88 bombers from the Grupo Aéreo de Bombardeo No. 13 in September 1990, the FAV considered that the need lay in light attack and counterinsurgency aircraft to combat drug trafficking and illegal mining. Thus, the general commander of the FAV, Division General Luis Monserrat Pérez, reported that they had selected the IA-58A Pucará (with Astazou engines), from which they aimed to buy 20 aircraft for a total of $60 million that included spare parts, engines and training for pilots and mechanics.

At the same time, Rockwell proposed a modernized version of the OV-10D, which they christened OV-10G, of which they would deliver a batch and also modernize the surviving OV-10Es. Although the FAV preferred the Pucará, the negotiations were halted again due to financing, when Venezuela proposed that the planes be offset against a loan granted by Venezuela to Argentina, which was not accepted by the FMA. Finally, the FAV ended up buying from the USAF a batch of 18 OV-10As without modernization, which were integrated into the Grupo Aéreo de Operaciones Especiales No. 15 based in Maracaibo, while the Canberra unit was equipped with Embraer AT-27 Tucanos and named Grupo Aéreo de Entrenamiento Táctico No. 13.

Also, around 1983, the Dominican Air Force expressed interest in 24 aircraft, although the idea came to nothing. Continuing with the intention of selling Pucará abroad, between 12 and 16 November 1984, Colonel Elías Alabirda Martiniuk and Captain Arnulfo Solni, of the Paraguayan Air Force, took the course to convert to the model, but no order was formalized.

The FMA, through Tecnología Aerospacial (TEA S.A.), created in 1985 to promote its products, began managing exports, which is why on 29 March of that year a contract was signed with Iraq for 20 planes with an option for another 20 for $3.8 million each, but due to pressure from Iran, a country that maintained good relations with Argentina, the contract was cancelled. Iran, in turn, was interested in the model and began negotiations to purchase 60 aircraft at a cost of $283 million. Although by decree No. 987/85 one plane was transferred to that country, it was never delivered.

In June, TEA quoted Bolivia for 20 planes in exchange for natural gas. The country had always been interested in the type, ideal for operation there due to its ability to operate on poorly prepared airfields and at low cost, and in 1986 a pre-contract was signed for 12 machines for $52 million, but again, the contract was not signed. In August a fresh offer was made, this time to Paraguay for eight Pucará in exchange for electricity from the Yaciretá hydroelectric dam, which Paraguay had built in conjunction with Argentina. Although Paraguay had a very modest combat fleet that was not suitable for its needs, having also few prepared airfields and a swampy and jungle terrain, to which the Pucará was perfectly adapted, the scarce resources available to the Paraguayan Air Force sunk the deal.

Meanwhile, in June 1985, by decree No. 333/85, the export of 50 aircraft, plus 50 fuel tanks and a batch of spare parts and tools, for a total of $159,730,000 to the Syrian Air Force, was authorized through Crowning International Corporation. According to the decree, the contract had already been signed, but it was cancelled shortly thereafter.

Offers continued with another of six aircraft to Zaire in October 1986 and another to Nigeria for 12 Pucarás and several Hughes 500D helicopters made in Argentina by RACA, all frustrated. The government also authorized the sale of the plane to Yugoslavia and China, although nothing was achieved either. Although there was interest in the aircraft, the Argentine economic situation offered few financing possibilities and caused buyers to doubt the ability of the FMA to provide effective after-sales support. During 1987 a pre-contract was signed with Zaire for six aircraft for a total value of $26 million, which also came to nought.

At the end of April 1987, five from the Iranian Air Force visited the FMA and then III Air Brigade to learn about the plane, as they were now evaluating the purchase of 50 aircraft, 25 of them used, for $160 million. This visit was followed on 21 May by three representatives from Mauritania, which was once again interested in the plane, although Argentine government policy prevented the sale from taking place.

Throughout the eighties, TEA S.A. made offers to the Ivory Coast, Saudi Arabia, El Salvador, Egypt (for 50 aircraft), the Philippines, Gabon, Honduras, Indonesia, Libya, Morocco, Nicaragua, South Africa, Singapore and Thailand. Finally, in

5T-MAB ready for shipment to Mauritania. (Archive José Martínez)

September 1991, a pre-contract was signed with Paraguay for four planes for $11.6 million, although the deal also fell through.

Many years later interest in the Pucará came from an unexpected country. In 2007, the US Navy had launched the Imminent Fury programme, with the objective of providing the forces deployed in Afghanistan with a light attack aircraft with ISR (Intelligence, Surveillance, and Reconnaissance) capability, which was what the special forces most demanded. Thus, in 2008 they bought an Embraer EMB-314 Super Tucano, which they evaluated but found that the Brazilian model had various combat deficiencies, such as being single-engine, with little armour, little endurance and little internal armament. Thus, they began analyzing options in twin-engined aircraft, which only existed in the OV-10 Bronco and the IA-58 Pucará, so in 2010 contacts were initiated between the US government and FAdeA and in 2011 US personnel visited the factory, with the intention of obtaining some aircraft and the licence to develop a new platform based on the Pucará. Unfortunately, there was no interest from FAdeA, considering that the company was not in a position to offer any aircraft or a licence, so there was no progress. Finally, although the Imminent Fury programme was cancelled in 2011, the US Navy moved forward in an agreement with NASA for the loan of two OV-10D+ Broncos that were modified to the OV-10G+ standard and extensively evaluated in Afghanistan in 2016 within the Combat Dragon II programme.

In 2019 there was another visit to FAdeA by interested parties in Pucará, this time from the United Arab Emirates. Although the company tried to interest them in the IA-63 Pampa, the visitors were more interested in buying the Pucará licence or aircraft made in Argentina but received a negative response.

Chapter 15

Uruguay

The history of Pucará in Uruguay began on 12 November 1980, after the visit from the 'Guaira' Escadrille of the Argentine Air Force that had paraded in Montevideo and carried out different exhibitions for the Uruguayan Air Force, which was looking for a replacement for the North American AT-6 Texan. Thus, the first export from Pucará was achieved, when six aircraft, with an option for another two, to be delivered as of April 1981, were sold to the Uruguayan Air Force for $9,329,443.27.

The airplanes had originally been manufactured within the batch for the Argentine Air Force and were assigned the Argentine serials A-542, A-543, A-544, A-546, A-547 and A-548, with construction numbers 042, 044, 045, 047, 048 and 049 respectively. Of these, A-542 came to be painted in Argentine colours. The aircraft were re-serialled FAU-220, FAU-222, FAU-223, FAU-221, FAU-224 and FAU-225 respectively and were sent to the facilities of Chincul company, in San Juan, to be painted with a scheme in two shades of green and light brown, with the belly in light grey. In addition, a Litton LTN 211-27 inertial navigator was added to them.

On 3 May, the Uruguayan crews travelled to the FMA, together with the maintenance team (made up of Second Lieutenant Arturo Nisivoccia and 45 technicians) to train on the plane. The first two Pucarás delivered to the FAU were FAU-220 and FAU-221, in a ceremony in Córdoba on 12 May 1981. At the same time, a group of pilots and mechanics from the FAU was sent to the FMA to train

Line-up of six Texans and five Pucarás at Durazno, 5 August 1983. (Archive Roberto Moreno)

FAU-220 before being delivered by the FMA. (Photo FMA)

On 19 November 1981 the planes made their first deployment to the grass runway of La Carolina firing range. (Photo Roberto Moreno)

Pucarás operating from a grass airstrip on a deployment out of Durazno in the 1980s.

Above: Pilots in front of FAU-225, which is armed with an AN-M64 bomb, 1987. The pilots are Héctor Luongo, Roberto Moreno and Jorge Chocho. (Photo Roberto Moreno)

Left: FAU-225 climbing. This was the only Pucará that was lost by the Uruguayan Air Force, in 1995.

204

Above: FAU-225 taxiing at Carrasco airport, Montevideo, in the 1980s.

Right: A Pucará armed with an AN-M64 bomb in the early 1990s. (Archive Gervasio Dambroriarena)

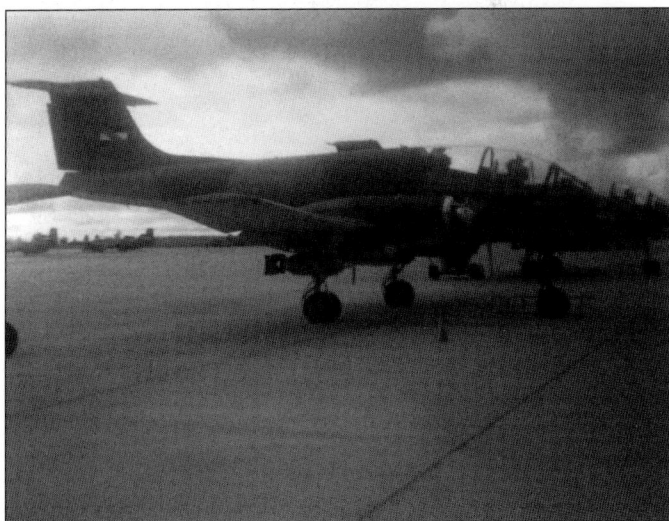

in the operation and maintenance of the aircraft and the first of them made the first solo flight on 28 May 1981 in FAU-221.

Shortly after, on 2 June, FAU-220 and -221 flew to Durazno, commanded by Major Daniel Barral, accompanied by Major Jorge Igarzábal of the FAA in the first and First Lieutenant Francisco Alonso with civilian Mr Blass in the second, arriving at 5:15 p.m. escorted by four T-6 Texans. Igarzábal was traveling to Uruguay as coordinator of the theoretical and practical course and as a flight instructor. Then seven Argentine technicians travelled to Durazno to provide maintenance instruction.

In the early 2000s, FAU-223 received this grey paint scheme, which was used for a few years. (Photo Cees-Jan van der Ende)

The planes became part of the Grupo de Aviación No. 1 Instruc Instrucción y Entrenamiento of Brigada Aérea II based at the Military Airfield Second Lieutenant M. W. Parrallada in Durazno, Uruguay, where they served throughout their career, under the local name of A-58. The unit had received in 1980 17 Texans, 17 T-34As and B Mentors, four Cessna U-17As and a Piper L-21.

On 27 July of that year, the first pilots trained in Uruguay, Second Lieutenants Nelson Juani and Odini, made their first solo flight, while on 1 September four planes did a flypast for the first time for the presidential review by Lieutenant-General (Retd.) Gregorio Álvarez.

FAU-222 was delivered on 15 July, FAU-223 on 19 August and FAU-224 on 23 September, the date on which the three planes flew to Uruguay commanded by Major Barral, First Lieutenant Francisco Alonso and Second Lieutenant Nelson Juani.

On 8 October, FAU-225 was delivered; FAU-221, -223 and -224 travelled to Córdoba and the next day, for the anniversary of the FMA, they paraded alongside FAU-220 (which was undergoing maintenance at the factory) and -225, along with the Pucará AX-04, A-530, -531, -532 and -533 of the FAA.

Shortly after, on 28 October, a CASA C-212 of the FAU collected from Córdoba the first batch of weapons, consisting of PG-50 and 125 bombs, INC-220 napalm, 20mm explosive ammunition and, on loan, an MER and two TERs that were returned during the Malvinas/Falklands War.

For the 25th anniversary of the Pucará in Uruguay, in 2006, FAU-223 received these special markings. (Photo FAU)

A-574 of the Argentine Air Force flying in Uruguay as FAU-226.

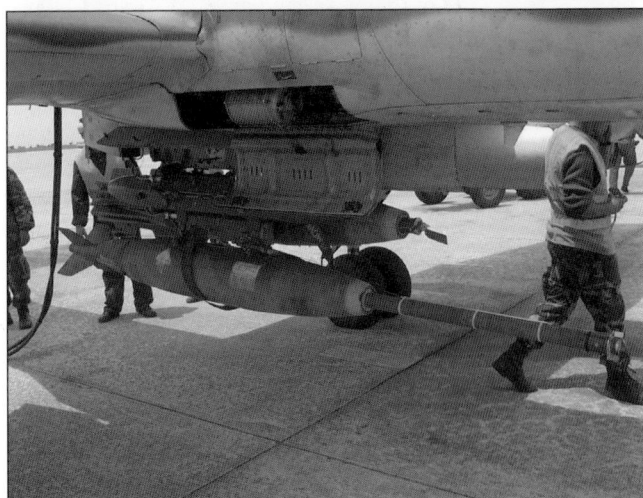

Mk.82 bombs on a TER in a Uruguayan Pucará, one of them with a fuse to explode at a set height from the ground.

In service

On 7 December, the first shooting exercise was conducted at the La Carolina range, next to the Rincón del Bonete dam, a few kilometres north of Durazno, with Major Barral accompanied by Major Igarzábal of the Argentine Air Force, with FAU-223 shooting with machine guns and guns, operating from the grass airfield at the firing range.

Given the new equipment received, on 22 December 1981, by Order of the General Command No. 2060, the unit's name was changed to Grupo de Aviación No. 1 (Ataque), also creating the Centro de Instrucción y Entrenamiento de Vuelo Avanzado (CIEVA, Advanced Flight Instruction and Training Centre), to which were transferred, on 24 March 1982, 15 T-34A Mentors, four Cessna U-17As and a Piper L-21, while two T-34Bs went to the Military School of Aeronautics. The Texans remained with the Pucará unit, although they were relegated to secondary tasks.

In addition to the weapons purchased in Argentina, the FAU initially used 250-kilogram AN-M64 bombs left over from the P-51D Mustang and PG-125 produced in Argentina, although they were later equipped with 500-pound Mk.82 and 250-pound Mk.81 bombs with normal tails or Snakeye-type braked tails, INC-220 napalm bombs, LAU-66 rocket launchers with 19 tubes and LAU-68 with seven, ARM-657 Mamboretás with 57mm Aspid rockets and AF/B-37K launchers for BDU-33/B practice bombs, to which they later adapted 12-pound practice bombs produced in Uruguay. Aspid rockets were used for both training and target marking.

LAU-68 rocket launcher on a Uruguayan Pucará.

On 17 March 1982 occurred the first deployment to Brigada Aérea No. 1 at Carrasco International Airport, in Montevideo, with the Sapo escadrille, to participate in the flypast for the FAU day. The escadrille was led by Major Barral, flying in FAU-224 together with Sergeant Marteluna, FAU-220 with Lieutenant Roberto Moreno and Corporal González, FAU-221 with Lieutenant Odini and Sergeant González (FAA), FAU-225 with Major Igarzábal (FAA) and Ensign Martínez, FAU-220 with Lieutenants Alonso and Grisolia and FAU-225 with Lieutenant Ruggeri and Sergeant Pitch (FAA).

LUU-2B/B illumination flares on the pylon of a Uruguayan Pucará.

In 2005, FAU-220 had a warthog head painted on the nose. This led to some similar nose art after that.

FAU-224 painted with the second design of warthog head.

During 1983 flights to different parts of Uruguayan territory were conducted, beginning on 22 September with Operation *Gala*, together with the Texans and a Fairchild FH-1100 for support, at Melo airport. This was followed by a deployment to Rivera, of the Tero 83.

By 1985, Grupo de Aviación No. 1 had the six Pucarás and Texans FAU-340, -350, -351, -363, -368, -370, -372, -373, -375, -378 and -379.

Meanwhile, in early 1986, an evaluation began on the use of Mk.24/SUU-25B lighting flares in four-tube containers, each with two flares, with the first launches on 10 April 1987. Tonhe flares had arrived in Uruguay along with the Cessna A-37Bs and were homologated for use in the Pucará. Later, LUU-2B/B lighting flares, two under each underwing pylon, were adopted. According to Roberto Moreno, a Pucará pilot at the time:

> the flares would orbit over the polygon and every few minutes we would launch flares. The other planes fired guns or rockets with machine guns. Another method was to illuminate the target with a campfire and shoot in the dark, without flares.

At the end of 1982, the Grupo de Artillería Antiaérea No. 1 of the Army based at Empalme Olmos, Canelones, conducted evaluations of the Pucará and how to act against artillery; artillerymen were also trained how to react against the aircraft.

Subsequently, in 1983, training was conducted with Batallón de Infantería Blindado 13, equipped with M-24 Chaffee light tanks, and the 14th and 15th

Two Uruguayan Pucarás flying with two Argentine ones over Brazil during Cruzex III in 2006.

Two Uruguayan Pucarás flying with three Brazilian Air Force Embraer Super Tucanos during *Cruzex* III.

In 2011, FAU-222 received a special paint scheme to mark the 30th anniversary of the type in Uruguay. As it was painted with water-based paint, it only lasted a few days.

Infantry Battalions with M-113 armoured vehicles, in live-fire exercises in the Sierra de las Ánimas, with the aircraft flying from the town of Treinta y Tres, where they carried out both the simulated attack on the vehicles and close air support missions.

Towards 1990 the Texans began to be relegated and the following year no longer flew, although they remained on strength, while the Pucará reached 10,000 hours from its entry into service.

On the occasion of the visit to Uruguay of the President of the United States, George Bush, in early December 1990, the General Command of the Uruguayan Air Force ordered the deployment of three IA-58s to Brigada Aérea No. 1 in Carrasco, to fulfil combat air patrols and as air escort of the helicopters of the presidential entourage, comprising three VH-60 Black Hawks of the Marines, five UH-60s of the US Army and two SH-60 Seahawks of the US Navy.

FAU-222 flying over the Rincón del Bonete dam on 18 November 2011. The plane has the final warthog head painted on the nose. This was applied to all the fleet and used until late 2013. (Photo Santiago Rivas)

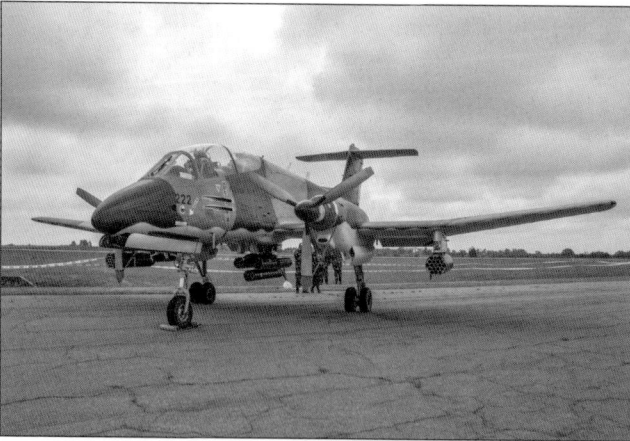

FAU-222 at Melilla airport, Montevideo, October 2013. The plane is armed with three LAU-68 and two LAU-61 rocket launchers. (Photo Santiago Rivas)

FAU-227 in flight near its base, 28 May 2013. (Photo Santiago Rivas)

In 2013, Pucarás took part in the *Cruzex* exercise for the last time at Natal Air Base, Brazil. They operated with many other types, including Super Tucanos from Brazil and Ecuador. (Photo Santiago Rivas)

Thus, on 3 December, the Pucará provided air escort with FAU-221 with Major Silveira and Captain García, FAU-223 with First Lieutenants Camaras and González, and FAU-225 with First Lieutenants Chocho and Marenco, taking off from Durazno and landing at Carrasco after an hour's flight, armed with guns and machine guns, in addition to carrying a 318-litre auxiliary tank.

The following day FAU-223 flew with Captain García and Major Silveira and FAU-225 with First Lieutenants Marenco and Chocho, operating between Carrasco and Punta del Este, then returning to Carrasco after 1.7 hours of flight, with the same weapons. Finally, on the 5th, they flew from Montevideo to Punta del Este, then to Colonia and returned to Durazno after flying over Montevideo, for a total of 2.3 hours, with FAU-225 with Major Silveira and Captain García, FAU-223 with First Lieutenants González y Cámaras, and FAU-221 with First Lieutenants Chocho and Marenco.

As the end of the Texan career was in sight, the FAU negotiated a contract for another four Pucarás in November 1991 that was never signed. However, the operation of the FAU Pucarás was maintained over time, despite budget cuts.

In 1993, with the accident of the Texan FAU-372, these planes were decommissioned, leaving only the IA-58s in Grupo de Aviación No. 1. Subsequently, on 27 April 1994, by decree No. 178/994, the name was changed to Escuadrón de Aviación No. 1 (Ataque).

FAU- 227 at night, Durazno, 2016. (Photo Santiago Rivas)

At Escuadrón No. 1

On 22 July 1993, the only loss of a Uruguayan Pucará occurred when FAU-225 crashed after carrying out combat manoeuvres at low altitude at the La Carolina firing range, falling into the waters of the Rincón del Bonete dam, with the loss of the two crew members, First Lieutenant (Av) Miguel Fodrini and Second Lieutenant (Av) Mario Roldós.

Throughout its operation, the exchange of information with III Air Brigade of the Argentine Air Force was constant, in addition to the FAU receiving support from the FMA and the CEV.

The Pucarás were regularly deployed to airports and airfields across the country, showing that they had no limitations to operating on any type of airfield, regardless of terrain or length. Thus, between 26 and 29 August 1996, three Pucarás deployed to the city of Salto along with five Cessna A-37Bs from Escuadrón No. 2, supported by a C-130B Hercules from Escuadrón No. 3 and a Cessna U-17 from Escuadrilla de Enlace of Brigada Aérea II. There, the Pucarás carried out attack missions against ground targets escorted by the A-37s, while other A-37s acted as adversaries and intercepted them.

The FAU, over time, changed the inspection schedule, adapting it to its needs and its own experience. The inspection carried out at 1,050 hours in the FAA was done at 1,200 hours in the FAU and those at 2,100 hours in the FAA were done at 2,400 hours in the FAU, while over time different elements were changed that differentiated the FAA aircraft from the Argentines', as a different model of GPS.

Flying low over the base, as seen from the control tower roof, in 2016. (Photo Santiago Rivas)

By the end of the 1990s the fleet of five Pucarás were suffering a low operational capacity, with FAU-221 out of service for some time. Thus, on 11 September 1998, the Argentine Air Force loaned A-574 to the FAU, which received the serial FAU-226, and operated in Uruguay until it was returned on 27 February 1999. The aircraft returned to Uruguay on 6 July 2000 and again operated as FAU-226 until 6 June 2001.

In March 1998, a cooperation and logistical exchange agreement had been signed between the FAA and the FAU, where the former promised to deliver two IA-58 Pucará airframes (A-605 and A-606) that were incomplete, in exchange for spare parts, two incomplete (formerly Spanish) T-34A Mentor airframes and two fully operational T-34As, with serials FAU-635 and FAU-646. In 2001, the latter flew to the FAA's Military Aviation School, while the A-605 was transported in a Uruguayan C-130B Hercules to Durazno in 1998.

There, the Pucará was completed with elements of FAU-221, which had been out of service due to a pending Major Cycle Inspection (ICM) after 2,400 flight hours and had been decommissioned, since it was considered more economical to assemble the new Pucará. Once delivered, it became FAU-221, although shortly afterwards it was re-serialled FAU-227, making the first flight on 14 April 1999 with Major Sergio González and First Lieutenant Rodolfo Pereyra. Meanwhile, A-606, after time at LMAASA without having been selected for service, with the roundels and the inscription 'Fuerza Aérea Argentina' covered up, had all the components that the Uruguayans needed removed and was again assigned to the FAA, although it was never completed.

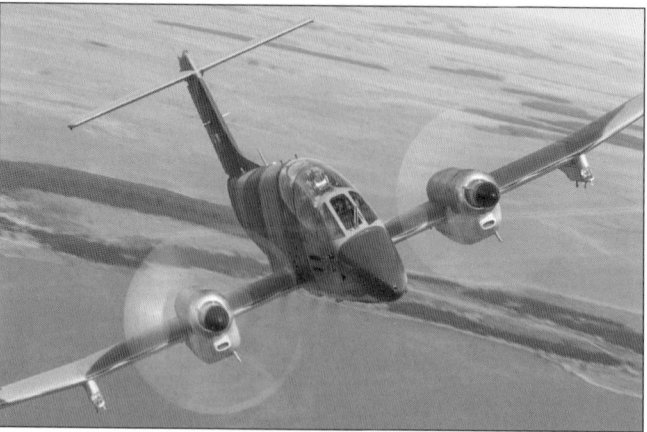

On August 2016, the last air-to-air photo shoot with the Uruguayan Pucarás took place, when FAU-227 posed for the camera. (Photos Santiago Rivas)

On 11 February 2002, the Argentine Air Force sent on loan Pucará A-571, which was also serialled FAU-226 to Uruguay where it served until 13 February 2003.

That year the Pucará carried out a series of deployments throughout Uruguay, with one to San Gregorio de Polanco with FAU-220,- 224, -226 and -227 between 26 and 30 March, another to Paysandú from 2 to 5 May with FAU-224, -226 and -227, to Rivera from 12 to 14 June with FAU-224 and -227, to Colonia from 3 to 6 July with FAU-220, -224 and -227, to Melo with FAU-220, -224 and -227 from 17 to 21 September, to Paysandú again from 23 to 26 October with FAU-220, -224 and -227, and finally to Vichadero from 11 to 13 December with FAU-220, -224 and -227.

On 13 June of that year, Escuadrón 1 took an important step when Ensign (Av) Carolina Arévalo became the first woman to make a solo flight in the Pucará. That day, together with Ensign (Av) María Eugenia Etcheverry (who flew A-37B), they also became the first female fighter pilots in Latin America. However, shortly after, Arévalo went on to fly helicopters in Escuadrón No. 5.

In 2006, the unit carried out what until then was its largest operational deployment when, between 21 August and 2 September 2006, three Pucarás were deployed along with three Cessna A-37Bs from Escuadrón No. 2, a CASA 212, an Embraer Bandeirante and an Embraer Brasilia, to Anápolis Air Base, in Brazil, to participate in Exercise *Cruzex III*, together with the Pucarás and A-4ARs of the Argentine Air Force, Chilean A-37Bs, Venezuelan VF-5As, F -16s and Mirage 50s, French Mirage 2000s and all types of combat aircraft of the Brazilian Air Force. There they were able to operate alongside the Pucarás of III Brigada Aérea and the Brazilian Super Tucanos.

The deployment to Brazil, but this time to the Natal Air Base, was repeated in 2008, when between 1 and 15 November, three aircraft were sent, along with three A-37Bs, on Exercise *Cruzex IV*, in which Argentina did not participate; Chile did with its F-5s, France with Mirage 2000s and Venezuela with F-16s. This was followed between 28 October and 19 November 2010 by *Cruzex V*, which saw the participation of French Dassault Rafales, F-16s from the United States and Chile and the different Brazilian models.

In addition, the FAU aircraft visited Argentina twice to participate in flypasts on the occasion of the Argentine Air Force Day. The first opportunity was in August 1998 when three aircraft were deployed to VII Brigada Aérea, in Moreno, Buenos Aires province, together with Pilatus PC-7s and Cessna A-37Bs; the second opportunity was for the centenary of military aviation in Argentina, on 10 August 2012, when FAU-222, -223, -224 and -227 aircraft were deployed to the Military Aviation School in Córdoba.

In order to improve the fleet's operations, at the beginning of 2008 an agreement was reached with the Colombian Air Force for the delivery of the three planes that Colombia owned and were out of service, to be used as spare parts. On 24 June, two officers and 10 non-commissioned officers were dispatched to Apiay Air Base in Colombia to disarm and load the fuselages and wings into containers, while the engines and other parts were carried in an FAU C-130B Hercules, culminating on 25 July. The planes were taken to Durazno disassembled and, although the possibility of putting the partially assembled FAC-2201 into flight was considered, the idea was finally discarded because all the airframes had corrosion from having been in the open for almost 20 years.

Shortly after, on 10 May 2010, the Pucarás reached a total of 20,000 flight hours.

Between 25 and 29 April 2011 the Pucarás participated in an exercise with Brazil, *Urubra*, in which the Pucarás operated from their base and the Brazilians did so from Santa María, carrying out border control flights and interception of illegal flights. The Brazilian Air Force participated with A-29 Super Tucano and Cessna 208B Grand Caravan aircraft and, along with the Pucarás, the Uruguayan Air Force participated with the A-37 Dragonfly, Pilatus PC-7, Cessna 206 and 310 and a Beechcraft B-58 Baron.

In the New Year of 2012, FAU-227 received new communication and navigation equipment, in addition to an EHSI Santed SN3500 that provided navigation information. This equipment was later installed in the other operational aircraft. Subsequently, in 2013, the cockpit instrumentation received modifications so that it could be operated with night vision goggles, reaching full night operational capacity in the middle of that year.

Meanwhile, on 12 April 2012, Second Lieutenant (Av) Stephanie Catherine Techera made her solo flight in a Pucará, becoming the second and last woman to pilot the model, since none of the other Pucará units had women among its pilots.

Further participation in the *Cruzex* exercises took place between 4 and 14 November 2013, where three Pucarás were again deployed to Natal along with three A-37s, with the support of a C-130B and a Brasilia, in which would be the last trip abroad for the Uruguayan Pucará. In addition to the Brazilian Air Force with almost all its units, F-16s from Chile, Venezuela and the United States, KC-135s from Chile and the United States, Colombian A-37Bs and a Boeing KC-767, a Canadian CC-130J Hercules and Ecuadorian Super Tucanos participated.

The lack of spare parts, especially for the Astazou XVI-G engines, led to the fleet's operability gradually declining and by 2016 only FAU-227 remained operational but suffering many problems. Thus, the decision was made to withdraw the aircraft from service definitively on 17 March 2017.

Pucará pilots and mechanics continue to consider it an excellent aircraft, robust and reliable, with a firepower and performance that no similar aircraft on the market today has. The Uruguayans, who tested it against Super Tucano on the *Cruzex* exercises, indicated that the Pucará was more reliable, thanks to its two engines, its greater firepower and greater endurance.

Despite being decommissioned, on 2 June 2019, FAU-227 was put into operation, and again in 2021, remaining in an almost operational condition. Currently, faced with the decision to withdraw them from service, their replacement has not yet been defined, despite having received several proposals, especially from Embraer Super Tucano.

Chapter 16

Colombia

Colombia is the country with the longest internal conflict in the Americas, with a war against communist guerrillas that officially began in 1964, but originated in the late 1940s. Since the late 1980s, the guerrillas of the Fuerzas Armadas Revolucionarias de Colombia (FARC) and the Ejército de Liberación Nacional (ELN) were also related to the drug traffickers who financed them.

Towards the end of the 1980s, the situation with the guerrillas in Colombia was very delicate, since they had managed to consolidate themselves in various areas of Colombian territory. At that time, the Colombian Air Force did not have adequate counterinsurgency aircraft, except for the 26 Cessna A-37B Dragonflys received between 1977 and 1980, plus some Lockheed T-33s of the 52 received by the force since 1954. They used the Dassault Mirage 5COA and IAI Kfir, although these were not suitable for providing close air support to troops on the ground. In addition, in 1986 it was decided to modify some of the Douglas C-47s as gunships, using the experience obtained by the United States Air Force and South Vietnam in Vietnam and that which was being experienced in El Salvador with its C-47s against the guerrillas. Thus, between 1987 and 1989 five C-47s were modified.

Major Germán Ribero jumps from his plane after his solo flight on the Pucará in Argentina. (Archive Germán Ribero)

Left: Germán Ribero receiving his handkerchief in squadron colours during graduation in Argentina. (Archive Germán Ribero)

Below: The three Colombian Pucarás at the Fábrica Militar de Aviones, Córdoba, before delivery. (Photo FMA)

However, the force needed aircraft with greater firepower, low speed, good endurance and armour, to provide close air support to ground units in an effective way. Recognizing the situation, at the beginning of 1989, the Argentine government offered the donation of the IA-58 Pucará constructor numbers 077, 079 and 080 to the Colombian Air Force (FAC), which had been completed in 1982 but were still in the factory. For unknown reasons, the aircraft 079, 080 and 081 were finally delivered, although the serial numbers were not changed administratively. Thus, 077, which was assigned the serialled A-576 for the Argentine Air Force, was re-serialled as A-580, while A-580 (c/n 081), which in 1985 had suffered an accident

TFAC-2203 before delivery. The planes were delivered with one 1,300-litre tank painted in blue. (Photo FMA)

When the planes arrived at Bogotá, an official ceremony took place in the presence of the Argentine ambassador. They then made the short flight to Apiay. From left: Germán Ribero, Germán Páez, Juan Carlos Ramírez and Jhon Gutiérrez.

FAC-2202 at Apiay, with a Douglas AC-47 Fantasma gunship behind. They flew together on night operations, with the Fantasma dropping illumination flares, as well as acting as a command post. (Photo J. Domínguez)

Pucará FAC-2202 at Apiay base in the early 1990s. (Photo J. Domínguez)

with 32 per cent damage and was in the FMA, after being repaired, was delivered to Colombia. The other two planes had assigned the serials A-578 and -579, which were ultimately not used.

The aircraft received a complete overhaul and were painted in Colombian colours, receiving the serials FAC-2201, -2202 and -2203 (previously A-580, -578 and -579 respectively).

The Colombian Air Force also began to negotiate the purchase of another nine Pucarás, to complete a squadron of 12 aircraft, but economic and political problems in both Argentina and Colombia delayed negotiations until, in December 1991, the United States delivered 12 Rockwell OV-10 Broncos to the FAC, followed by another three in 1993, ending negotiations for more Pucarás.

When the three Pucarás (mentioned above) were donated, a commission of four pilots was organized under the command of Lieutenant-Colonel German Páez Huertas, together with the Majors Jhon Jairo Gutiérrez and Jorge Ribero and Captain Juan Carlos Ramírez. In addition, 15 technicians under the command of Major Montaño would be trained in the maintenance of the plane. Towards August 1989, the Colombian personnel travelled to Argentina. Germán Páez, who was commander of Comando Aéreo de Combate No. 2 (CACOM-2) at CT Luis Francisco Gómez Niño Air Base in Apiay, remembers:

> They received us in Buenos Aires and took us to Reconquista in a Guaraní from the Argentine Air Force. Upon arrival we met the commander and they introduced us to the group of pilots and instructors. We settled in and started the ground course. I was going to receive the Pucará instructor course – I was the only one who did that course. On the ground course we got to know the plane and its systems and we started the flight course. We had a permanent

instructor, but they rotated us with others. As I was the oldest and I needed to finish the course faster, I was the first to qualify. I flew solo and then I continued in the more advanced missions in terms of training, instrument flight, navigation and tactical navigations. I don't remember the solo flight as something very pleasant because our Argentine friends used to tease us. I was the first to receive the celebration of the solo flight when I got to the platform ... at a certain moment I was tied up and received what they called a '*manteada*' [being slapped around]. The celebration ended with the commitment that I did not warn my colleagues, because it was the surprise for them: they were flying and when they arrived back one by one, they were received in the same way. We continued with the training, I finished my basic course and then I did the instructor course.

On his part, Ramírez recalls that

the Colombian Air Force chose two pilots from the AT-33, Germán Ribero and myself, and from the A-37, Páez and Captain Gutiérrez. We travelled to Buenos Aires, and the next day we had medical tests at El Palomar and then we were transported to Reconquista. We started the ground course, which lasted between two to three weeks, and then came the flight phase, where they gave us acrobatics and instruments training, before we continued with the advanced phase of using the weapons. As we were experienced in instrument flight, the sessions were cut from five or six to just one, the only part of the course that was cut. In aerobatics, I was struck by the fact that I had never flown a twin-engine plane with a shut-down engine and that it could do aerobatics.

Germán Ribero says that

At that time the CACOM-2 command operated T-33s and AC-47s, which were not yet re-engined. With the T-33 our mission was to control the north coast of Colombia, because at that time the gringos came down from the Bahamas or Florida in DC-3s or DC-6s to the upper part of La Guajira and there they loaded their planes with marijuana to take it north. They moved us from Apiay, in Villavicencio, to Barranquilla, where there was another command with A-37s; the T-33s carried out patrol missions and aircraft destruction when they were intercepted. I had to intercept and destroy planes on the ground on the north coast. Being there, in 1989, despite the fact that the T-33s had undergone a modernization stage, they were ending their operational life, especially the turbines, and the acquisition of spare parts was increasingly complicated.

Regarding the possible purchase of more Pucarás, Ribero explains that

> it was a squadron of 12 airplanes, but with the passing of time the political landscape changed and the idea fizzled out because of Argentine issues, which changed the government; a government-to-government negotiation was taking place. The hook was for us to operate those three planes, which were giving good results, so that they would later complete the squadron.

Regarding training, Ribero adds:

> In the end we had a very pleasant experience, because being pilots from another country, when it came to air-to-ground at low altitude, which was what we did the most, you want to hit the target. I remember that the polygon we used was outside the standard of what we operated, because the one that we operate in Colombia is a two-minute flight from the base. In Reconquista we had to fly about 40 minutes. In Apiay the polygon is at the same base. What most caught my attention was that every time they hit the target, the Argentine pilots sang 'Viva la patria!' [Long live the homeland]. In the air-to-ground and low-level part, we hit where we had to hit and that made a good impression on them; we were already experienced pilots and obviously the plane as a stable platform, especially for dropping bombs, was a marvel.

Ferry flight

The planes would be ferried in flight, so the pilots initially studied the possibility of departing from Reconquista to the northwest, passing through Bolivia to make a stopover in Arica or Antofagasta, but they abandoned the idea because they had to fly above 24,000 feet and could have problems. Thus, they decided to fly to Santiago de Chile and then go north through the Pacific. Páez says that a C-130 Hercules from the Colombian Air Force arrived at Reconquista and, after receiving the planes in Córdoba on 13 December, they were taken to Reconquista, with Páez flying FAC-2201, Ribero FAC-2202 and Ramírez in FAC-2203. On the 16th, Ramírez and Gutiérrez made a local flight in FAC-2202 and -2203 respectively, so that the four pilots had already flown the Colombian planes.

From there they left on 17 December at 8 o'clock in the morning. 'I was leading, along with Captain Gutiérrez, and the other two on their planes. We crossed the mountain range; in Santiago we refuelled and went to Antofagasta,' says Páez, while Ramírez remembers:

> We went down to Malargüe town, then we crossed the lowest mountain range, and then to Santiago. We slept there and the next

day we went to Antofagasta, where we refuelled; then over the coastal mountain range and we reached Arica where we had a problem with the Peruvians, who did not want to let us follow the coast. We lost about 40 minutes. We left Arica for Lima, spent the night and the next day to Guayaquil in Ecuador and from there to Colombia; we stopped in Cali to load fuel and then went on to Bogotá.

They crossed the Andes Mountains at 22,000 feet, with a storm front that was approaching and for about three minutes they were inside the storm, with strong turbulence and ice formation, but they were able to overcome it without the situation getting more complicated. After 4:30 hours of flight, they finally landed in Santiago. The next day they made the four-hour flight to Antofagasta and then continued to Lima, but the Peruvian controller indicated a route that involved flying more than 200 miles over the sea and the planes did not carry survival equipment for flight over water. The planes continued to Arica, where they requested authorization to fly to Lima over the coast, although this took almost 40 minutes, in which the planes kept orbiting at 18,000 feet above the city's stadium.

From Lima they took off the following day, having to enter cloud at 100 feet, penetrating the layer at 3,000 feet, with the three planes reuniting at 3,500 feet. Upon arriving at Guayaquil, they were informed that they were not authorized to land. After reviewing the situation, they saw that they had enough fuel to continue to Cali, so they climbed to 22,000 feet and continued the flight, landing 5:30 hours after leaving Lima.

After refuelling in Cali, they flew the remaining 450 kilometres at 22,000 feet, flying over the mountains in bad weather and landing in Bogotá on 19 December, with an 18-knot crosswind, forcing them to abandon the initial idea of landing in formation. Ribero adds:

> The next day was the ceremony for the delivery of the planes at Comando Aéreo de Transporte (CATAM) in Bogotá. They held the welcoming ceremony; President Virgilio Barco was present and the representative of the Argentine government came too. The next day we took the planes to the Villavicencio base and began to train pilots.

In the CACOM-2

As soon as they arrived, they joined the Escuadrón de Operaciones Especiales 314 together with the Douglas AC-47 *Fantasma* and Germán Páez began training two pilots, starting with Pablo García. In June 1990, a demonstration of the plane was organized at the Colombian Army Military Fort of Tolemaida. Páez recalls that

> at the College of War there was a demonstration of an attack on a guerrilla group. They invited us to participate, and we went in with

rockets and guns. They were impressed because we came in through the canyons, very low, and then we pounced, bombing and strafing or firing rockets and destroyed the targets that had been set for us. The general commander told me that we would land at Tolemaida, and he was very interested in looking at the plane. I showed them the benefits it had against drug trafficking and counterinsurgency. The fact that they were armoured was a comfort to the pilots. We used Mk.82 bombs. We used the conventional weapons used by the Air Force, rockets and 20mm guns.

Although the planes were delivered with a small batch of 20mm ammunition, this was finished shortly thereafter and no additional batches were purchased, as the Colombian Air Force did not use 20mm ammunition in other aircraft. Ramírez explains:

> The Pucará arrived in Colombia with a large 1,300-litre tank, four 7.62 machine guns and two 20mm guns. In Colombia there was no money to buy ammunition for the guns, which would have been excellent to use in the interception of aircraft.

As neither MER nor TER were purchased, the typical configuration used was the ventral tank and a 70mm rocket launcher on each wing, which could be either a 7-tube LAU 68 or a 19-tube LAU 61. In addition, they utilized the 7.62mm machine guns.

Shortly after the arrival of the Pucará, the AT-33s were retired from service, making the new planes all the more necessary. However, in the first half of 1990, they were used for training and exercises.

Exercise in Palanquero

In January 1990, an exercise was carried out at Comando Aéreo de Combate No. 1 at Palanquero base, the main FAC fighter unit. In addition to the Dassault Mirages and IAI Kfirs of the unit, Cessna A-37Bs, the Pucarás and other FAC aircraft were added, as well as USAF pilots who flew the A-37Bs. Ribero explains that the objective was to train the FAC in defending the perimeter of the base, making interceptions at a distance with the Mirages, while the attack planes did interdiction.

> There were two missions, one in the morning and one in the afternoon, and from Palanquero, a theatre of operations was created. There was a defender and an aggressor and we were on the defensive side, with the Mirage and the Kfir in the interceptor part, the A-37 to defend the base and us in the shorter range. It was one more exercise,

to learn the appropriate techniques, regardless of the performance of your plane, to have the ability to identify the target and to know how an aircraft is intercepted.

Ramírez, for his part, says that the A-37s that acted as the enemy were manned by USAF pilots who were later to provide training.

We engaged with the A-37s and the engagements were titanic. There was the pride of the pilot of the A-37 and that of the Pucará to see who fell first, to get in line behind the other; the gringos became desperate and shouted, 'Knock it off' to suspend the exercise. We were still engaged and we reached very low speeds, 60 knots, with the engines at full power, to grab something, to have a chance to shoot and obviously we hit them.

Operation *Casa Verde*

Although in theory there had been a ceasefire agreement between the Colombian government and the FARC since 1984, the actions of the terrorist group had been escalating since 1988, but became especially relevant as of September 1990. This led to the government of the recently assumed César Gaviria to institute Operation *Colombia*, better known as *Casa Verde*, to counter the offensive by the FARC central command, in the area of La Uribe, in the department of Meta, about 150 kilometres south of Bogotá and about 120 to the southwest from the base of Apiay.

The operation would involve a series of air assaults by FAC helicopters carrying various Army units, which would attack a series of FARC camps and training units,

Subteniente Pablo García, one of the first pilots trained in Colombia, in the cockpit of FAC-2202. (Photo J. Domínguez)

FAC-2203 at CATAM on the day of their arrival in Colombia.

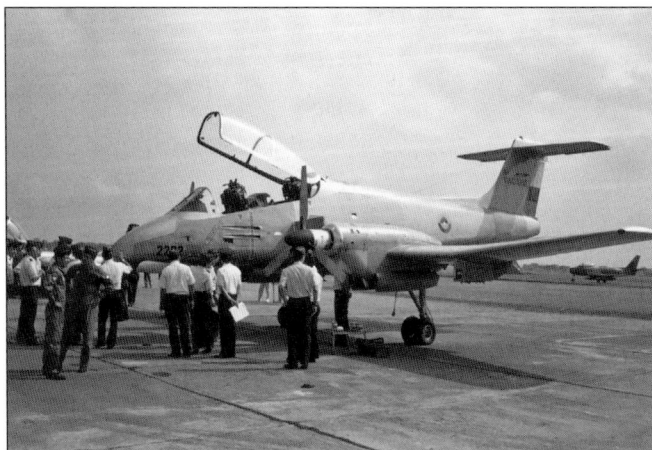

FAC-2202 at the Escuela Militar de Aviación Marco Fidel Suárez, Cali, during a presentation for reserve officers based at Cali.

Photos of Broncos and Pucarás together are rare. Here, an OV-10 taxies in front of a Pucará and a Tucano in 1995, when the Uruguayans went to Apiay to return the Pucarás to service. (Photo Roberto Moreno)

including the headquarters, located in a building with a green roof that gave the place its name, Casa Verde.

On 9 December at dawn, the planes that would provide air support to the helicopter landings began to take off, beginning at 7:17 a.m. with two Kfirs from Palanquero, which at 0805 made the first bombing run, followed by nine A-37s and two AC-47s. Although the Pucarás did not participate in the first attack, they did so in the second. Ramírez says that 'the operations were of support, escorting the logistics cargo aircraft. We made our entrance with rockets, the helicopters came in, made their landings and we all left'. At La Uribe there was a very small airstrip where the Douglas C-47s (DC-3s) would land to fetch resupplies for the troops, but these became guerrilla targets. Ramírez again:

> We started formation flights with the DC-3s. Before we started, we made an entrance with rockets and machine guns, firing into the security perimeter. Those rockets made a lot of noise when they hit the ground. We the escorted the DC-3s in. From Apiay to Uribe it was 20 minutes. There were many DC-3s all with multiple strikes, but while the Pucarás were there, there was not one attack, which means that the use of the plane was dissuasive. We spent about eight months doing that mission.

In addition, he says that they performed softening-up missions with rockets, two planes in tandem, to prepare the ground for the helicopter landings

> before the helicopters came in, because the place is mountainous. Then came the landings; you stayed as top cover because often the helicopters in the LZs were still being shot at. They called us sometimes and sometimes the guerrillas resisted the urge to shoot at the helicopter troops because the Pucarás were up too, which provided security to the ground troops. The weapons scheme that we did with the Pucará was the same as the AT-33, which had two hard points. We normally carried 250-pound bombs and machine guns. At times we launched rockets, but we liked the bombs more: they were louder.

Ramírez explains that the flares fired by ground troops directed them onto their targets: 'We entered with rockets and machine guns and we stayed in place until the landing was completed. These missions lasted a maximum of an hour and a half, always from Apiay.'

Germán Ribero adds that they worked as a team with the A-37s.

> We entered first, we softened up, the helicopter gunships entered, Bell 212s and Hughes 500s, then us with the machine guns and then the A-37 with rockets or bombs of 500 or 1,000 pounds … the army officers felt comforted when the Pucarás arrived, they felt safer.

Shortly after, they also carried out missions in the Casanare area, near the border with Venezuela, operating from Yopal base.

Over the sea

Tensions with Nicaragua over the sovereignty of the islands of San Andrés, Providencia and Santa Catalina, several keys and the surrounding ocean, had generated tensions between both countries over the years, especially since in 1980 Nicaragua declared null and void the treaty signed in 1928 and began to claim sovereignty over the contested area.

On the other hand, the Caribbean had become one of the preferred routes for drug traffickers to transport drugs from Colombia to the United States, and Colombia lacked adequate aircraft for maritime patrol. Thus, in 1990, it was decided to deploy a Pucará to Barranquilla to carry out maritime patrol missions and then to San Andrés. German Ribero says that

> there was the idea of moving the planes to San Andrés, given that the Nicaraguans, every time they are politically shaken in the interior of their country, the first thing they do is say that they are going to take the islands.

Ramírez adds that they went to San Andrés:

> They were long flights: from Apiay to San Andrés it was about three hours and forty minutes. I did it with a co-pilot in Cartagena. The endurance is impressive, and we always flew with the 1,300-litre ventral tank. The flight was very long and we had to watch the water; we were two crew members, not always pilots. Sometimes the technician would go in the rear cabin.

According to him, this deployment was done with a single plane. Six-hour missions were carried out, sometimes with a stopover in Cartagena, covering the almost 750 kilometres of sea that separates San Andrés from Barranquilla. Adds Ramírez:

> We were flying with the rocket launchers, at 15,000 feet. Before any novelty, one would go down, communicate with the Navy and inquire about the boat that was there. We went up and down until the patrol time was up and then we returned to San Andrés. Each maritime patrol sortie was between four and six hours. We brought along two one-litre bottles each, one full [of water] and one empty [for urine]. Oxygen was not too much of an issue because we were flying at 15,000 feet, so did not consume so much. We had this limitation with oxygen because we used the liquid oxygen system. They supplied

oxygen, but the idea was to fly low so as not to have to consume too much. At that time, we also provided training, I think to three or four pilots.

In total they stayed for about six months, until well into 1991, alternating with the Cessna A-37Bs based in Barranquilla, and always with a single Pucará deployed in San Andrés.

By then, Germán Páez became the commander of CACOM-2, Germán Ribero became the commander of Escuadrón de Operaciones Especiales 314 and Juan Carlos Ramírez the head of combat operations.

Protecting Marandúa

In 1990, the Colonel Luis Arturo Rodríguez Meneses Air Base in Marandúa, Vichada, in eastern Colombia, was an aerodrome with few facilities, dependent on the Comando Aéreo de Combate No. 2 of Apiay, but 570 kilometres from the latter and only 120 from the border with Venezuela. The place was only accessible by air and had little infrastructure, which made it an interesting target for the guerrillas, who saw there an outpost of the FAC from which they launched operations against them. Thus, they began to carry out night attacks against the base, so the Escuadrón de Operaciones Especiales 314 was sent to provide support. The operations were carried out with an AC-47 Fantasma that acted as a command post, provided support and also launched lighting flares. Ramírez says that

> Marandúa was a very incipient base, and it was very frequent for subversive groups to attack it and we had to constantly go out to defend it. It was a flight of more or less two hours from Villavicencio, late at night; at any hour they would call us and we would go out to try to soften them up. Several times we went out the lights of the Pucará's formation flight took on great importance. At that time, no combat aircraft had them, and we flew very comfortably.

As they were long missions, there were always two pilots. The Fantasma was already over the area and was acting as a command post. Adds Ribero:

> They flew with an officer as a liaison; he was the commander of the operation and directed the orchestra. One night we had to leave Apiay for Marandúa base. They called us out around 7 at night, because they were attacking at Marandúa. We arrived at the base after midnight, and the weather was bad. This time I was very impressed. The troops on the ground guided us in and marked the targets. We spent more than two hours over the target, and we still had more than an hour: the plane had a spectacular endurance.

Above: A Pucará flies over the hills near Apiay. (Photo Peter Steinemann)

Left: Two Pucarás with two Cessna A-37B Dragonflys and three AT-33s in the background, Apiay, 1990. (Photo Peter Steinemann)

During these missions, the AC-47 launched flares to illuminate the target and indicated direction and distance of it, after which the Pucará attacked with rockets and machine guns, saturating the area, which, added to the fact that the guerrillas knew that the aircraft remained orbiting above the base, led to the attack being suspended.

Out of service

By 1991, given the fact that the FAC did not buy spare parts for the airplanes and the situation of the FMA in Argentina had become too complicated to be able to provide them in a timely manner, the Pucará began to experience operational problems. At the same time, the economic situation in Argentina generated doubts for the FAC of the possibility of a contract being fulfilled if the nine additional planes needed to complete the squadron were purchased. The United States, as it had done previously with the frustrated sale to Venezuela, offered to donate a squadron of 12 Rockwell OV-10 Broncos to replace the Pucará. This donation was accepted and the planes arrived in Apiay in December 1991.

The small fleet of Pucarás was impacted as no spare parts had been purchased, so they stopped flying before the end of the year. Since the planes were in good condition, at the end of 1994, an agreement was signed with the Uruguayan Air Force through which the latter sent pilots and technicians to recover the planes and train new crews. Roberto Moreno, from the Uruguayan Air Force, explains that the agreement implied

> the transfer to Colombia of a Uruguayan technical team to evaluate the status of the IA-58 Pucará flight equipment and carry out the repairs that were necessary for the return to airworthy condition of the three IA-58 aircraft, within a period of no more than 30 days. In addition were the necessary flight courses for the training of four new IA-58 pilots. The technicians who went first were appointed on an official basis to Colombia by the head of the material section of the FAU Escuadrón Aéreo No. 1, Captain (Av.) Nelson Riambau, followed later by three pilots, Major (Av.) José T. Odini, commander of Escuadrón Aéreo No. 1 and captains (Av.) Sergio González and Héctor Luongo.

The team arrived in early 1995 and having evaluated the condition of the planes, it was found that they had not been well looked after. FAC-2201 was abandoned, with multiple components missing, including the right engine. The technicians began with washing of the planes, since they had been out in the open for many months, continuing with maintenance and fine-tuning. As they were made ready, the necessary ground tests (fixed points) and the flights of verification, acceptance and delivery of the aircraft were carried out, for use in the flight training of the new Colombian pilots, whose theoretical courses were in the meantime being conducted with the arrival of the FAU instructor pilots.

Captain Juan Durán 'Chacal' (pilot of T-33A), Lieutenants Cuan and Jaime Clavijo (pilots of OV-10A Bronco) and Second Lieutenant 'Apache' Landines (EMB-312 Tucano pilot) were designated to conduct the training course on the IA-58 Pucará. Captain Héctor Luongo was in charge of monitoring the maintenance, aimed at putting the aircraft back into the air, the execution of fixed points (ground tests) and maintenance flights, in addition to collaborating as a flight instructor, replacing the squadron commander, on his frequent trips to Bogotá as liaison with the FAC command. Luongo says:

> My mission was to monitor and commission all three, although I ended up doing my thing and supporting the flight instruction. In short, I did the flight checks for each plane, plus instruction to a student, Lieutenant Cuan, in instruments and basic shooting.

The commissioning of the aircraft was more complex than expected and it was not possible to do it simultaneously for all three aircraft, so FAC-2202 was delivered

A Colombian Pucará armed with seven-tube rocket launchers, 1990. (Photo Juan Carlos Ramírez via Javier Ordoñez Jimenez)

first, followed by FAC-2203 and finally FAC-2201, but all within the stipulated timeframe.

FAC-2203 had problems with setting up the left engine because switches which are accessed through an inspection cover had been tampered with; these are located on the extremity, near the leading edge of the wing, so the engine did not exceed 40 per cent RPM. Once the problem was resolved, the test flight was made, at a minimum level of 070 (7,000 feet), in a sector assigned to the south of the base.

With FAC-2202 Luongo describes a landing gear retraction failure:

> We had completed the ground checks, the fixed point tests and FAC-2202 was ready for its test flight. We took off, rotation, brakes, gear lever up and then a new problem cropped up: the gear lever could not be brought back to place it in the up position – therefore the hydraulic pressure passage for the retraction of the gear was not enabled. This fact in itself did not constitute an emergency situation, since the landing gear was down and stuck, but we notified Apiay Tower and prepared to return when we heard on the radio of an OV-10 Bronco reporting a landing gear indication unlocked, declaring an emergency. We suggested to the air traffic controller that we could fly in formation with the OV-10 and observe if any leg of the gear was retracted or semi-extended, which the ATC agreed to and

FAC-2202 at the Military Aviation School in Cali, together with the school's Stearman PT-76, which was kept operational for flypasts and airshows. (Archive Javier Ordoñez Jimenez)

instructed the Bronco to stay vertical. We flew by his side, inspecting the position of the legs of the gear and we found nothing remiss, so he was instructed to land, which was carried out without incident. The non-rising of the gear at take-off was only a failure of the lever system. Operationally it was fine.

During one training flight, the oil system seal broke in one of the engines of a Pucará and the plane lost all its oil, but was able to be saved despite having operated for a few minutes without oil. Luongo also says that

the radios and navigation equipment gave us headaches, to the point that it was necessary to send an avionics specialist from the Maintenance Service, in Carrasco, Montevideo. That technician had to completely review the wiring of the communication and navigation system, welding, etc. He pasted the plans on the inner side of the dome and on the instrument panel on the skirt and he only had to raise his head to read and compare the plans with what he had in front of him. His work was incredible. The equipment had failed in every way imaginable; for example, having established communication with the tower, suddenly everything went dead. It was a tough task to be able to put all those systems back together until the planes returned to flight order. The VHF, VOR and NDB had serious wiring problems; they had been tampered with by someone who was clueless about what they were doing.

This was also due to the fact that they had been fitted with T-33A intercoms, to improve communication between the crew, since it was argued that it was a weak point in the Pucará. Luongo again:

> You could clearly see that there were non-commissioned officers who did not want the Pucará. Probably because all their experience came from the USAF and for the first time in their aeronautical careers, they had come across a different plane, with different engines, with different technical documentation. But a few put their prejudices aside and learned to love it, especially the gunsmiths.

The then Lieutenant Jaime Clavijo was one of the FAC pilots who received training. He had experience flying the Douglas DC-3, Embraer Tucano and later the OV-10 Bronco. He had asked to fly the A-37, but when the agreement with Uruguay was reached, he was assigned to do the course on the Pucará:

> They presented a good course in a very professional way and then, due to the versatility of the plane, we began to vigorously sell the idea that it was an ideal plane for the fight against the guerrillas at that time. Unfortunately, I don't know if there was a lack of vision on the part of our commanders to take advantage of all the aircraft's capabilities and we only had the opportunity to do one real mission, which went off very successfully. The Pucará was the plane that everyone wanted to fly at Villavicencio base. There were the Tucanos which were small, the OV-10 which was small and there was the Pucará which was the big, warrior plane that everyone would want to fly. At that time, it was an escadrille attached to the OV-10 squadron, but it was very underutilized.

Back in combat

After the Uruguayans left, the unit kept on training, but was not authorized for combat. Clavijo explains that they did tests with the 20mm guns at Palanquero range: 'it was a real spectacle and we dropped the practice bombs, the BDU-33, they were the only bombs we had the chance to drop. We were dying to drop bombs in the internal conflict.'

However, since at one point the OV-10s were almost all out of service, a single combat mission with two Pucarás was authorized. Clavijo says that it was

> a mission against the guerrillas on the eastern plains, very close to the Meta River. At that time, OV-10 combat sorties were permanent fixtures, because the guerrillas had battered and captured some towns;

later they took refuge in areas protected by the indigenous reserves. It was very difficult to hunt them down. It was a time when the OV-10s were also found wanting and the authorities were forced to use the Pucará, but they only authorized us to fire the 7.62mm machine guns. For us in the Pucará escadrille this was better than nothing because we felt very cooped up at the base, seeing that everyone was in combat, and we wanted to be in on the action. On that mission we went out with Lieutenant Cuan and we were able to help the army, which was being attacked in a town called Puerto Rico.

Clavijo says that the Pucará was evaluated for maritime patrols, both from the coast of Cali and from San Andrés, but the idea was abandoned.

Since the recovery by the Uruguayans, the planes flew during 1995, but since no new spare parts had been purchased, little by little they went out of service again and by the end of the year they stopped flying permanently. In total, they had flown about 1,670 hours from delivery to the FAC in Córdoba until their final retirement. Over the years there would be another Uruguayan mission, with the same purpose, but the planes were never put into service. Sometime later, an attempt was made to coordinate with the Argentine Air Force to provide training and to obtain spare parts, but this did not prove possible.

Subsequent negotiations agreed to the return of the three planes to Argentina, including an exchange for a retired plane from the FAA to be exhibited at the museum of the Colombian Air Force. The lack of funds from both countries, added to the marked deterioration of the Colombian Pucarás, parked in the open air, determined the lack of interest in sealing the deal, despite the fact that Pucará ex-A-518 had already been painted in FAC colours.

Finally, in May 2003, an agreement was signed with the Uruguayan Air Force whereby the FAC delivered the three decommissioned aircraft and some spare parts and, as a consideration, the FAU provided training for an FAC officer, all of which was carried out in 2008.

Pucará versus Bronco

Having two aircraft produced for the same mission, the Pucará has always been compared to the Rockwell OV-10 Bronco, with which it competed in failed sales to Venezuela and Colombia. Until today, very few pilots had the opportunity to fly both planes and only Jaime Clavijo, from Colombia, was able to fly both in combat. Asked about how he compares them, he explained that

the Bronco is an aircraft with different capabilities, and although they say it is competition, the Pucará has a versatility that the OV-10 does not have. The OV-10 has a lot of take-off weight restriction, the engines are counter-rotating, and an engine failure is quite critical on short runways, while the Pucará has a lot of power, more speed and take-off weight. The Pucará is better with the armament capacity as well. The OV-10 has slightly more range, consumes less fuel, and has belly-mount 180- and 230-gallon tanks. The Pucará, if I include all the weapons, has little chance of going very far. The versatility of the Pucará allows more ammunition to be loaded and unloaded when attacking, which makes it more responsive than the OV-10. Due to the shape of its cabin, it has a lot of visibility, but from the knees up one is more exposed, but it allows better visibility when delivering weapons.

The performance is superior in the Pucará; in the OV-10 with a single engine you are very restricted in height, your ceiling is lowered a lot, and you cannot cross the mountain ranges of Colombia. In the Pucará if an engine is shut down and, without a load, you can overfly the Colombian mountain ranges. That kind of thing gives the pilot more peace of mind.

The only disadvantage of the Pucará is logistics, that guarantee that the planes will be in service for longer. They are very well-designed airplanes but the engines are the karma of the maintenance personnel. The two models are very good, but I prefer the Pucará.

On the other hand, on 20 February 1995, Captain (Air) Héctor Luongo of the Uruguayan Air Force had the opportunity to evaluate the OV-10 Bronco in flight during its deployment at Apiay, and to establish specific parameters for comparing performance with the IA-58 Pucará:

On 20 February 1995, I was invited to participate as an observer pilot on a training flight on OV-10A FAC-2219, with Lieutenant Félix Antonio Sarracino Botero in charge. We took off from Apiay Air Base to remain in sector. It was a very enjoyable experience. I could see on the horizon, above the helix cone, the majestic Andes Mountains. The plane is a first cousin to the IA-58, but in some ways, it is inferior: when performing a series of manoeuvres, consisting of loops, left and right barrels, reversals, Immelmanns, etc. it was impossible not to lose height (this does not happen in the IA-58, which maintains height throughout the entire aerobatic series). The principles of regulation of the engines were similar to many turboprops and different from the Astazou, the speeds of manoeuvres were similar but generally slower: it is a rougher aircraft, less aerodynamically refined.

This difference between the engines caused different flight procedures between one plane and another and, while in the IA-58, after take-off the RPM is kept

Argentine Pucará A-518 was painted in Colombian colours in 2000 as it was planned for delivery to the Colombian Air Force Museum, but the exchange for three Colombian Pucarás never took place. (Photo Santiago Rivas)

at maximum, in the OV-10 they are reduced to the range of cruising flight. This motivated one of the students, perhaps because he came from the OV-10, to reduce the RPM to 82 per cent after take-off in an IA-58, with all the risk that this implies for the life of the turbine. Fortunately, nothing happened apart from a fright and the instructor's correction.

Chapter 17

Sri Lanka

This was the last export of the Pucará and, according to Commodore Carlos Argente, who was at the factory at the time, everything arose when in 1992 a telephone call was received from Belgium by the company's commercial manager, engineer Francisco Luciano, the caller asking if there was a Pucará for sale. Given the positive response, the negotiation was advanced directly to between the factory and the Sri Lankan government. Having also evaluated the Embraer Tucano and the Pilatus PC-7, the aircraft met the expectations of the Sinhalese, especially in terms of firepower and precision. In November 1992, an export contract was signed and the aircraft, from c/n 100 to 103 inclusive, were sold to Sri Lanka for $11 million,

The Sri Lanka Air Force (SLAF) needed the plane to fight the guerrillas of the Liberation Tigers of Tamil Eelam (LTTE) group, which were seeking independence in the north and east of the island. Supported by India, the Tamil Tigers started their insurrection in 1983, which by the late 1980s had escalated and developed into a full-blown civil war. In addition to some transports and helicopters, the SLAF was only equipped with eight SIAI Marchetti SF260TPs (turboprop) and nine SF260W Warriors (piston) for training and light attack.

The four Pucarás received a Trimble GPS and communications equipment of a different model from that used by Argentina, which is why initially the FMA named them IA-58SL, but later IA-58L.

Three pilots, Group Captain Shirantha Goonetilleke, Squadron Leader Pamunu Mahamalage and Flight Lieutenant Priyantha Adikaram, along with 12 others, including engineers, mechanics and specialists, travelled to Argentina before the end of 1992 and received training at the Área de Material Córdoba, with Argentine Air Force planes, flying 15 hours each. Among the pilots was Flight Lieutenant Priyantha Adikaram, who remembers that they had two instructors, Captains Omar Elías and Guillermo Alsúa, who later travelled to Sri Lanka to set up the aircraft together with Commodore Carlos Argente and the civilian personnel Alberto Pitch.

Adikaram recalls that 'three pilots and four engineers went to Argentina and there were eight other people who went, including gunsmiths, to learn about weapons. The total of the personnel was fifteen'. They included rocket launches as part of the training, but Priyantha remembers that he only launched one. After a month and a half at Córdoba, the Sri Lankan staff returned to their country.

The planes were then transported in the I Brigada Aérea FAA C-130H Hercules to Katunayake base in Sri Lanka.

'The same instructors came to Sri Lanka and we did quite a few training flights as well. They first did the test flights after commissioning the planes. Then we did some training flights. We were also trained to fly from the back seat, as instructors,' adds Adikaram and says that the training in Sri Lanka lasted one month, but the Argentine staff spent a total of six months in the country. Of the three pilots, only Adikaram was trained as an instructor.

On 28 December 1992, CA-601 and -602 aircraft were delivered by the workshop. CA-601 was sent on 30 December in the L-100-30 Hercules serialled LV-APW of the Argentine Air Force, followed by CA-602 on 11 January 1993. CA-603 followed on 2 March 1994 and in April CA-604.

In Sri Lanka they were assigned to the 1st Flying Training Wing of Anduradhapura together with the Siai Marchetti SF-260TP and -W for

Due to the size of the Pucará, only one could be loaded on a Hercules. Here, one of the first two sent to Sri Lanka is loaded at FMA. (Photo FMA)

training and light attack; some de Havilland Chipmunks were still operational. CA-602 was re-serialled shortly after arriving as CA-605.

Adikaram says that 'from the ground attack role it made a big difference, due to a higher load capacity than the Siai Marchetti'. As soon as the training was over, the planes began to carry out combat operations, while Adikaram also dedicated himself to training new pilots.

Squadron Leader Uditha Danwaththa was one of the first pilots to train on the plane and recalls:

> I had my rating in 1993 after completing my training. So, I had my first combat mission in 1993. We were eight pilots in total. We were using the plane primarily for air support against terrorists. The Sri Lankan Army had to gain ground, advancing on the ground, and the Sri Lankan Air Force was the supporting arm for them. We had

many missions to support the Army and we had the capacity to carry rockets, 7.62mm machine guns, 150kg and 250kg bombs and we also used 20mm guns.

In addition, he says that he participated in some test flights led by Guillermo Alsúa, flying in the back seat to familiarize himself with the plane. 'I was in the rear seat. So there he told me, "Ok, this is this, this is that."' Adikaram also highlights the fact that the Pucará had armour and ejection seats, while the SF260 did not, which gave them greater survivability.

The greatest guerrilla activity occurred in the vicinity of the city of Jaffna in the extreme north of the island, and in Mullaitivu, Alampil and Trimcomalee, in the northeast. For this reason, for the initial operations they deployed to the north and east of the country, starting with Air Station Mullaitivu, in the northeast of the island, and then also to Palali Air Base in Jaffna, and Vavuniya. The Palali base was the only government-held area in the extreme north of the country and was surrounded by guerrilla-dominated territory.

As explained by the Air Chief Marshal (Retd.) Kolitha A. Gunatilleke 'those places depended on the requirement at the time, they used to go and use them for small operations. But the main base was Anuradhapura in the centre of the country.' Gunatilleke was another of the pilots trained in Sri Lanka by Adikaram in 1993. 'I did a little more training by myself. Priyantha took my exam and after a while, maybe a month or so, I was flying in combat. I had flown a lot with the Siai Marchetti,' he says.

On 13 October 1993, CA-601 suffered an accident when the nosewheel retracted when the aircraft was stopped and a mechanic mistakenly operated the gear lever. The incident occurred in the town of Jaffna and was later repaired.

Among the early missions are those carried out on 25 July 1993, during defence of an Army unit in Welioya. At that time, the Sri Lankan government was developing plans for Operation *Riviresa* to recapture the city of Jaffna, which was in

Captain Carlos Alzúa, Flight Lieutenant Priyantha Adikaram and an Argentine mechanic at Córdoba during the training of the Sri Lankan pilots. (Archive Priyantha Adikaram)

Squadron Leader Uditha Danwaththa with a Pucará armed with two seven-tube 70mm rocket launchers. (Archive Uditha Danwaththa)

CA-604 refuelling at Anuradhapura Air Base; it is armed with 19-tube 70mm rocket launchers. (Photo Peter Steinemann via Carlos Ay)

the hands of the guerrillas, but the enemy learned of these plans and launched a pre-emptive attack against the Army positions and the Sri Lankan Navy in the Kilaly area and attempted to occupy their positions in Poonaryn in the early morning of 11 November 1993, launching a boat assault across the Kilaly lagoon.

Danwaththa recounts how in one of the following missions, on 11 November 1993, during a mission in support of the Nagadivanthurai naval detachment in Pooneryn, he was hit by enemy small-arms fire:

> I was shot in November 1993; in the south of Jaffna, there is a lagoon, where the north and the south were connected by that lagoon. So, it was strategically a very important area and near the Army base is a nearby Navy base. We sent two planes to Jaffna Air Force Base. So that

morning we detected the enemy at 2:45 in the morning. The army was there and we could see all the tracer bullets. The attack was near the air base. We fired with rockets, guns and bombs. So, on my fourth mission, I was wounded, two shots in the leg. I didn't have to eject because my engines were fine – they had 100 per cent engine performance, so I managed to land in Jaffna. What happened on landing was that I had no brakes or hydraulics. Fortunately, my radio was working, so I radioed the base saying they had hit me and I made an emergency landing. I managed to get the aircraft back. They came looking for me and in no time, they sent me to the hospital. And they operated on me, because I had two bullets to my right knee. Had it not been for the armour plate it would have been vital damage, because some of the bullets were stopped thanks to the armour plate, because the protection part was done perfectly. There were nine hits on the plane. They repaired the aircraft; our team deployed to the air force base. The plane needed an engine change, so they replaced the aircraft's engine, repaired all the damage, and the aircraft was back in operation shortly thereafter. But in my case, I had to stay two months in the hospital.

It was on my fifth mission, and we started early in the morning. After landing I was able to brake, but I had no nosewheel steering, then no reversible pitch and no brakes. Somehow, I managed to control the rudder, but when the speed slows down, the rudder stops working, but I managed to stop on the runway. Generally, after completing a mission, we had a bit of time on the ground, and a briefing on the next objective and next take-off time decided by the operations commander. The routine on the ground was to refuel the aircraft, rearm it and leave in half an hour.

Danwaththa adds:

We operated alone – although the plane has two seats, we operated with only one pilot. There was a Navy ship that was trying to make a landing on the beach, to reinforce the army troops. And there were four enemy boats. They appeared from different places and came to attack the Navy ship and there were a good number of Army troops inside the ship. So, I completely destroyed two enemy boats. There were two attack boats and two others supported them. I managed to destroy the other two boats, there was an explosion, I fired with rockets and the boats exploded. And when I went for the third, they shot from below and hit me. It was an area of lagoon, sea and lagoon, and the land was in the middle. So, for the most part, they fired from the boats.

The Pucará attacks were on the Kilaly lagoon, launching the rockets from a height of 500 feet, although they were not enough to stop the LTTE attack. The enemy

CA-604 flying with a SIAI Marchetti SF260TP. The Pucará is armed with four 19-tube 70mm rocket launchers, having a triple ejector rack on the pylon under the belly. (Photo Peter Steinemann via Carlos Ay)

occupied the naval detachment and swept the army defences in the area, capturing about 200 soldiers who were then executed. The rest of the personnel managed to escape to the Elephant Pass military camp.

That night, 52 men from the LTTE's elite unit, the Black Tigers, attempted to enter Palaly air base, but were driven back and the Sri Lanka Army was able to hold their positions. On 14 November, the Navy launched a landing and managed to recapture the Nagadivanthurai naval detachment.

The Argentine personnel stayed for several months in Sri Lanka, giving assistance, according to Horacio Argente, who stayed there for a year and a half, although the pilots were only there for six months. Four Argentines were sent to the Palali base to provide support during the operations. Argente recalls that, on one occasion, one of the Pucarás was on a 150-hour inspection at that base when, in the middle of the night, they were informed that there was a guerrilla attack on the nearby beach. 'They took the jacks out of the plane for inspection, they left it ready and went to shoot,' he says, adding that this was the plane used by Danwaththa.

> They hit him on the nose, broke the hydraulic pipe and hit the pilot on the thigh. It didn't lower the nose gear, but he did release it by gravity. The SLAF commander called us to go and inspect the plane … the Sinhalese were very skilled, they wanted to buy the tools from the Pucará, which were piled up at the back of the factory, but there was no interest from the factory. They also wanted to buy bombs.

Kolitha A Gunatilleke explains that the Tamils used a fleet of boats for attacks and also to carry weapons from India. 'The Navy did everything it could to handle this,

CA-605, former CA-602, armed with 250kg Mk.82 bombs, together with two other Pucarás at Anuradhapura Air Base. (Photo Peter Steinemann via Carlos Ay)

but there was a lot of arms smuggling during the war. And we were often deployed, especially on the east coast,' he says. Adikaram, for his part, adds, 'I have carried out quite a few reconnaissance missions, but I did not come across any LTTE ships. So, we used to do surveillance and observation. And if we weren't sure, we called the Navy to investigate.'

Operations continued throughout 1993 and 1994. On 23 April 1994, two Pucarás and two Chengdu F-7 jet fighters (Chinese version of the MiG-21) were used in close air support operations throughout seven hours of very heavy fighting in the vicinity of Batticaloa, although in general that year there were not so many major combat operations.

The threat of the SA-7

Until 1995 the guerrillas only used small arms against aircraft but the increasing firepower of the SLAF with the Pucarás and the F-7s led them to search for more effective weapons, obtaining SA-7 Strela missiles. Thus, on 28 April 1995, the LTTE achieved their first victory: Avro HS-748 serialled CR-835 of the SLAF took off from Palaly with Squadron Leader Pamunu Mahamalage at the controls (Pucará pilots also flew transport airplanes, due to the shortage of pilots); the plane was hit in the left engine and caught fire, crashing shortly after and killing all 51 occupants. The following day, Priyantha Adikaram took off as co-pilot of HS-748 serialled

Above and below: Pucarás CA-604 and -605 flying armed, one with bombs and the other with rocket launchers. (Photos Peter Steinemann via Carlos Ay)

CR-834, commanded by Squadron Leader Sujeewa Pathirarhna, but on a stopover in Anuradhapura, Adikaram was replaced. The plane was carrying a team led by Pucará pilot Group Captain Shirantha Gunathilake, who was going to Palaly to investigate the shootdown of the previous day. As they approached Palaly, the pilot reported that they had been hit by a missile and the plane crashed seconds later, killing its 54 occupants. This was a significant change in the war: without flares to deceive the missiles, the planes were extremely vulnerable.

In early July, the Sri Lankan Armed Forces launched Operation *Leap Forward* against the Tamils north of Jaffna, seeking to expand the perimeter of the controlled area around the Palaly air base, in the area of the towns of Navaly, Valikaamam and Sandilipay. On the afternoon of 9 July, a Pucará attacked the Catholic Church of Saint Peter in Navaly, where it was believed that guerrillas were taking refuge, but in reality, there were civilians, 65 of whom died in the bombing. Speaking to *Time* magazine, Jaffna Bishop Thomas Savundaranayagam, who had already urged Sinhalese President Chandrika Kumaratunga to stop bombing religious places of worship, said:

> The army has warned civilians to clear the southwest of their base in Palaly, recommending churches and temples as havens. At 4:30 p.m., a Pucará fighter plane made in Argentina flew towards the church of Navaly, three kilometres from the combat zone, and bombarded the sanctuary and the adjacent courtyard. Saint Peter's Church in Navaly and the adjoining Saint Peter School, where hundreds of people had sought refuge, were destroyed. Fifty-six bodies were recovered from the rubble, many of whom were women and children. The final death toll in Navaly was about 120.

The *Leap Forward* operation continued over the following days and on 14 July 1995, Pucará serialled CA-601 took off from Palaly to participate in the fighting at Sandilipay, about 10 kilometres east of the base. Danwaththa recalls:

> Our base was Anuradhapura and we were asked to go to Jaffna because some of the terrorists had infiltrated the air force base. I was the operations commander at the time. We went to Jaffna early in the morning, then my friend flew out on the first mission; he had deployed with me. After the briefing, my colleague went out on the first mission and I was in the control tower. He took off and when he was about 2,000 feet, maybe 2,500, they fired a missile at him. I saw the whole situation from a distance. When I saw that the missile was going towards him – the SAMs are very visible, you see the smoke trail – I screamed on the radio, but he didn't react, and the missile hit the left wing. I saw the missile hit the plane and half of the left wing broke off. I yelled on the radio, 'Eject, eject, eject!' But I still don't know why he didn't eject. The plane fell and hit the ground. We were

very close and, on the battlefront, we were very active; when you lose someone like that you can't help but feel sad about it. We had to send two helicopters to retrieve the body. And to this day it still springs to mind: 'Why didn't he eject?' He had two ejection handles. His name was Flight Lieutenant Dilhan Perera.

This shootdown was followed by a Shaanxi Y-8 on 18 November and an Antonov An-32B on 22 November, which led the SLAF to completely change tactics: while trying to avoid the SAMs, it was decided to buy fighter jets, which could attack with greater height and speed, making it more difficult for the enemy to hit them. Thus, in 1995, six IAI Kfir C2/TC2, were purchased, which arrived in January 1996.

More combat operations

Meanwhile, on 28 September 1995, Operation *Thunder Strike* was launched, which weakened the LTTE, so that on 17 October, Operation *Riviresa I* began with the occupation of the Valikaamam area, with air support from the Pucarás and other aircraft, and with the recovery of the city of Jaffna on 2 December of that year.

Gunatilleke explains that he flew very few missions in the Pucará, since he was only in the unit for a short time:

> One that I remember is that the army had their airmobile unit and they had information about a terrorist training camp. The army used to ask the air force for helicopters, maybe six or seven, to assault this target by air, because we didn't control the ground. So, they would often call us. When the helicopters were approaching at dawn, to neutralize the target, then they would also call for close air support. I did two missions that time, but I think the initial information was not correct. So, when the army arrived, they found a small number of weapons and ammunition and a few LTTE guards guarding them, but it was not as large as expected. They never hit me in the Pucará.

Adikaram recalls his most interesting mission, against an enemy camp:

> It was when we got information that said 23 of the terrorist leaders were meeting. I was carrying rockets and the terrorists were all lined up. I went and fired the rockets at the LTTE guns, and they were firing at me, but, since I knew they had anti-aircraft guns and everything, after firing I came out very low to the height of the trees and I saw some guys with guns, but as the plane was very low, they couldn't shoot me. I had another pilot with me and he saw everything, he was reporting on the weapons, the people with weapons and everything.

He adds that he was hit on a mission:

> I have the pieces of the bullet with me, not in my body, but in the armour plates. A bullet hit the ejection seat, but we had armour, so it hit the armour, but the pieces are still with me … Sometimes we used to do combat air patrols when the army was going to carry out operations, to provide support if they called us. Those sorties were the longest, the rest of the sorties were of a maximum of 45 minutes

because they always operated close to the battlefield. In the case of the patrols, he explains that they lasted an hour and a half or more. Gunatilleke adds that 'Sri Lanka is not a large country, so from the base to the furthest point in flight time with the Pucará., it would have been about 25 minutes. So, the deployment flights took about 15 to 20 minutes'.

Adikaram and Gunatilleke report that they also conducted night missions. The former recalls that

> mainly when the army was in operations we knew where the front line was. And on certain occasions we also used flares to indicate the location of the target. The Pucará used a combination of weapons depending on the target – there was no fixed configuration of weapons.

Gunatilleke adds that

> the flares were launched on these missions by the army. Basically, to indicate their position or the front line. And they could be seen from a distance, so we knew where our own forces were and then the distance and position of the target. In the conflict, as it escalated, we had to modify and adapt to various conditions to support the army. I don't recall piloting Pucarás on those missions, but when we flew with the Siai Marchetti, the army had several small camps located at various locations and the LTTE used to surround and attack them. There was a place, I think it was after the arrival of the Pucarás, where we lost perhaps a thousand soldiers. Those missions happened often – it was very difficult, because they couldn't fire the flares or even turn on the lights, because they couldn't defend themselves against the enemy. Then, there was also darkness and then it was very difficult to know where the army was, but we knew the terrain and from afar we were calculating distances. And then our soldiers went on to adopt a method where they dig a large well, maybe 25 feet deep, in the centre of the camp. And inside that well they lit a fire, so that we could see it from above but not from ground level. So, we get used to coordinating that way. We had to think outside the box.

On one occasion they had to fly continuously for four days, together with the SF-260, making attacks day and night. Adikaram says that

> the only time we rested was when we were rearming There was an example where the enemy was firing flares. The terrorists were firing flares for some reason and we could see them very clearly. They fired in the opposite direction and gave away their positions. We were six or seven pilots, so we could return to the base to load weapons. And then another pair came in. That was continuous, four pilots attacking the target while others were returning to base and another pair was on the ground rearming. I don't remember the number of sorties.

Gunatilleke adds that

> we probably violated all the rules we had about pilots, but it had to be done – we couldn't tell the army that we wanted to rest. We flew with one pilot. We did not have the luxury of taking two pilots. We didn't have many pilots.

Adikaram adds: 'Only once do I remember a mission with another pilot in the rear cabin.' Gunatilleke says that

> depending on what was happening, how the information was reaching us and how much support was required, we generally flew in pairs. The selection of weapons depended on the target and the intelligence: the air base decided on that and told us which weapons to use. We generally used Mk.82 bombs.

Regarding the appreciation of the plane by the ground troops, Gunatilleke says:

> I was one of the first pilots to fly the Siai Marchetti and even that was something very important for the army, because before that we only used helicopters. Everyone was talking about it. So, when we arrived with the Pucará they liked it even more.

Adikaram adds: 'We used a combination of escadrilles as well, with Pucarás and Siai Marchettis, and the soldiers always preferred the Pucarás,' among other things, because of its firepower and the ability to carry a lot of weapons, which allowed the pilots to do multiple strafing runs. Because the plane had basic communications systems, the guerrillas interfered with the VHF signal, so the Air Force had to change the equipment for more advanced systems.

After losing Jaffna, the LTTE regrouped in early 1996 and on 18 July of that year launched Operation *Unceasing Waves*, occupying the military base of Mullaitivu, in the northeast of the island, surrounded by the sea to the east, a lagoon to the west and north and jungle to the south. The government then launched Operation *Thrivida Pahara* to recover the base and rescue the 6th Battalion of the Vijayabahu Infantry Regiment, who were besieged in the centre. The Pucarás, together with the Kfirs and Mi-24 helicopters, launched attacks against the LTTE troops, while an air assault began on Alampil, south of the base, using Mi-17 helicopters escorted by Mi-24s; however, a Kfir assault resulted in a blue-on-blue incident with 80 government casualties, dead and wounded. Towards nightfall, the 6th Battalion collapsed and the base was occupied by the enemy. An attempt to carry out an amphibious assault the following day failed, with the loss of a Navy patrol boat, destroyed by an LTTE suicide boat. Although on the 23rd the base was recaptured, it had been completely destroyed, and the government decided to abandon it on the 24th and 25th.

Final operations with Pucará

On 7 February 1997, a Pucará sank the cargo ship *Caribbean Queen* that was carrying weapons for the rebels.

At 2232 on Sunday, 15 March 1997, CA-604 took off from Anuradhapura Air Base. Flight Lieutenant Udeni Rajapakse was on a night raid mission targeting a group of guerrillas gathering in western Batticaloa, as requested by the Army. Recalls Rajapakse:

> I had the rank of flight lieutenant and was the operations commander of the 1st Flying Training Wing at Anuradhapura, flying Pucarás. On 15 March, we were on a mission between Trinco[malee[and the Batticaloa coast to attack a large LTTE meeting. The mission was very detailed and the ground crew and pilot had been on standby since the afternoon. However, it was another pilot who was nominated to fly, not me.*

The pilot designated to fly was a married officer. By 1930 there was still no flight order, so Rajapakse took over the duty so the pilot could be with his family. That day, nine SLAF planes had been hit by the enemy. Around 2200, Rajapakse was given his mission orders.

> I was in the air from Anuradhapura at 10.32 p.m. Due to the missile threat, we were asked to maintain cruising altitude of 10,000 feet. When I was reaching the desired altitude, I heard a thunderous explosion. A dazzling light lit up the whole area. The left wing of Pucará broke off and separated.

---

* http://archives.sundayobserver.lk/2008/05/18/spe03.asp

Rajapakse lost total control of the aircraft which began to roll; at the same time that he was left without communications. 'I had to think fast because I had so little time to do everything,' he says. Due to the amount of gravity from the roll of the plane, he could not easily reach the ejection handle. 'As we were taught in our training, I dragged my hands against my body (from the knees up) and reached the ejection handle just above my head. I pulled the handle,' adding that he later passed out and woke up when he was parachuting. 'I was going down, but, for a moment, I doubted if I was alive or not.' He had lost his left glove and his handkerchief. In the distance he saw a glow – the remains of the Pucará in flames.

> I felt safe and was very aware of what was going to happen next. Exactly at the moment of ejection I knew where the plane was, as when we were flying, especially at night, we were instructed to navigate foot by foot. We had to be one hundred per cent sure of the navigation. The moonlight was guiding me. I saw the city of Hingurakgoda and another city. I recognized the west of Kavudulla.

He made it to the ground with something of a jolt and unclipped his parachute.

> I didn't even bother getting my survival pack, as both it and the parachute were red and white, glowing in the moonlight, and would be good markers for the enemy in the distance. My boots were damaged so I took them off. To check my physical condition, I climbed a tree. I was pleased. In the event of an attack by a wild animal, I could run and protect myself.

He walked to Kavudulla and heard that two SLAF helicopters were looking for him, alarming some wild boars who bolted and forced him to climb a tree.

> I had all the signalling devices to tell the helicopters where I was. But I didn't want to use them because I was pretty sure I could find my way back. I also thought that if the pilots did not see my signals, it would have been in vain, but if the enemy saw them, which probably they would, then I'd have a problem.

Helicopters were flying near the wreckage and one flew over him. Once the moonlight diminished due to the clouds, he continued walking. He thought about resting a bit and then starting the journey at dawn, but when the clouds moved off, he took the plunge to move on. Suddenly, Rajapakse saw a beam of light, coming from a parked vehicle, and saw shadows moving through the beam. At first, he didn't know if they were friend or foe.

> There were two vehicles. I heard them speak in Sinhalese and recognized that they were from the armed forces. It was about

300 metres away. I knew that I had to be careful, since at that time everyone thought that I was dead. So, if I was too hasty, I would have been shot, mistaken for an LTTE guerrilla. So, I slowly approached them and then I raised my voice.

After indicating who he was, he began to walk with his hands up as the conversation continued. 'I asked them to turn the vehicle around and shine the light on me. They did and then they recognized me.' Flight Lieutenant Aruna Jayathilaka recognized him and they took him to Hingurakgoda.

The shootdown had been 10 minutes after take-off and 30 minutes from the target; he was flying at 220 knots and the aircraft had crashed into a dry riverbed near Hatharaskotuwa (off the town of Trincomalee). He landed 500 metres from the wreckage of his plane, becoming the first SLAF pilot to eject during a mission. The cause of the loss of the plane could not be determined, but it is believed that it was a missile.

This loss further demonstrated the aircraft's vulnerability to anti-aircraft missiles. Gunatilleke explains that with the Pucará they began to try other tactics to reduce their vulnerability: 'In jungle areas we were bombing from about 12,000 feet, over a huge area. So, one of our bosses wanted us to try a low-level attack, but that's how we lost a Pucará to a missile.' The problem in high-altitude attacks was poor precision and, when they dove, it was still the low speed of the plane which led to coming within the range of the missiles for a longer time, so the attacks began to be carried out almost exclusively by Kfirs and F-7s.

However, the remaining two aircraft participated in Operation *Jayasikurui* in May, which began on the 13th, which sought to open a land corridor to Jaffna, from Vavuniya, passing through the town of Kilinochchi, which was also in government hands. The start of the operation was preceded by air strikes and artillery fire. During the operation, 232 sorties were made by IAI Kfirs, 127 by Mi-24 helicopters and 13 by Pucarás. Gunatilleke says that at that time

> we asked Israel if they could help us with some flare launchers which they did with various models, such as the transport planes we had. But in the Pucará it was something completely new, so they had to start from scratch and only for one or two planes, to do a completely new project, I think it was not worth it.

Thus, given the vulnerability of the plane and the growing problems in obtaining spare parts, and with a fleet of only two planes, the Pucarás were grounded in 1998 and were decommissioned in 1999. Currently the two are preserved in the museum of the Sri Lanka Air Force at the Ratmalana base.

Chapter 18

United Kingdom

Although it was not a sale, at the end of the Malvinas/Falklands War, the Royal Air Force took over several abandoned Pucará aircraft with different degrees of damage. As soon as the war began, the RAF saw that it knew very little about the Pucará and that it could be a threat to British troops. For this reason, when the fighting ended, given that the British were not sure that the war would continue with Argentine attacks from the continent, they put emphasis, among other things, on knowing everything they could about Pucará. Wing Commander John Davis of the Technical Intelligence (Air) Department of the Ministry of Defence (MoD) received the order, on 14 June, to go to the islands:

> My boss told me to go down to the Falklands and I took with me an armament specialist and a radar specialist. Our idea was to look at all the technical intelligence, look at as many of the crashed aeroplanes as possible to see what kit they had, look at all the ground side, look at the armament side – for example, the Exocets that were on the island – and send home as much kit as we thought would be useful.[*]

Davis travelled in a Hercules to the islands a few days later and toured both BAM Malvinas, BAM Cóndor and the EAN Calderón, studying the existing airplanes and looking for technical documentation, which they did not find, since on the islands only frontline maintenance was carried out.

'In looking at all of them, we found only one that was whole,' says John Davis. 'All the rest had been sabotaged by the SAS at some time beforehand. We commandeered this one, plus two "Christmas tree" aeroplanes.' The complete airframe was A-515, which still had rocket launchers installed under the wings, while the aircraft intended for use for spare parts were A-533 and A-549.

A-515 was loaded with a Chinook on the ship *Atlantic Causeway*, together with A-549, on 10 July and on 27 July 1982 they arrived in England. They were followed by A-533 on the *Tor Caledonia* on 20 August and A-522 and -528 on the *Contender Bezant* on 23 September.

---

[*] 'Flying the Pucará: The Boscombe Down Verdict', Ben Dunnell, *The Aviation Historian* No. 8.

A-528 being unloaded in the UK from the *Contender Bezant*, with A-522 already on the pier.

ZD-485 with Sqn Ldr Russell Peart of A&AEE at the controls.

ZD-485 was flown for 25 hours during trials; 50 hours were planned.

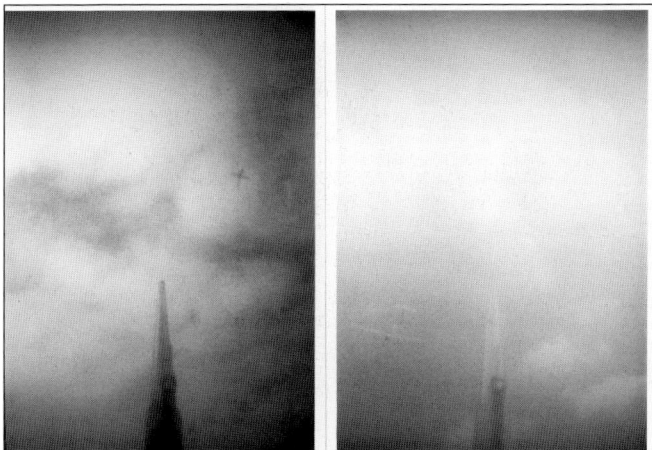

ZD-485 seen from the gun camera of Sea Harrier XZ459 commanded by Flt Lt David Morgan of No. 899 Naval Air Squadron during air combat trials between the two models, 18 July 1983. (Photo David Morgan)

ZD-485 at the 1983 Air Tattoo.

Aircraft A-515, A-533 and A-549 were brought overland on 1 August 1982 to the Aeroplane & Armament Experimental Establishment (A&AEE) at Boscombe Down for commissioning. The aircraft received the British serial ZD-485, while A-533 received the serial ZD-486 and A-549 became ZD-487, although the latter two were never painted.

Work began immediately to recover A-515. 'It needed a huge amount of restoration,' adds Squadron Leader Tony Banfield, then a test pilot in A&AEE's B Squadron. 'They brought it back as deck cargo,' Tony recalls, 'so it had got a lot of salt in it. The A&AEE trials engineers, and there were some very clever people there, virtually took it apart.'

In March 1983, Squadron Leader Russell Peart of A&AEE A Squadron found the handwritten Pucará flight reference cards, which are now housed in the RAF Museum. For the purposes of the Boscombe tests, the aircraft would be limited to a maximum speed of 350 knots; for inverted flight the limit was 160 knots, while

A-517 in the United States, 2020. (Photo Mitchell Enríquez via Carlos Ay)

The front part of A-533, currently owned by Gordon Ramsey in the UK. (Photo Gordon Ramsey)

A-529 was preserved for many years at RAF Mount Pleasant, until it was scrapped and its remains thrown into a lagoon.

with the undercarriage down it was 150 knots and 140 knots with flaps down. A maximum of 3.5 g was imposed for the initial flights, which was later increased to 5 g, while the negative g limit of the aircraft was −1.5. No more than 30 seconds of continual negative-g flight were to be made. Stall entry was to take place no lower than 10,000 feet (3,050 metres), and stalls discontinued by 7,000 feet (2,130 metres). Aerobatic manoeuvres permitted were rolls, loops, stall turns and Immelmanns, spins being prohibited.

On 22 February 1983, the taxiing tests began and on 28 April Squadron Leader Peart made the first flight of an RAF Pucará. It was the first Latin American aircraft in service in the RAF (the second was the Brazilian-designed Shorts Tucano).

'We did a lot of radar simulation work,' Banfield said, 'and we discovered that the radar returns from those huge turboprop propellers, together with the sound that they made in warning of their approach, meant that against Rapiers it would have been like a pheasant shoot.' These observations were made at the Larkhill firing range on the Salisbury Plain; and, on 23 June 1983, mock attacks on a Rapier battery took place.

In total, Tony Banfield flew 7:10 hours in the Pucará, 4:40 hours of that time as captain. 'It was a fun aircraft to fly – a splendid aerobatic aircraft,' he says of the IA-58:

> If you were doing a stall-turn you could virtually do a cartwheel if you chopped the inboard engine, like Jan Zurakowski used to do in the Meteor. I could never get all the way round, though ... In respect of carrying out its task, it was more or less useless. Although it was very heavily armed, and everyone feared it, when you put it in the dive, the trim-change as speed increased was enormous. In order to hold it you had to trim, and you had to take your hand off the throttle to do that, so you couldn't do your radar-ranging and things like that. In addition, as speed increased the controls became heavier and heavier and heavier, and you virtually had to use two hands on the stick to move the ailerons, so actually aiming the thing was very difficult. It wasn't fit for purpose.

It is evident that the British evaluated it as an attack aircraft in conventional conflicts, in a scenario against an enemy well equipped with air defences, for which the Pucará had not been designed, since that it was a counterinsurgency aircraft for asymmetric conflicts.

John Davis flew the plane on 10 June 1983 for 40 minutes with Russell Peart, concentrating primarily on take-offs and landings, and naturally took command himself:

> An interesting plane. Quite easy to fly, relatively good controls, but got very, very heavy as the speed increased – it was similar in that respect to an early-mark Canberra. But, generally speaking, quite

pleasant, with lots of room in the cockpit. We did both hard and grass runway operations at Boscombe; it's very rugged.

Peart was at the helm when the Pucará took on a variety of British military aircraft models for mock-combat testing. Records in the RAF Museum show that '1-v-1' combat with Westland Puma and Sea King helicopters took place from 27 to 28 June 1983, followed by air-to-air combat against two McDonnell Douglas F-4 Phantoms on 12 July, although the results of those encounters are not public.

Then, on 18 July 1983, a simulated combat of different performance was carried out with a Sea Harrier commanded by Flight Lieutenant David Morgan, veteran of the Malvinas/Falklands War. Morgan flew from Yeovilton in Sea Harrier XZ459 of No. 899 Naval Air Squadron, while the Pucará operated from Boscombe Down. According to Morgan:

> I flew them on 18 July 1983 from RAF Boscombe Down. There were two phases, the first to assess the ability of the Sea Harrier to pick up the Pucara on the Blue Fox radar. The large propellers proved to be very good radar reflectors and I achieved pick-ups in excess of 18 miles from most aspects at medium level. Low-level pick-ups were in the region of 10 miles, if I remember correctly.
>
> The second phase was air combat. Initially, I maintained high energy and made missile attacks from a position of great height advantage. The missile locked very well out to a range of about six miles against a land background and held lock throughout the attack, even though the Pucará managed to turn to achieve an almost head-on pass by the time I was at minimum range. This was repeated many times until I got bored and tried a low-speed guns attack. At 300 knots with full flap, I initially managed to turn with the Pucará and maintain a guns solution but after about 120° of turn, had to pull high to avoid overshooting. At this stage the Pucará reversed his turn and very nearly managed to achieve a guns kill on me! The Pucará was a very good AIM-9L target because the jet efflux was visible from all aspects.

On 21 July, the Pucará was taken to Greenham Common to participate in the International Air Tattoo event on the 23rd and 24th of that month, returning the day after its only in-flight presentation in public. After completing the tests at Boscombe Down, only 25 of the planned 50 hours had been flown, for which maintenance had been done. Says John Davis:

> We had an aeroplane there, serviceable, and pilots who could fly it. My thought was to offer it to the RAF so that, in the summer of 1983, it and a Harrier could fly around all the RAF open days and 'At Home' days to show the Harrier and the Pucará side by side. This was

rejected at a very high level by the Ministry of Defence, on the basis that they couldn't afford it. So, what we ended up doing was filling it up with every litre of fuel possible, planning a cross-country round every unit in the south of England, and dropping it off at Cosford.

Thus, on 9 September 1983, it stopped flying after landing at the RAF Museum in Cosford, where it is now part of the museum collection.

Other Pucarás

A-517 was sold to Grampian Helicopters International and registered as G-BLRP in December 1984, with the aim of taking it to England, although the serial was never painted and it never flew again; in 1985 it was loaded into two containers, one 20 foot and the other 40 foot, and was carried by the ship *Monsunen* from Goose Green to Stanley. There it remained until 1987, when it was taken to England. Rodney Butterfield bought it in 1989 and in 1990 took it, in two 40-foot containers, from Oxfordshire to Forest City, North Carolina, in the United States, where it remains today awaiting restoration. In the containers there is also the cockpit canopy of A-509 and a cover of the front end of A-529, in addition to components of other aircraft.

A-522, taken to be displayed in the St Athan Museum and then to the Fleet Air Arm Museum in Yeovilton, received the RAF 8768M maintenance identification which was never painted. On 24 July 1994, it was transferred to the North East Air Museum in Sunderland (Northumberland).

A-528 received maintenance identification RAF 8769M and was taken first to Abingdon, then to the RAF Museum in Cosford, later returning to Abingdon, after spending some time, in 1985, at the Museum of Army Flying in Middle Wallop; on 24 July 1994 it was loaned to the Norfolk & Suffolk Aviation Museum in Flixton. These two machines had also been used to provide spare parts for ZD-485.

Regarding the ZD-486, formerly A-533, it was integrated into the Museum of Army Flying in Middle Wallop, but years later it was sold for scrap by Hanningfield Metals of Stock of Essex. Tony Dyer convinced the company to preserve the cabin, which in 2004 was sold to Gordon Ramsey, who partially restored it and keeps it preserved.

The ZD-487, formerly A-549, was taken to the Imperial War Museum in Duxford, where it is on display to this day. The rest of the Pucarás that remained in the hands of the British at the end of the war remained in the islands, where A-529 was for many years a monument at RAF Mount Pleasant base, until it was scrapped and its remains thrown in a lagoon, along with those of an F-4 Phantom that was also a monument, both badly damaged by the marine environment. A-514, -532 and -552 were left on the islands, along with others in varying degrees of deterioration, but they were destroyed over time, being used in live-firing exercises on the islands.

Appendix

Technical Specifications

Engines	2 x Turbomeca Astazou XVIG turboprops of 978hp (720KWh) each that move two Ratier Forest 23 LF-379 three-bladed propellers of 2.59m diameter and variable pitch
Length	14.25m
Wingspan	14.5m
Wing surface	30.3m²
Height	5.36m
Wing chord	2.24m
Stabilizer span	4.7m
Fuselage width	1.32m
Empty weight	4,020kg
Maximum weapons weight, including ammunition for the guns	1,620kg
MTOW	6,800kg
Maximum payload	2,780kg
Internal fuel	1,000kg
External fuel	1,280kg
Maximum dive speed	750km/h
Maximum horizontal speed	520km/h
Maximum cruise speed	485km/h
Stall speed	142.5km/h
Climb rate	1,080m/min
Service ceiling	27,165ft
Service ceiling with one engine	17,532ft
Take-off run	300m
Take-off run with 15m obstacle	700m
Landing run	200m
Landing run with 15m obstacle	603m
Range at cruise speed	1,400km
Maximum range	3,042km

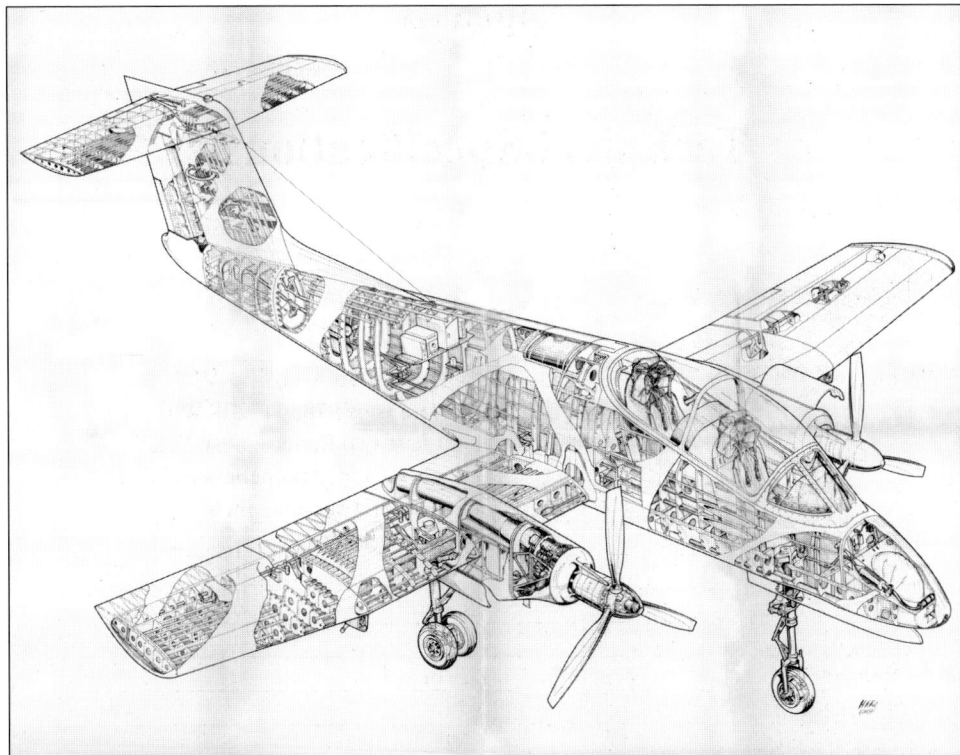

IA-58A Pucará cutaway drawn by Héctor Ruiz. (Archive Eduardo Ruiz)

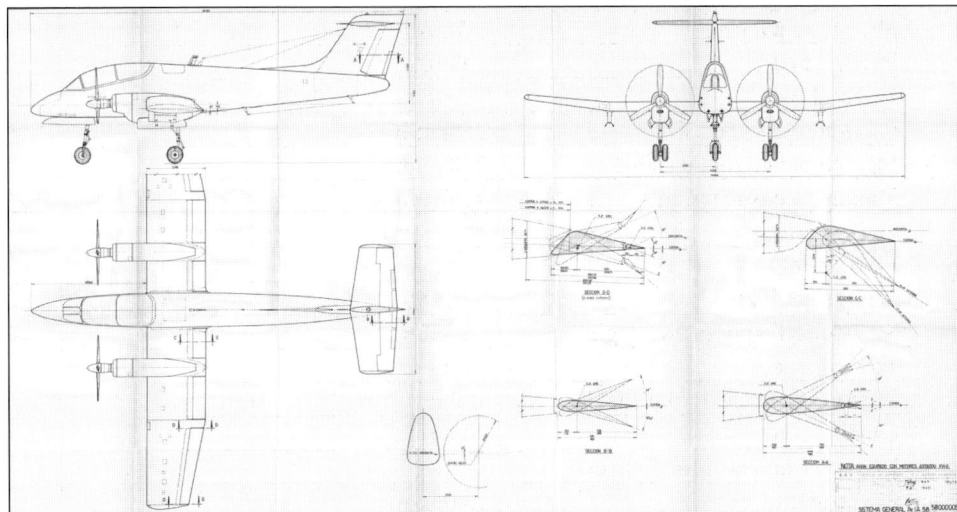

Three views of the IA-58A Pucará from a factory plan.

263

View of the pilot's cockpit.

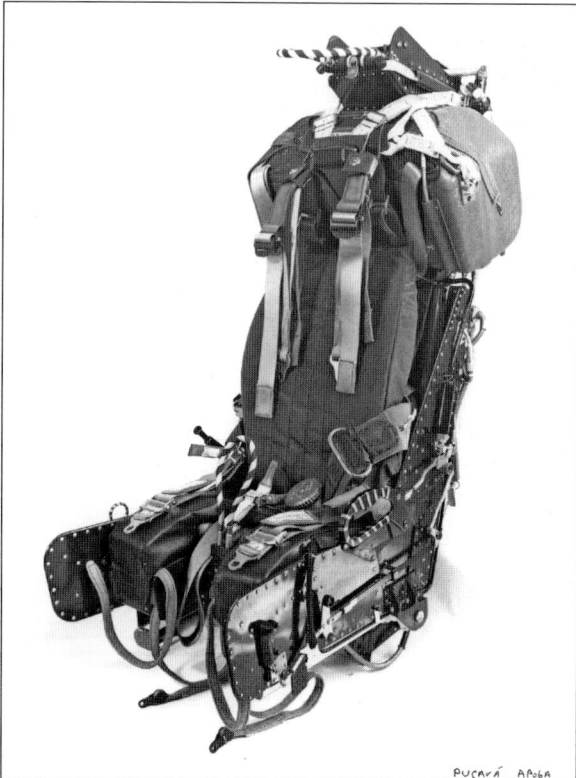

Martin Baker Mk.6HA seat
in the Pucará. (Archive Bryan
Willburn)

264

KRW-24C photo-reconnaissance pod on the belly of a Pucará.

Pucará simulator at III Brigada Aérea, developed by the unit. (Photo Santiago Rivas)

Bibliography

'A proposal to conduct a pre-prototype conceptual study for a utility transport utilizing a maximum number of Pucará IA-66 components, the Córdoba', prepared by Volpar Inc. September 1980.

'Análisis del Proyecto IA-67 "Córdoba"', Fábrica Militar de Aviones, 1981.

Aeroespacio magazine, various issues.

Alas magazine, various issues.

Amores, *Eduardo, Fuerza Aérea Argentina, Guía de aeronaves militares, 1912–2006.* Dirección de Estudios Históricos of the FAA, Buenos Aires, 2007.

Bound, Graham, *Falkland Islanders at War*, Pen & Sword Books, Barnsley, 2002.

Burden, Rodney et al, *Falklands: The Air War*, British Aviation Research Group, London, 1986.

Carballo, Pablo Marcos, *Dios y los Halcones*, Editorial Abril, Buenos Aires, 1983.

Carballo, Pablo Marcos, *Halcones sobre Malvinas*, Ediciones del Cruzamante, Buenos Aires, 1984.

Comando de Material, *Memoirs of the Fábrica Militar de Aviones*, III Brigada Aérea & IX Brigada Aérea.

Dunnell, Ben, 'Flying the Pucará: The Boscombe Down Verdict', *The Aviation Historian* No. 8.

Especificación General Avión IA-53 versión COIN, Capitán ingeniero Justo Demetrio Díaz, ingeniero aeronáutico Billy Juan Mauricio Montico, FMA, Córdoba, December de 1966.

Factory manuals of the IA-58, IA-58C & IA-66.

FAdeA Central Archive.

Historia de la Fuerza Aérea Argentina, Tomo VI, *La Guerra de Malvinas*, Volumes 1 & 2, Dirección de Estudios Históricos de la FAA, Buenos Aires, 2000.

Maruri Juan, teniente 1° (Av) (R) (ed. S. Rivas), *Historia de la Fuerza Aérea Uruguaya*, edited by the author, Montevideo, 2007.

McManners, Hugh, *Forgotten Voices of the Falklands*, Ebury Publishing, England, 2008.

Morgan, David, *Hostile Skies: The Battle for the Falklands*, Phoenix, 2007.

Principi, M. D., Principi, A. C., Rodríguez, G. M., Manno, R. H. & Oviedo, J. O., 'Diseño mejorado de pantalla multi función para la nueva versión del sistema de navegación de la aeronave Pucará'.

BIBLIOGRAPHY

Ramsey, Gordon, *Falklands Then and Now*, Battle of Britain International Ltd, Essex, 2009.

Rengel, Gonzalo Sebastián 'El FMA IA-60' at www.zona-militar.com/2015/08/11/fma-ia-60/

Rengel, Gonzalo Sebastián, 1Los IA-58 Pucará a reacción' at www.zona-militar.com/2016/01/25/los-ia-58-Pucará-a-reaccion/

Ward, Nigel, *Sea Harrier Over the Falklands: A Maverick at War*, BCA, London, 1992.

Acknowledgements

Brigadier Horacio Oréfice, Brigadier César Cunietti, Brigadier Alberto Vianna, Brigadier Miguel Cruzado, Brigadier Alejandro Moresi, Comodoro Miguel Navarro, Comodoro Gabriel Pavlovcic, Comodoro Juan Manuel Cimatti, Comodoro Carlos Tomba, Comodoro Roberto Vila, Comodoro Roberto Címbaro, Comodoro Carlos Horacio Argente, Comodoro Rubén Sassone, Comodoro Raúl Páez, Mayor Sebastián Ardiles, Geselino Garbini, Martín Liva, Teo Maza, Guillermo Rasia, Suboficial Alejandro Marcori, Suboficial Sergio Schoenfeld, Suboficial Martín Neme, Suboficial Matías Paczkowski, Darío Gambini, Coronel Hugo Parentini (FAU), Mayor Wilfredo Guedes (FAU), Mayor Marcelo Lorenze (FAU), Pablo Souza (FAU), Ricardo Moreirazerpa (FAU), Stephanie Catherine Techera (FAU), Roberto Moreno (FAU), Iván Salaberry (FAU), Pedro Cardeillac (FAU), Germán Páez (FAC), Germán Ribero (FAC), Juan Carlos Ramírez (FAC), Jaime Clavijo (FAC), Uditha Danwaththa (Sri Lankan Air Force), Air Chief Marshal Kolitha A. Gunatilleke (Sri Lankan Air Force), Captain Priyantha Adikaram (Sri Lankan Air Force), Flt Lt David Morgan (RAF), Eduardo Ruiz (FAdeA), José Martínez, Buddhika Dissanayake, Hernán Casciani, Lisandro Amorelli, Jona Zorzón, Gonzalo Rengel, Cees-Jan van der Ende, Sergio Bellomo, Jorge F. Núñez Padín, Sergio Baroni, Jorge Leonardi, Gabriel Lladó, Javier Franco, Gonzalo Altamirano, Sergio García Pedroche, Mauro Bia, Gervasio Dambroriarena, Marcelo Buteler (FixView), Juan Remedi (FAdeA), Federico Bima (FAdeA), Sebastián Ugarte (FAdeA), José Ignacio Bertea, Rodrigo Jiménez Sch., Álvaro Romero, Carlos Maggi, Ben Dunnell, Juan Martín Rivas & Javier Ordoñez Jimenez.

Index